looking good

looking good

the liberation of fashion

clara pierre

READER'S DIGEST PRESS

DISTRIBUTED BY THOMAS Y. CROWELL COMPANY

NEW YORK | 1976

This book is for my family
and particularly
for André

Manufactured in the United States of America

Library of Congress Cataloging in Publication Data

Pierre, Clara.
  Looking good.

  Includes index.
  1. Fashion.   2. Clothing and dress.
3. Beauty, Personal.   I. Title.
TT507.P52 1976   646'.34   76–22191

ISBN 0–88349–093–5

10 9 8 7 6 5 4 3 2 1

acknowledgments

The opportunity to discuss my ideas with some of the great Paris designers helped the concept of this book spring to life. I am especially grateful for the time I spent with Yves St. Laurent, André Courrèges, Louis Féraud, and Vicky Tiel.

Monsieur Bernard Lanvin made it possible for me to go "backstage" at his family's couture house in order to observe the *ne plus ultra* of dressmaking, and to see how perfume is manufactured at the Lanvin fragrance headquarters outside Paris.

In this country, Claire Hellawell McDaniel of Lanvin–Charles of the Ritz opened many doors for me, including the elegant portals of The Greenhouse spa in Dallas, as well as those of her own company's cosmetics factory in New Jersey.

The personnel of many stores across the country, especially those of Neiman-Marcus in Dallas, were also generous with their time.

I benefited enormously from a spirited exchange of views

with the doyenne of American fashion, Diana Vreeland; even to disagree with her is an honor.

Grateful acknowledgment is due Mrs. Vreeland's own special province, the Costume Institute at the Metropolitan Museum of Art, which was my writing home while the book was in progress. Gordon Stone, the Institute's librarian, was a helpful presence, a fund of knowledge, and a fount of anecdotes on the subject of dress.

My thanks to Hy Cohen, whose faith in me manages to survive innumerable cups of rot-gut coffee (dark, with sugar). And to Dorothy Murray of "Saturday Review" who typed the manuscript with intelligence and interest.

Among those who, through their writings, stimulated my thoughts about the history and psychology of fashion are Bernard Rudofsky, Bruno du Roselle, and the late James Laver.

But the people who most helped this book to be are my parents and particularly my mother, who spent countless hours suggesting, correcting, looking up facts, xeroxing, and catalysing ideas.

contents

The law of fashion is a law of life.

Justice Oliver Wendell Holmes

Clothes, as despicable as we think them, are unspeakably significant. Clothes, from the king's mantle downwards, are Emblematic.

Thomas Carlyle, "Sartor Resartus"

Style is the dress of thoughts.

Earl of Chesterfield

All fashions seem trivial but *are* serious.

Sir Kenneth Clark

Fashion reflects an era. If, 2000 years from now, people want to know about us, they'll look at our clothes.

Norman Norell

chapter 1

you wear what you are

Do you think you follow fashion? Quite the reverse, actually: Fashion follows you. Clothes are the way you dress your self-image. They are, quite literally, a second skin, a completion of personality. *You* do the choosing. What you choose to wear, how you wear it, what you neglect or choose not to wear, all say a lot about what kind of individual you are.

Do you think fashion has gone out of style? That no one pays it any attention in today's world? Make no mistake—fashion is a very serious matter indeed; it only looks trivial. For clothes, as Thomas Carlyle once wrote, are emblematic. They stand for other things, if only we know how to read them.

Fashion—with its attendant arts of cosmetics and body culture—has the power to recall us to ourselves. Take as simple an accouterment as lipstick. Think back to the first time you used it and see what it summons up. The savor of an era is there, in ways intensely personal and collective at the same time. I remember furtive applications of Tangee "Natural" in the girls' locker room immediately upon arrival at my secondary school each morning. Tangee's product was purchasable at Woolworth's and a far cry from the more expensive spread of our dreams. It had the consistency of orange-flavored gelatin and was apt to break off at the base. Lipstick was not allowed, but it was unofficially tolerated. Meanwhile, Revlon waited in the wings until we became seniors, and could drive to school and were permitted coffee at recess instead of chocolate milk. Acne receded and our lips blossomed with "Persian Melon" and "Powder Pink." The more adventurous among us wore "Orchids to You" or "Fire and Ice" to dances.

Today we view the fifties with nostalgia, the last decade in this century when we could feel at one with our times and what we were. The cap-sleeved Ship'n Shores, the waist cinchers and Merry Widows, the Capezio flats and crinolines stiffened with sugar water can now be found at thrift shops and boutiques in New York's East Village and along the upper reaches of Madison Avenue. Certain neglected pharmacies no doubt still have, in dusty drawers, remnants of "Certainly Red" and "Edwardian Rose," their tubes now oxidized from gold to gunmetal gray. They represent a world that was.

The farther back one goes in history, the easier it becomes to get below the surface of a society by scanning what it wore. Even the merest glance at the dresses of the Victorian era tells us a lot about what women have been liberated from. For the new middle classes, the second half of the last century was an age of great possessions. This is apparent from the number of accessories women wore: hats and bonnets, fussy pocketbooks, parasols, net gloves, cloaks, capes, shawls, mantles, aprons, muffs, boots. They were veritable Christmas trees, carriers of the baubles of status earned by their husbands and families, and they were themselves mainly ornamental.

A look below the surface is even more revealing, telling us much about Victorian woman's high tolerance for pain and about her patience. The complexity of her undergarments is truly baffling: corsets steam-molded on whalebone or metal, bustles, hard crinolines. Underlinen included, at a minimum, a chemise and five or six petticoats. Additional padding, "English garters," hoops, bust improvers, insertions, corset covers, drawers, "combinations," frills could all be had in the appropriate horsehair, silk, wool, linen, cotton, or satin. Each piece required, of course, several fittings. Not only was each separate costume an architectural labyrinth, it had to be changed according to occasion and time of day. A lady of fashion could spend most of her life getting in and out of garments at the proper moments. Should one want an accurate visual frieze of the Victorian era, one has only to leaf through *Godey's Ladies' Book*. It is all there: the modest bearing, the chaste and downcast eyes, the pouter-pigeon stance, how a woman's age dictated her hair style, how the fabrics she chose measured her prosperity, how men appeared to her (usually on bended knee, or peering around doors, bearing flowers).

It is true—fashion is our social barometer. It gives a sense of moment to our lives and ushers us back to ourselves, handing us a mirror image. Clothes incorporate for us our own unique span in time, if we look at them knowledgeably. When we pay close enough attention to them, clothes provide one way of sorting out the chaos that living "now" always means. There are countless other ways of defining what we are, of reading our soundings, taking our pulse. But fashion is one of the best ways precisely because, as Cecil Beaton says, it's so fleeting. Is it not so that those products of popular culture that seem least enduring—a snatch of song, a shoe, a film, a newspaper clipping—always seem to re-create an era better than the monumental work of art that stands outside as well as in its own time? Our current love affair with the thirties, for example, may rest on nothing more than a white piano, a few Bogart films, and a handful of feathers. (Then again, it may be the result of our total lack of identifiable style in contemporary clothes. Our ransacking of the attics of the past may be telling us that we are having a serious identity problem.)

Yet fashion is its own worst enemy. Because good fashion is necessarily of the moment, it must self-destruct, leaving itself as a kind of carapace of time. Because fashion's chief principle is change, it arrests the instant by going on to the next frippery, and then to the next, until we can have, if we know how to assemble it, a playback in slow motion of what we have just been through. Anatole France knew just how telling fashion can be when he wrote, "If I were allowed to choose from the books that will be published one hundred years after my death, do you know which one I would want to read? By no means would I select a novel from that future library—I simply would take up a fashion magazine so that I could see how women dress one century after my departure. Because these rags would tell me more about future humanity than all the philosophers, novelists, prophets, and scholars."

So fashion remains the catalog of our follies, as funny and ephemeral and true as Andy Warhol's soup cans, and as much a by-product of popular art. But Warhol packaged our commercial foibles; fashion packages people.

Finally, it must be remembered that clothes are as unpredictable as humans, and can transmit irony at the speed of light. Clothes can mean status in a democracy; they can be indices of herd instinct among the very rich; they act as instruments of social protest in a commune, as public relations for a limp ego, sexual direction signals, security blankets, come-ons; clothes are commercial, trendy, audacious, languorous, boring, witty. The one thing clothes almost never are is just clothes.

In fashion, real news is rare; most of it has to be manufactured. During the last half century or so, there have been perhaps four or five major changes in the way women have dressed. There was Chanel, pure and simple. Then Dior's 1947 New Look altered the shape of things to come for at least a decade. Courrèges's brand of architectural chic was news in 1963. Carnaby Street, the mini, and the Youthquake shook up the sixties. The lean years between bouts of news give fashion hounds and manufacturers their chance to phantasize and dream up trends, and occasionally they come up with a platform heel or a fur boa. Then, in ways not amenable to anyone's control, the real world has its crack at fashion too. The counterculture of the sixties, in head-on conflict with the establishment over the war in Viet Nam, spawned such diversities as the universal blue jean, granny glasses, and the ubiquitous overall. Not least of all, the fashion press has always done its bit to create fads, and so have the other props of modern life: jet travel, movies, the media, new leisure sports, the economic ticker tapes, the Pill, moon walks, and the women's movement.

But the biggest influence on how women look is also the least news. It has been happening gradually over the past fifty years and its effects, which are altogether revolutionary, will last long beyond this era. It's called the liberation of the body. One of its results is that a new physical type of woman has emerged. She is a hybrid of the boyishly angular twenties and the more rounded and muscular body type called endomorph. Before the tango and tennis and tubular dresses were the rage, we were all, men and women alike, mostly endomorphs, which means in modern terms that we inclined toward stoutness. The opulent expanse of upper arms and chest found on any demimondaine of the Belle Epoque testifies to that ideal. A thin woman was a fashion failure; her form bespoke poverty, chilblains, and probable lack of immunity to disease. The post-World War I fashion plate was not thin by any means. She simply had her buttresses and stays removed, the stuffing shaken out of her bosom and hips, and what was left redistributed along a relatively straight line between collar and knees. Indeed, characteristic women of the time, photographed by the great camera portraitist Hoyningen-Heune, all had long heavy arms and bodies, a curiously cylindrical aspect to their flesh. What they evidently lavished great care on was outline: of lips, of brows, of maniacally waved and metallically gleaming hair, of silhouette made to look slender by stance.

Our modern mesomorph of medium body build has retained some of the twenties' tendency toward the cylindrical. But she looks more like a Giacometti than a Léger. What changed her shape most has been the twin obsessions of dieting and physical fitness. Both began, as did almost everything for modern womanhood, right after World War I. At first women bandaged their breasts, strapped themselves into girdles, and refused to face the fact that extraneous compression could not achieve what a new inner discipline called slimming could. The incentive to be slender was everywhere—in the look of skyscrapers, in the sleek sports cars, in the revved-up dances, the craze for horseracing and tennis. "Fast" referred not only to behavior; it was becoming a way of being. As early as 1913 Colette described the physical fitness freak as *l'élève sé-rieuse*, who even exercises in secret, doubling and tripling the number of times prescribed for each movement. Such folly occasionally ended in enforced rest by intervention of a physician.

Similar discomforts lay in wait for zealous followers of the sixties' fitness religion, which gave us the victim of famine as cultural idol, with Twiggy as its ninety-eight-pound superstar. If you couldn't achieve the goal by not eating, it could always be done by overexercising. The majority of those who reached ninety-eight pounds and lived to look in the mirror started the climb back up the scale of reason. The seventies are thin, but not sick. What we *are* is a nation of health maniacs. Our new ideal is neither undersized child nor overgrown matron, but the woman in between—old enough to have children of her own but not too old to be a skydiving or champion tennis pro. Billie Jean King with a home life; in effect, mesomorphic woman in the athletic age.

When did her body begin to change on its own, and not as a result of various and profitable engineering feats carried out by underwear manufacturers? Though women did not give them all the credit they deserved, the genies of early modern medicine did much to improve female looks. Vitamins were discovered in 1911. Soon vitamin D was isolated, and rickets no longer deformed legs. We began to grow taller children whose teeth and bones were stronger and who could sail through early life unmarred by disfiguring deficiency diseases. Knowing what we know today, it seems odd that the connection between health and good looks has been accepted publicly only within the last ten or fifteen years. But it was not until May of 1957 that this country's most influential beauty authority, *Vogue* magazine, came out with its first statement about health: ". . . we think a woman ought first to realize that no matter what her makeup skill, no matter how remarkable the genius in the cosmetic bottle . . . the making of an astonishing number of beauty flaws . . . may be nutritional in source." So said *Vogue*'s editorial—and thousands cheered. Oh, there had been brief appearances of "Dr. Beauty" in its pages before. Warnings against overexposure to the sun. Posture and waist-whittling exercises. Various eccentric diets. Sensible diets for Mrs. Exeter (*Vogue*'s prototype "lady of a certain age," who was put to rest long before population-age statistics warned of her decline). Fillers, mostly. Or advertisements for Larsen's Swedish Milk Diet alongside Warner's Merry Widows. In 1956 there had been an attempt to put together a "*Vogue* Diet Authority," which made a brief appearance in its pages and then dissolved. Nonetheless, the mid-fifties marked the first time a fashion publication had attempted a medical symposium composed of such eminent professionals as Drs. Ancel Keys, Jean Mayer, and John R. Brobeck.

In terms of success, *Vogue*'s medical breakthrough was anything but sudden. The medical profession has long been notorious for its (no doubt unconscious) compliance with abusive or ridiculous fashions. Our grandmothers' whalebone body cages displaced inner organs and caused every ailment from fainting spells to miscarriages without raising many doctors' eyebrows. The waist cincher that followed Dior's New Look similarly escaped medical notice, as did the stiletto heels and toes of the late fifties. The doctors were *men*, after all, and presumably as seducible by a wasp waist as any other males. In the end, physicians merely helped to swell the conventional wisdom on the subject of underclothes.

Take pantie girdles, for example. In 1946, *Vogue* announced that the pantie girdle was "not a garment to be done without." If you were thin, *Vogue* went on, a pantie girdle was a "substitute for faultless natural muscular control." And if you were not built with reedlike conformation, the pantie girdle would step into the breach, getting on with the job it was created to do. No doctor spoke up then to warn readers that the odiously named garment would actually reduce the effectiveness of one's own musculature. Even a decade later, *Vogue*'s find for the March 1, 1956, issue was "the apricot all-in-one." It covered the situation from armpits to hip bottom, cost $22.50, and was indeed the color of apricot purée. One's muscles were not destined to be one's very own until the late 1950's.

Once physicians took a more objective look at the situation, medicine and beauty slowly became more closely allied. The good doctors did not have an easy time of it in an era which still assumed that to be beautiful you had to suffer at least a little. But soon a *modus vivendi* grew between medical experts and the fashion magazines. Sometimes these publications ignored the doctors and sometimes the doctors overlooked the

THE GREAT VICTORIAN CORSET, circa 1874... (From *Victorian Costume and Costume Accessories,* by Anne Buck, Universe Books, New York, 1970.)

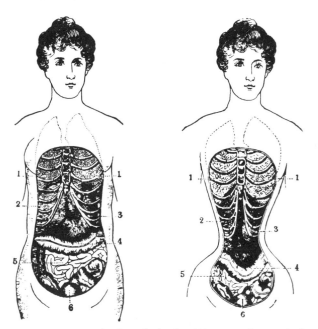

AND ITS EFFECTS on the female body. (From *Reform–Moden–Album,* 1904; used by B. Rudofsky in *Are Clothes Modern?* Paul Theobald, Chicago, 1947.)

more injurious caprices of fashion. On the whole, though, the New Look and its requisite waist nipper and pointed bosom-pouter were dinosaurs—the last throwbacks to a time when underwear was relied upon for control of the female figure. From the late fifties on it was to become apparent that exercise could accomplish what yards of Lycra Spandex couldn't.

Today, liberated bodies have served notice that muscles can stand, sit, and walk alone. The refusal to be passive has created a look of its own. The athletic mesomorph laughs at under-clothes and lives in leotards. If her house has many rooms, one of them may be a gymnasium. She has a winter sport and at least one for summer. She will try anything new once. Her bicycle is likely to be parked in the hallway, where a side table used to take up space. Her office lunch hour is more likely to be spent on a slant board than at a coffee-shop counter. Her makeup is applied with wizardlike efficiency in five minutes each morning. Every product she puts on her face is likely to have one of the following words on its label: "transparent," "gloss," "nonallergenic," "biodegradable," "organic," "light-weight," or "gel." As for what she wears, her kind of fashion is born of a life-style as big as all outdoors. The Chanel slippers she loved in the sixties, as beautiful as they were, tended to disintegrate in rain. Now she has rubber Wellingtons that rise to mid-calf, the kind that English grooms use for mucking out stalls. Such footgear acknowledges that there is such a thing as weather, and that it exists on the way to offices as well as while hiking in the woods.

Weather is fashion's new discovery. Raincoats can be worn to the theater. Safari cloth is indeed cool. Shoulder duffels hold snug and dry everything a city dweller needs in the High Sierras or down Fifth Avenue. All-weather clothes are all-activity clothes as well. What are the possibilities? The kind of pants that bicycle to work, get through a day at the office without complaint, and then go out to dinner. Dresses that can play lunch-hour tennis. Jeans tough enough for riding, devoid of the nailheads and appliqués of days gone by. Backpacker's equipment that will hold up under the stresses of *city* mud, rain, and snow. All-season sandals. (The plastic kind imported from France are a start in the right direction, as they can take the moisture in stride. For cold, one sees stout stockings worn with strapped platforms of buffalo hide.) Already the line between active sportswear and "fashion" is blurring: In France, *le sweatshirt* comes in everything from springy cotton knits to evening satins. Our athletic mesomorph has been haunting the good sports outfitters for years now: Miller Harness Company supplies her stocks, shirts, hacking jackets, and aforementioned Wellingtons; Army and Navy surplus, her rain gear and a handsome wind jacket for playing touch football in Central Park; Kreeger's, her walking shoes, Norwegian hand-knit socks, and canvas bags. Soon Seventh Avenue will be producing them for her.

Will the Swiss Army knife be the fashion accessory of the future? It's not a facetious question. Americans are good at manufacturing sportswear and know how to wear it. Women will soon be sick of looking like decorator showrooms or a carte blanche for designer initials. Clothes have come a long way, but what they can still afford to give is a physical sense of the body's uses, a machine-made simplicity that doesn't recall the machine itself, with a place reserved for individualism and (why not?) eccentricity. Since designers and manufacturers are quick to learn what women really want, the height of urban street sophistication may soon resemble the Appalachian Trail on a crowded weekend.

The message from black designers is strong as well. They have ego. They have a daring color sense. They have a whole new range of synthetic fabrics at their disposal with which to cut costs. Their mannequins are built like Masai warrior maidens, and they can dance. All of which adds up to a new look of flash and bravado currently gleaming on city streets. Maybe that's what women really want. But whatever it is we want, we all need a rest from hard chic—and from the restrictions of the structured garment. The liberated body demands liberated fashion, a new concept which rejects fashion per se and which traces its beginnings to the counter-culture of the sixties.

chapter 2

sixties
counterchic

It was the counterculture that first stepped outside, slamming the door on chic. When kids began to leave home it was as often to hitch or bike across country as to go to college. Some walked alone or in pairs from California to Maine, armed only with Boy Scout mess kits and trekking boots. Their preparation came first from books and then from experience; they owned their bodies and whatever they carried—that was enough. The image of the backpacker with his world in his knapsack was one of the most vivid icons of the counterculture. And so it remains part of our personal baggage, since we are, every one, no matter what our age, children of the sixties.

Simply being alive now has made us all immigrants in time, cut loose forever from the world that was before the cataclysm of 1939. For those born after the war, who were just reaching adolescence in the early sixties, there were additional factors to cope with. As Margaret Mead has pointed out, a young person of ten or fifteen years ago grew up expecting change: It was all he knew. The gulf naturally separating children from parents and grandparents was further widened by a series of events that cut off young people from their own history. These events, taken singly, were hard enough to understand, but coming as they did, one on top of the other, their effect was explosive. The two decades between 1940 and the launching of the sixties took on an almost ominous momentum. There was first and foremost the Bomb, then preparation for what was to become Sputnik. Discoveries on terra firma included everything from advances in cell biochemistry to the invention of the computer. There was a dawning awareness of those earth problems that are still with us: the destruction of our natural environment, the breakdown of cities, acceleration of population growth, the food crisis, the fact that distribution and consumption were replacing production as prime concerns of the advanced countries. Meanwhile, what is collectively known as the "media" (anything that gets messages across, whether by wire or wing, print or photo) encouraged the world to respond more quickly to its own doings. The advent of jet travel increased the general velocity. Finally, industry was discovering and developing both new energy sources and synthetic raw materials.

To grow into adulthood as live monitors of all these factors was the fate of postwar youth. They entered the sixties with antennae waving. The creation of a teen-age culture was not due just to their sheer numbers, though they were increasing at the rate of twelve million a year. The baby boom wasn't responsible for those mass emigrations from home base any more than it could be held to account for the twist. What happened was that, pried loose from their parents by a widened generation gap, the kids had only their peer groups to rely on. They found, in a society whose sands were constantly shifting beneath their feet, the one relatively stable factor in their lives—each other. At that age, there is always security in numbers; in the sixties the need for that kind of security became the basis for a way of living. Communes and crash pads linked youth all over the United States. The neonomads bailed out in Berkeley and the East Village, crashed in New England and Taos communes, and kept the wires humming between East and West coasts with their underground newsletters and magazines. They built their pleasure domes wherever the psychic weather was warm.

Soon it became apparent that, alongside an early youth consumer boom, there was an ironic opposing ethic, that of owning nothing. Counterculturists became experts on self-sufficiency, survival, marginal living, growing it at home, and doing-it-yourself. They devised ways of recycling old clothing and building furniture that could be stashed in a trailer for the next move. The nationwide rise in vandalism, rip-offs, and crime (and the cost of insurance) made furnishing with costly possessions seem silly. They turned their backs on what seemed to have become more and more a national preoccupation, the seeking of refuge in sleek objects. They refused to respond to the messages from Madison Avenue. Their revolt took on, at times, a high moral tone, encouraged by a smattering of antimaterialism from the Eastern religions. But by and large, they really meant it. A flat statement by James Hennessey and Victor Papanek in *Nomadic Furniture #2* sums it up: "Young people . . . have turned around clothing and their needs for furniture so that uncluttered personal freedom becomes the goal, rather than an object-laden showplace." For the first time on such a large scale, ways of doing things, dress, and patterns of conduct were arising from within the youth cult itself and fast spreading to the masses.

News about life-styles was transmitted with the speed of light. Young people in small towns across the country grew their hair and bought love beads in no time, because these artifacts of counterculture were easily seized upon. But long hair and love beads do not a social revolution make. There is always the danger of thinking that because the jeans are raggy enough, because one has caught the lingo, one is participating in a movement to change something. Yes, we have learned a few tricks from the kids of the sixties, but most of the basic tenets of our culture remain. Our avidity for material goods is intact. We will consume, like Brillat-Savarin's gourmande mother, until we die.

Yet part of the legacy of the counterculture remains. It blends with a tendency already strong in American culture—mobility. The image of the nomad, free to strap his belongings to his back and take off, had become a national insignia almost as soon as Conestoga wagons started out for the Old West. Jack Kerouac bummed his wheels in the fifties and the counterculture's neonomads were direct descendants of the Beat Generation, crossbred with *Easy Rider*. In the sixties, mobility was signaled by the self-decorated minibus or by piggybacking a boxcar. Today, truckin' is still the name of the game, with the pickup taking over as cult object. But whether the means is bike, rail, or ordinary auto, the urge to move still winds its leitmotif through the country. For this kind of life, possessions make little sense.

The desire to own little has other charms and deeper roots, however. It has become a symbol for something much farther below the surface. For what the kids of the sixties were doing was mounting a giant protest against the complexity of contemporary life. Their angst was everybody's. It is true that slogans like "back to nature" have always provided an easy antidote to overworked societies. But justification of the yearning for simplicity was certainly ample. Didn't Oscar Wilde say that simplicity is the last resort of complicated people? He was right, insofar as we seem to be living in an age in which the height of sophistication is in knowing how to live like a peasant again.

Simple lives we have not. Our era is destructive in addition to being complex. We have been occupied with dismantling old structures both figurative and real. We tear down buildings, whole sections of cities, organized faith and ways of thought, the family unit. Our art has broken up what we see into fragments of a merely optical reality. We prefer Oriental philosophies to our old ones, and we like having no set religion better than salvaging bits and pieces of the outworn ones.

We have been forced to start all over again with ourselves—and we have begun at the body. For bodies are where it all begins. We are tuned in to the point of limitless curiosity about how our hearts and brains work; whether it is possible to arrest death in a deep freeze or create life in a glass tube. We are concerned with food: how to grow enough for everyone, how to feed ourselves in a more satisfactory—and less chemical—way. We explore how to protect our bodies with experimental ways of clothing and sheltering. And we have learned how to read a new language: body talk, or the signals by which we indicate ourselves to each other. We have become quite simply, on one level, bodies in communication with one another. This is a good foundation for salving the wounds of a cruel postindustrial "progress." Slowly, we are recoiling from a consumerism gone mad. Perhaps we shall all end up, happier and much the wiser, like the couple in Alain Tanner's film *Rétour d'Afrique* who remained in a room devoid of anything but themselves, having sold every stick of furniture before an expected trip that didn't materialize. For the old personal elegance and material well-being that were once the privilege of kings and queens and courtiers are today merely the height of what is within everyone's reach. Medicine, grooming aids, gadgets are available to all; the general level of taste in dress is definitely on the rise. At present the more difficult attainment has become the knowledge of how to reduce life to fewer elements in order to enjoy it more. As long as people think they want twenty varieties of soapflakes, our inflated economy will continue to grind them out. But meanwhile, those who have already had the choices are beginning to renounce them. The flower children had seen abundance in the suburbs, and it hadn't brought them happiness. Less, they were discovering, was indeed more.

Meanwhile, back at the drawing boards of Seventh Avenue more was certainly getting to be less and less in terms of body covering. A fashion trend was literally on the rise, culminating in the micro-miniskirt and hot pants of the infamous winter season of 1970. If anything characterizes the decade brought to a close by the demise of the mini, it was this example of garment-center chutzpa. Clothes were a charade led by Mary

Quant, Courrèges, Giorgio Di Sant'Angelo, and joined by every two-bit designer in the business. They gave us metallic goddesses in vinyl spacesuits and plastic bubble helmets, fringed leather Indian costumes and gypsies, Poor Boys and Rich Hippies. Magazines like *Vogue* and *Harper's Bazaar* did fashion shots on location everywhere from the Himalayas to garbage dumps. It was the age of false poverty that brought us $300 silver evening dresses staged against slagheaps or riverside cranes. And the cash registers roared with approval. Bras were burned and unconfined bosoms bobbed in public streets. Unisex beckoned to all with its long hair, handbags, and safari suits. Pop, kitsch, what the French call *folklorique,* and the natural look all coexisted in a splendid circus of inventiveness. It was more than enough to alarm the gray-flannel-suit crowd, which issued warnings and ultimatums to its wayward but undaunted employees. This one came from the upper echelons of Dell Publishing Company: "Bare feet, bare midriffs, bare backs, halter necklines, spaghetti straps, micro-miniskirts, shorts and culottes, tank tops, T-shirts, undershirts, AND SUCH, which are in the fashion picture, may be acceptable modes of dress (or lack of it) for picnics, poolside, beach and cookouts, but they are totally UNacceptable in an office environment. . . ."

Clearly, something major was happening to cause all this clothes unrest. Why should all hell break loose in a prosperous postindustrial society which could have lulled itself to sleep over a beer in front of the telly? Why did people choose to look like freaks, celebrate happenings, flock to the nearest underground movies? Why could you no longer tell the wife of a Boston banker from a professional "danseuse"? Everyone had joined the circus. And in the process, fashion had literally come out of the closet. It was no longer a mark of gentility to wear a proper little Chanel copy or a Davidow. It was just dowdy. All those manufacturers of suburbanite tweeds like John Meyer and Villager rescued themselves at the last moment only by making long kooky things in black rayon instead of Donegal. For in the sixties, the old desire for social superiority began to be translated into the *need to be different.*

This was what the clothes revolution was all about, and why it took such extraordinary form. Given momentum by a technology that could provide the goods quickly, given a media network that could transmit the desire for such goods fast to a waiting public that could afford them, the stage was set. In an essentially democratic time beset by questions of man-versus-machine machismo, the impulse was strong to distinguish oneself from the masses, to frame the ego with clothes. Clothes provided the most available, logical, and ultimately the cheapest way to do just that. But the contest wasn't any longer for the most expensive way of dressing—it was for the most individual.

Social climbing, mind you, was not dead. It was just perverse, in a way that came naturally to the sixties. The methodology as well as the aims of the climber had changed. There was a rush for the backhanded, underground superiority of being first with the most, soonest. . . . First to wear, to do, to be seen at . . . The New York taxi magnate and art collector Robert Scull and his wife, Ethel, excelled at this sort of superiority. Their renown was packaged by Halston and Andy Warhol, then broadcast by *New York Times* accounts of their parties for liberal causes. If Ethel Scull inherited Baby Jane Holzer's title as queen of pop people back in the late sixties, it was because she understood that being genuinely outré usually wins the spotlight. And the spotlight was what you had to have a lot of if you wanted to make it in the new society. The Sculls' finest public hour came with the auctioning off of their pop art collection in November 1973, a gesture that simultaneously announced the interment of the Warhol era and the new rage for divesting oneself of collections of any sort—"the new simplicity," they said. It is entirely fitting that a documentary film was shot of the event.

The snobbistics of the sixties took on another and even more contorted expression in the guise of "radical chic." The famous Black Panther party given by the Leonard Bernsteins and castigated by the journalist Tom Wolfe was a particularly poignant case of instant media exposure. With the advent of the Panthers, the cocktail party circuit was stopped dead in the middle of its morning-at-the-hairdresser's, little-luncheon routine by its contact with "real people." Those Panther wives were elegant as all get out in their Yoruba turbans, just as Wolfe reported, without benefit of hours before the dressing table mirror. One ultrafashionable New York socialite was heard to remark that she was now against fashion because "the sophistication of the baby blacks made me rethink my attitudes." If the Bernstein party gave pause to aggressive liberals, would-be swingers, and other dabblers in ego, it did put a new kind of class consciousness into the public domain.

In a self-professed democracy, herd instinct is strong. Once the inverted snobbism of the sixties caught on, it was picked up in no time at all by the fashion industry. The very latest in revolutionary wear began pouring off the mills and out of the cutting rooms: guerrilla shirts, bullet belts, camouflage patterns. Egalitarianism had not been such a fashionable cause célèbre since the French Revolution. Every sort of group provided stimulus, from the bearded, khaki-clad "Barbudos" or revolutionaries of Fidel Castro's Cuba, to the blue-suited workers of Mao Tse-tung's China. French laborers' *bleus du travail* were imported to the United States by a sophisticated outfitter in New Hampshire; Mountain Artisan patchworks became the last word in expensive chic on New York's Madison Avenue. Artifacts of Appalachian destitutes, African dashikis, fabrics from Bedford-Stuyvesant: All these are sartorial alignments with the poor, bought by the rich, sophisticated—and guilty. The worker's boot has become a symbol among the young. Companies like Frye manufacture it for those who can afford its welded seams and tough, no-nonsense look. A glorification of "real" work: this is the secret and real meaning of the hippie-sponsored jeans, farmer overalls, peasant smocks, and lumber jackets, all of which are still with us.

Along with the counterculture move toward egalitarianism is another summons to change. It comes from the young Beau Brummels of today, the urban blacks and Spanish-Americans. They have what might be called Flash—a downright unreal eye for style. Style is all of content for the New Dudes. It's the "meanest" way to make one's presence felt, and these kids are self-conscious in the best sense. They *are* somebody, man, and they want to be *noticed*. Their use of color and materials could put a painter to shame. Flash is, very specifically, ghetto elegance: Badman, Batman, grommets, studs, fur-covered Superfly hats stung with motto buttons, stabbed with rhinestone-initialed stickpins. Leather armor—not the Ace flying jackets cracked at the elbow or the vicious vinyls of the Teddy boy era, not the bad black Hell's Angels motorcycle outfits, but leather sharp and lean, cut like an Edwardian's, in panels that graze the heels; deeply back-vented, high-armholed, double-breasted slabs of Naugehyde worn with a cocked cap or a hair rake and a leer.

Leather is tough, durable, and means business. The brand of violence it connotes is of the classier sort. Under this shell is the tightest pair of pants that ever bunched a high-assed bottom, so tight that they come up off the boot in back. Whatever the Dude wears, he makes his own. But whether cravated or turtlenecked, bowlered or capped, sneakered or platformed, the true New Dude is never without his hat and cane. Or his single gold ear stud and silver cross. Or his special footgear.

His shoes are real seagoing vessels, as accurately engineered and rigged as models of galleons in the Hispanic Society Museum. Like those ships, shoes are their own emblem, no longer a mere accessory to movement or means for setting the rest of the body afloat. Shoes are discussed and bought like works of art; they are as hard-edged and vinylized as ski boots, and almost as heavy. You don't catch any Dudes wearing Earth Shoes. Theirs are high as skyscrapers floating on a marshmallow cloud, blunt as bludgeons, and sometimes sparked with silver stars on azure and vermilion backgrounds. Theirs have imitation styrofoam soles—a concession to comfort and the last word in cool.

In winter, the with-it Dude changes leatherette for a rabbit-fur greatcoat, or perhaps a panné velvet baseball jacket for subway or bike riding. Wherever he is, style is in evidence. Wasn't it Maurice de Bosdari who said that a truly elegant woman is so obsessed with her clothes and jewels, she must think day and night of the impression she makes with them? So, too, with the Dude, whose clothes are as much himself as the incandescent shell is the scarab or its fabulous tail the peacock. Dress is all ego, anyway—and the New Dude is not the first to know it. Nor to use it to stir up, frighten, and amaze those in authority whom he not-so-secretly disparages.

Today's dandy wants to be counted. He is part of a popular liberation movement like so many others. Whereas in the past dandyism was taken up by those whom it was intended to offend, i.e., the aristocracy, the modern urban Dude is bent on expressing his own version of *épater le bourgeois. Le bourgeois*, mind you, has to stand in for an aristocracy that has ceased to function in modern society; and the bourgeoisie, intent on the maintenance of its gray-flannel standards, is not about to pick up the sartorial habits of a group whose existence it would rather not cheer on. Naturally there are those whose jaunty stance as individuals outside the middle class excuses them from worry about such things. For example, the outstanding female dandy of the camp world of rock-music aborigines, darling of the Beautiful People, is that anachronism of elegance, Bianca Jagger. Her primitive, dark profile contrasts nicely with the regency cane that has become her trademark. And then there is the enfant terrible of the world of new journalism, the white-suited tattersall-vested Tom Wolfe himself.

By and large, though, identifying rungs on the social ladder by dress no longer works. The classifying traits—such as beards or Afros—more often relate to movements than to background. How have we arrived at this semihomogenized state? When there *was* an aristocracy, the impetus to imitate was strong. Especially in this country's early years, everyone copied the upper classes, who were then forced to alter what they wore just enough to maintain themselves apart. When the dress of lower classes is ossified, as it was in the European peasantry, pressure on the aristocracy to change its styles is greatly diminished. America, however, having always allowed shifts in and out of the class structure, provided a different sort of atmosphere. At first, the ruling classes here followed the example of their English and French peers in matters of dress. This was handed on—with modifications—to the new country's rapidly rising middle classes. With the beginning of ready-to-wear manufacturing around the turn of the century, getting clothes to purchasers was possible within a very short time frame. Design piracy was to provide the backbone for the new clothing industry. When the procedure of setting new styles and copying them for the masses escalated to such speed that the two blurred, it became almost impossible to distinguish a person's background or how much money he had merely by what he was wearing. In a sleight-of-hand way, the ready-to-wear revolution may have contributed to making a democracy at least *look* more as though its citizens were truly created equal. In any case, it certainly shortened the old cycle that every piece of clothing repeats: First it is new, then it begins to look ordinary, and finally, whether worn out or not, it appears old.

Many dress historians have tried to analyze the factor of change in fashion. Some accuse the designers and manufacturers of inventing change just to keep the industry alive. Fashion journalism has come equally under fire. But the fact is that women don't have to buy new clothes on a continuing basis. The designer-industry-advertising conspiracy theory may make it easier to rationalize expenditure, but the answer is more likely that women *want* change. Clothes are second skins. The easiest way to make oneself feel new is to wear a new dress. Undeniably, for some women, clothes and shopping for them are the equivalent of a sort of perpetual search for some idealized self. But even for the nonneurotic purchaser, it is nevertheless true that familiarity, in the shape of an old dress on the hanger, breeds contempt. Then there is the art of keeping men interested. If the mini-midi crisis of recent history did nothing else, it mobilized men into vociferous opinions on women's appearance. No sooner had they got used to the sight of thousands of female thighs on the scene than skirts descended abruptly, curtaining everything except an occasional pair of platform shoes. The "shifting erogenous zone" had, for once, shifted too quickly, and the decibel level of male protests went up accordingly.

What with women promoting change in clothing styles as the stuff of their own advantage, it is unlikely that they will ever accept uniforms as a solution to the "fashion problem." Not that the uniform idea doesn't have its sponsors, even among dress designers. Norman Norell said in a 1967 interview, "The main trouble with fashion today is that there are too many clothes designed, too many choices. . . . My idea of chic is that everyone in the world would have the same dress and the chicest woman would be whoever could do the best thing with it." At the other end of the design spectrum is the supercontemporary Rudi Gernreich of mono-kini fame, who claims that the Chinese workers' cotton pajamas are the world's most perfect garment. They are cheap, durable, and never go out of style. Sociologist Bernard Rudofsky's solution to the obsolescence problem is to make clothing according to one or two basic patterns, like the Greek chiton or Roman toga, which would fit everyone. The wearer's individuality would be expressed in the body itself, its stance and gestures, rather than by garments. Rudofsky has even proposed guest

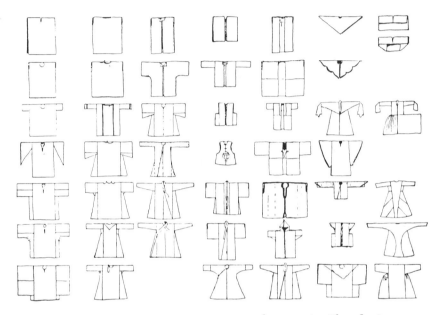

ORIENTAL DRESS HAS CHANGED LITTLE over the centuries. These basic
forms remain because of their ultimate practicality. They inspire
what could be—but so rarely is—a modern simplicity in Western
dress. (From Tilke: *Orientalische Kostüme,* used by B. Rudofsky
in *Are Clothes Modern?* Paul Theobald, Chicago, 1947.)

robes to be kept ready by the considerate host for anyone who visits him, thereby eliminating to some extent the traveler's luggage problem. Claire McCardell devised clothes in the forties that were made from primary geometric shapes. Her designs were simple, classic, easily manufactured without fabric waste, and not doomed to an early demise by an excess of detail.

Other cultures had the answer long ago. The huipil of Yucatan is a garment of genius. Shaped like a white cotton pillowcase, embroidered richly at yoke and hem, the wealth of its wearer is distinguishable only by the amount of gold jewelry she wears, and occasionally by silk, rather than cotton, embroidery. In the streets of Merida, the eye is drawn immediately to the faces of women, as their clothing varies so little. Men abide by the same system: White cotton trousers and open-necked shirts seem to turn the cities of southern Mexico into a giant tropical hospital full of white-clad interns and nurses.

But it was left to the hippies of the 1960's to take multipurpose patterns of great originality and put them into widespread use here. The idea of adapting one basic shape—like the caftan—to a multiplicity of uses sprang up simultaneously in such diverse locales as Vermont communes, Tangiers, and at the New Life Pattern Company, a one-woman operation in New York City. The latter, run by Moisha Kubinyi, is a business based on the T-shirt and variations of the caftan sewn without lapels, buttonholes, inner tailoring, or set sleeves. Depending on the fabric chosen, these prototypes can go from ballroom to beach, and are certainly among the most adaptable garments of our time. Other designers have explored the possibilities offered by draping rather than cutting from even

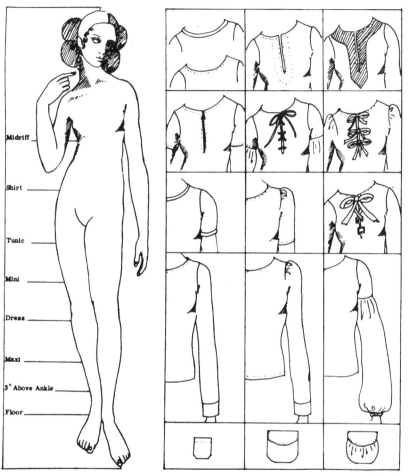

TODY, SOME MANUFACTURERS are beginning to base their designs on ancient prototypes. Clothes made from New Life Patterns permit many variations on a single theme, but retain an age–old simplicity. (Moisha Kubinyi)

the simplest of patterns. Draped clothes eliminate the steps of cutting and piecing; size is not a problem. Such garments are stored flat instead of hung, can be machine-laundered, and can still fulfill all the demands of formal-informal activities.

Then there are the American "concept" clothes of Design Community. Originated by American Peter Kent from a boutique-restaurant-commune in Corsica, the Community now operates between Morocco, where the fabrics are woven, and a loft in Manhattan's Chelsea district. Design Community garments are still made without zippers, snaps, facings or linings. At the beginning, Kent and his co-designer could not afford industrial fittings. It was easier to use self-ties from the fabric. And then it occurred to them that ties were more beautiful than manufactured fastenings. Part of a whole new breed of original thinkers on the subject of clothes, Peter Kent writes about his coterie, "We are a *Whole Earth Catalogue.* Our work has nothing to do with fashion except in the sense that we make garments. It is a reflection of the way we live. It *is* the way we live. . . ." Indeed, the notion of an actual catalog of simple patterns that can be adapted for any size, shape and use, much along the lines of Ms. Kubinyi's, is a prevalent one among new designers. But before this sort of thinking could happen, a major reassessment of how we looked was necessary.

It was the flower children who were the first to serve notice that our way of dressing, among other things, was getting too complex. This they did by ignoring fashion completely. Their own limited finances dictated reliance on durable fabric (denim) and on cheaply produced long dresses which looked as different as possible from current modes and recalled instead the days when homesteading women were heroines. These neopioneers and nomads unwittingly sent fashion into a tailspin, precisely because of their scorn of style. They did what no professional designer at the time could do because their disinterest corresponded profoundly with that of a public that had other issues on its mind: presidential assassinations, Viet Nam, and the mini-revolutions in universities all over the world, among other concerns. Designers were still too dazzled by their own creations to see their way out of the maze of status initials, gold chains, and layered looks into the kind of casualness women really wanted. It was not until Halston emerged in 1968 with his flowing caftans and unlined body dresses that the right chord was struck—for those who could afford his clothes.

Today, Halston remains well beyond the means of most and is unknown to the rest. The problem of simplicity is still with us. We have repeatedly gone back to the past for "inspiration," and always with disastrous results. Last time around, the quest for ideas led to the thirties. But Art Deco is not exactly what it says; it is decoration *without* art, ornament without substantial form change. Hoodwinked by our infatuation, we have been led through all the superficialities of latter-day Egyptian embellishment: fabrics printed with side-turned figures, stylized profiles, flat animals with wings; machine-turned Bakelite jewelry to offset the cold slink of satin. The realization that Deco lends itself well only to office buildings and bars has been long in coming. If Deco possesses any merit at all it may be in the way it makes the beholder feel: Harlowish and slithery, a remembered champagne glass perpetually in hand. For the rest, it is a copyist's paradise, providing an elaborate smokescreen for what is really the matter with contemporary fashion: It is too complicated for today and too frightened about tomorrow to have any clear direction at all.

With luck, the thirties revival may teach us that roaming around the past as a substitute for thinking about the future should be regarded with suspicion. At the very least, such a revival instructs us in the paucity of our own invention. Should other eras continue to haunt us, may it be in spirit alone. For spirit, with regard to clothes, really does have a lot to say if we can listen.

If in the mid-seventies we long to release the body from its wrappings as we say we do, why not take nature at her word and start at the beginning, with the body? Things have been moving in this direction for the last few years, but we need to think more about perfecting the body's health. Let us, furthermore, give up tailoring. If limbs are ever to be free, garment construction must abandon the old encasement method. How else to clothe the body? The designers mentioned are on the right track. Think of sheets. Squares of beautiful fabric to be draped, hung on the body so that the *wearing* of a dress is the thing. Imagine if every woman were to be handed a bed sheet from which to construct her look. No zippers, buttons, or fastenings of any kind except a brooch or fibula. Once weaned from the old cut-piece-and-sew method, we would all learn how to drape. Obviously, the body itself, as prime expression of our individuality, would become even more important than it is now. The lost arts of stance, movement, gesture, would all take on new significance. Prime areas for fantasy and adornment would be hair, face, feet, hands. Our clothes of today are too fussy for jewelry, but against a square of beautiful fabric, what could not be displayed!

Despite the fashion obsession of the sixties, however, the cry had already gone up: The body was back—and along with it a rediscovery of the senses. The body became an instrument for "getting in touch." The physical self was explored in detail by Esalen group leaders, bioenergeticists, and disciples of Ida Rolf. Treatises were written on touching, on breathing, on gynecological self-examination. There was a stream of best-selling recipe books on sex, while adventurers in other varieties of erotica expounded the "sensuous art of massage."

If you hadn't "met" your body yet, massage was the way to make its acquaintance. A plethora of techniques invaded a field once dominated by the Swedish method. Now there were experts from Japan, India, and California all in there competing. Like Yoga, massage was being exploited not just as a means of relaxation, but as another route to knowing the body.

Americans have always regarded self-improvement as an inalienable right; physical self-improvement became really "in" only during the sixties, placing it on a par with university extension courses as a means of mind-body expansion. As a substitute for social ambition, the new gymnastics was quite acceptable; in leotards, everyone at least *looks* equal. The results, moreover, were visible ones that fulfilled at least the second half of the Duchess of Windsor's dictum that you can never be too rich or too thin. That was the trouble. Improvement soon translated into emaciation. The proverbial bag of bones began to be a generally applauded method of repackaging oneself. The Duchess of Windsor was the (barely) animated embodiment of her own rule. It took a full decade for women to prove to themselves that she was wrong. Medically speaking, you *can* be too thin. (What's more, the social conscience of the seventies has taught us that you can be too rich as well.)

From the vantage point of the late fifties and early sixties, the truly liberated body was a long way off. Thin was in, and that was that. Women hardly had time to buy a new bathroom scale and decide which diet to crash. They had bought the superthin image along with the lock on the refrigerator door.

chapter 3

fear of fat

At what point did dieting turn the corner from health concern into national obsession? The trend began as soon as women were sprung from their corsets back in the early part of the century. Monarchs of Paris fashion kept the momentum going with hobble skirts and a passion for tiny waists, until the French expression *gardez la ligne* became commonplace. But it was the twenties that launched the full-scale attack on excess flab. You couldn't dance like Irene Castle if your body was boosting excess baggage. Josephine Baker's spare form, looking as though it were carved from a single piece of ebony, was the rage. In the jazz age, woman's preoccupation was keeping her own version of the "new shape" as flat as possible, both fore and aft. Measurements became important. Whereas, in 1917, a scale advertised in *Vogue* announced its effectiveness as a way of keeping one's eye on one's weight for health reasons alone, it was not until the early twenties that the calorie was a known quantity and reducing was something women *had* to do. By then, dieting for looks instead of mere well-being was already a national craze. *Vogue*'s postwar decree became a way of life: "Bust—flat. Waist—au naturel. Hips—none." Moreover, in order to be young and fashionable, it was desirable to look poor—within limits. Both states of mind were new. In the Edwardian era youth was never a liability, but neither was it a condition to be coveted, let alone preserved. In 1920, however, when the suffragettes had won their vote, the world must have seemed young all over again to women. The war behind them, economic and political equality beckoned ahead. For reasons of identification, perhaps, women evidenced a desire to look as much as possible like men. Fashion followed suit and women followed regimes. The pancake silhouette, cloche pulled down well over the face, made all females look somehow the same age, whether they were fifteen or fifty. Youth and slenderness became inextricably associated in imagination if not in fact. As to looking poor, that became fashionable through the good offices of Chanel, whose caved-in suits and little black cocktail dresses were the emblems of the age. Her jerseys clung to the body and emphasized slenderness better than traditional fabrics. Jersey was a democratic cloth, unresponsive to ornament and totally unsuited to the kind of display and magnificence that had characterized the creations of Poiret and his pre-World War I confrères. Jersey was practical and cheap, it connoted the new equality, but more than that, it provided the very first examples of "body dressing" in this century.

As popular as it had already become in the thirties, dieting at first was devoid of any but the most superficial nutritional knowledge. Women were on their own about what to eat, or they relied on their physician's scanty knowledge. Health farms in Europe were devoted to cures for physical ailments or nervous disorders. Overweight had not yet become a medical problem on a scale large enough to interest the spas, whose attention was still fixed on providing royalty, harried business-men, and overworked cocottes with luxurious respite from the stressful world outside. But slowly science was publicizing its views on balanced meals and the dangers of starches and overgarnished dishes. Escoffier's multicoursed menus had gone out of style with the Edwardian era. Simplicity and speed were in. American eating habits were changing rapidly.

The fast-food concept may be said to have begun as early as 1914, when the first cafeteria opened in Los Angeles. Auto-mats and diners followed in profusion, and 1941 marked the first drive-in restaurant where sandwiches were served by drum majorettes. Working women ate lunch alongside men in canteens. In America's upper classes, dressing for dinner became an anachronism in all but the most resolutely stuffy circles. Velocity, the sheer speed at which things were moving, was altering life at its most basic; it was shortening mealtimes, thus cutting into the hours formerly employed in the acquisi-tion of excess avoirdupois.

The new search for shape provided the momentum for a series of weight-related discoveries that we take for granted today. In 1938, for example, the notion that suppression of fats leads to weight loss was first publicized. A decade later marked the advent of the first diuretics. In 1950, thyroid extract was first used in connection with obesity. The next two years saw the invention of appetite-cutting medicines and biscuits. And by the early 1960's, dieting had become a way of life. Clothes were cut with high armholes and fit close to the body.

The decades between the twenties and sixties saw a bewildering succession of diets, some sound, most unbalanced, a few frankly dangerous: banana diets, grapefruit diets, ice-cream diets, the Du Pont low-carbohydrate diet, the Duke rice diet, the Mayo Clinic diet, the Hambletonian diet, Gaylord Hauser's raw vegetable diet, the Drinking Man's diet, the Air Force diet, Dr. Stillman's, Dr. Atkins' and Dr. Yudkin's diets, the Dr. Soloman Easy No-Risk diet, Dr. Friedman's advice to "grab your mate, not your plate," Mary Ann Crenshaw's Lecithin, Cider Vinegar, and B_6 diet. And as a last resort, supervised starvation or intestinal bypass surgery. On and on it goes, straight into the seventies and no doubt beyond, borne on wings of the fast buck. Most of the gimmicks are addressed either to particular addictions (such as ice cream, bananas) or encourage the dieter to keep on feeding his little indulgences (alcohol) in the hope they will diminish his major ones. For some promoters, the financial risks seem well worth taking in an industry that has ballooned to over $10 billion a year. The lucky ones who backed safe diets merely got rich; those less lucky spent their proceeds in legal hassles. Still others are undergoing Nader-like raids on their weight-loss pills or gadgetry.

Some methods, highly successful as well as lucrative, do address themselves to the whole fat person and his problem instead of to food alone. These use the group therapy system:

Weight Watchers, TOPS (Take Off Pounds Sensibly), Overeaters Anonymous, the behavior modification method. But no matter how the fat problem is attacked, the basic premise remains the same: Diets are a quick fix for what is invariably a long-term concern, both the individual's and the nation's.

The forties, fifties, and early sixties put up with the advent of fast food until, having become a behemoth industry, it threatened our national health. By the mid-sixties the food industry, against all admonitions from nutritionists, had loosed an incredible flood of junk food on the market. By the time of the White House Conference on Food, Nutrition, and Health in 1969, the poor quality of food eaten by the American public was creating headlines. And fat. The obesity problem had become a major concern to health professionals. Thirty percent of the American population is now considered overweight. In no other society of such affluence is the diet so inadequate and food so abused. And in no other country is obesity so despised. The battle of the bulge is being waged unceasingly—by doctors, journalists, pharmaceutical manufacturers—against the junk food industry, against the psychological predisposition to overeating, against nutritional ignorance.

"Organic" food, previously considered to be on the lunatic fringe of our eating habits, came to the fore in a massive attack against the fatty hamburgers and chemical malteds of our roadside stands, against junk food, bleached flour, white sugar, too much carbohydrate, and the increasing mechanization of eating in general. This countercultural thrust did make a dent in our feeding patterns and in our consciousness of nutrition. The organic food movement also pointed up dramatically the dangers of overconsumption of animal protein and sugar, both of which are held suspect in this country's high incidence of obesity and heart attack. In no other country are there still to be found such extremes of fat and thin. It might almost be said that no other nation attaches so much importance to weight control. Insurance company charts, weight limitations for certain professions, physicians' scoldings, and the embarrassment of searching for properly fitting clothes all conspire to increase the psychological imperative for slenderness.

But health concerns served only as further hype for the diet hysteria. Before the sixties had arrived at middle age, dieting had taken on the proportions of a nationwide contest. Within a certain set of women, fear of fat was becoming a disease. Outrageous and dangerous methods for losing weight were in practice in superskinny circles. Amphetamines, diuretics, Ex-Lax were going down some of the most sophisticated throats. So were fingers. The rediscovery of vomiting after overeating —the ancient Roman method—was fast becoming a conditioned reflex. For the confirmed food addict, hypnosis was having a field day; European sleep clinics promised weight loss through snoozing; English fat farms administered high-colonic enemas; American and South American plastic surgeons wielded the knife. Weight doctors' offices were as crowded as gyms and exercise salons. Mrs. Gloria Vanderbilt Cooper was photographed at ninety-eight pounds by *Women's Wear Daily.* It was reported that her husband was unhappy about her looks. But to fashion leaders, the drive to out-skinny their friends supplied relentless motivation to diet, bringing the competition for poundlessness to an all-time pitch.

The mid-sixties, moreover, was the era of Youthquake. The frenzy to look young had seized matrons of all sizes and ages. While the legitimately youthful were into brown rice life-styles and didn't mind being a little plump, their mothers had swallowed the media pronouncements hook, line, and sinker. They became slaves to a cult that was aggressively packaged and displayed by all the circuitry available to the worlds of fashion, advertising, and film. Evidently the only way to reach the nirvana of youth was by counting calories. As a marketing device, the diet line worked with devastating success. The most complimentary thing one could say to a woman of fashion in the 1960's was "You've lost weight." For the magic diet formula to work, its efficacy had to be acknowledged by others. And proof that it was working, support for its cause, came mostly from other women, while the opinions of husbands like Mrs. Cooper's were being ignored. Thus the mania flourished and was enshrined by the images we lived with every day, the advertising icons of the sixties projected by a media gone wild with enthusiasm for fatlessness. The word "diet" on the cover of a magazine produced a Pavlovian reaction on the part of women purchasers. Editors soon discovered that it sold more copies than sex.

Signs of the diet disease were everywhere. They were part of a psychology of perfection which comes from the inability of individuals to see themselves as they really are. That this inability can acquire the dimensions of a psychopathic condition seems almost incredible, but it can and often does. Anorexia nervosa is just such a disease. The occasional teen-ager who begins by a little innocent crash dieting can, if predisposed to the ailment, end up dying from self-starvation. Compulsive noneating, the almost total refusal of food, and its accompanying binge and vomiting sessions, is symptomatic of this sickness, which was first described to the public by psychoanalyst Dr. Hilde Bruch in her book *Eating Disorders*. Since then the popular press has published many alarmist accounts by and about young women who have suffered anorexia. Although no statistics exist on the frequency of the disease, most doctors with urban practices have encountered it in some form or another and find it definitely on the rise. The most striking feature of the affliction is that it is characteristic of bright, otherwise attractive, achievement-oriented girls.

The central pathology in anorexia, just as in any relentless pursuit of extreme thinness, is the inability to form a realistic picture of the self. *Fausses maigres,* as the French call those who force their weight down below what is natural for the body structure, are characteristically women who cannot rely on their own inner resources, who are constantly in search of affirmation of themselves from the outside world. They may have basic identity problems that threaten to put them out of control; hence the incredible rigidity with which they deny themselves food. A body can adjust to this only by its eventual inability to feel hunger. The superthin woman may lack a satisfactory sexual identity; one of the common symptoms of anorexia is the complete absence of menstrual periods. She may need to assert her power over others and unconsciously hit upon being thin as a way of proving her own superiority, willpower, and social acceptance. In any case, she rarely is able to see herself as other people see her. At eighty or a hundred pounds she looks beautiful to herself and is unable to gain weight for fear of relinquishing the only control she feels she has over her own body and its life. This is her reward, the sole measure of her self-esteem, and one of the only ways in which she is able to know herself. Perfectionism plays a role here, too, for it is most often those women who have been "ideal" children, students, and, later, wives who seem most susceptible to the superthin syndrome.

Part of this syndrome is a carry-over from the 1950's. In those days, the ideal was elegance, which, in turn, may have owed a lot to the surface polish, the newness and lack of muss, the movieland look of the preceding decade. In any case, the fifties fashion magazines set us all to dreaming of the mysteries of elegance. Public figures with Almanach de Gotha names were hired to define elegance for American readers. There were lists of things to do or to buy in order to achieve it. Whatever it was, elegance was a quality to be cultivated by the sweat of one's brow if one was not born with it. Unlike "good bones," this quality, the fashion journals seemed to be saying, could be had by observation, by hard work or, if one was lucky, by breathing the right air. Above all, it could be had by being thin.

Audrey Hepburn, her attenuated silhouette unmistakable in a concave Givenchy, was the idol of elegance in the late fifties and early sixties. Close on her heels came Jacqueline Kennedy, and the reign of breeding and the semiwhisper was in. Mrs. Kennedy's counterpart was the upper-middle-class Park Avenue housewife for whom elegance meant buying expensive clothes, cultivating an inexpensive figure, and being groomed to the point of absolutism, where any impulsive movement, any stray hair, or any possibility of adapting to imperfections in the weather was severely trammeled. Her hair was by Kenneth, her face by Pablo, her figure by Kounovsky, and her personality, if she had any left, did not project itself beyond those restrictions. Indeed, she was those restrictions. She shopped at Valentino for her size eights. When the scales recorded an ounce above 110, she ceased to shop until the scales behaved. She never entered stores where it was possible to make a mistake on a label, where one might be taken in by unchic merchandise. Much of her effort went into making sure this never happened. While shopping, her face wore a look of hunted envy. The haute boutiques of Madison Avenue were jammed with women in their forties and fifties, impeccable in sleeveless wools labeled "nifty" by *Bazaar*, hems well above the kneecap, double rows of brass buttons on the chest, bracketed by lizard handbags and shoes. These women had admirable backbones and bodies desiccated by a decade of dieting. Their discipline was evident in the set mouth, in a grit-your-teeth perfection which looked as though someone had gone over them with lacquer from a spray can. One mused that their clothes would remain upright if they walked out of them. One feared for these ladies in times of natural disaster, like wind or rain—or trying on a turtlenecked sweater over Kenneth's $25 "do." These women could be assigned almost any age but child, and they were all in search of some mythological chronology, some magical year set as far back in time as each woman's need dictated.

It was American women who seemed to be going through most of the agony of trying to stay youthful. The buying of clothes, the cultivation of the figure were ordeals at which they worked hard. Did they perhaps not see *themselves* when they tried on clothes, but only another image, a hope for something else? Were they not pleased—the ones of overaverage income —to be the healthiest and probably the slenderest race of women on earth, with every possible help emerging, on their behalf, from laboratories and salons all over the country? But when they looked into the glass it was with anger that they stared back at themselves. Perhaps they had hoped to solve the problem of how to look by enthroning perfect grooming as the solution. Anyone with a trim outline can get away with practically anything, such is our national reverence for the clean and neat. (Note that this is not what in Europe is called *soignée*. There, it means more than "cared for"—a *soignée* woman still looks that way with her hair a mess.) Our good grooming is perfectionism to the point of stasis, as though a fixative had immobilized the whole body. This was the look of women whose lives were confined. You could be sure that they were up to nothing at all. Their lives were ruled by don'ts: no dessert; no entrances without makeup; "no greens, can't wear green"; no children running around those *House and Garden* interiors to mess up the furniture; no large animals—only lap dogs. Until ten years ago women seemed imprisoned by perfectionism, much of it from lack of knowing the self well enough to say "yes" to its dictates. This feminine failing was compounded, in the early sixties, by the fact that women *prided* themselves on looking as the fashion press intended them to look. We have, still, the same psychology about food and wine. We have learned to admire only the product that is standardized. American vineyards advertise that their wines taste the same no matter where they were bottled. The FDA rules our taste buds by the same methods. What has always been the goal in American industry was, in the sixties, merely extended to the ideal human shape.

Why, in Europe, were things so different? France is a country that glories in its three hundred varieties of cheese, in good and bad wine years. Clothes, even in industrialized France, have always been regarded as an essentially anti-assembly line matter. Why else would a woman buy a ready-to-wear dress but change its belt or collar before donning it, much as she would fiddle with a recipe? In France, how one looks is still intensely personalized, whereas, in this country, uniformity has been one way of becoming part of society. European women talk with their hands. Their hair is messy. Things don't match. They know *ce qui me va*, what becomes *me*. They are in perpetual motion, but there is discipline. The difference has been that the discipline is in their lives, not in their faces.

To some extent, European influence was just beginning to affect the way American women wanted to look by the mid-sixties. The Italians, with their turbulent hair, black-smudged eyeshadows, and pale lipstick, were making news. Suddenly, in a *Vogue* editorial entitled "The Changing Eye," it was noticed that standards of beauty were multiplying. There was to be no more of the Dresden look of perfectionism, no labored artifice. Mannequinlike hauteur was out. Models began to move in their clothes in the pages of fashion magazines. People still talked about elegance, the word was still around, lip service was given to it as an ideal, but it stopped being the drop-dead goal to strive for.

Part of the reason for the demise of artificial elegance was that the desire for perfection always comes from lack of confidence. The conformist fifties and early sixties, when everyone took comfort in being lost in the crowd, were over. The initiative in clothes design had devolved, at last, on America. American women were shedding their uncertainties about dress. Today a certain elegance survives, but it represents the aspiration of only a very small—and older—minority of women. By and large, elegance is no longer much associated with clothes, but has instead been reduced to an ephemeral social quality. As such, it has gone the way of manners and other vanishing standards. When it comes to a way to look, the words "style" and "dash" have taken its place in the fashion vocabulary. In our time, American women are almost indistinguishable from their European counterparts in this matter of style. But until the sixties were half over, Americans were different. They were apprenticing, learning how to trust being themselves.

On the question of figures, however, we still seem to be hung up on perfection. Lessons learned from Europe about movement and vitality in clothes have yet to be completely absorbed by American bodies. Our confusion about weight is evident in the extent of the obsession itself. For years European aestheticians, cellulite experts, and plastic surgeons have exploited the American woman's insecurity about her figure. With characteristic savoir faire, the French have exported their methods for firming and reducing or increasing one's measurements to this country, where they have been received with the usual reverence for continental mystique. The list of "cures" offered the American woman is staggering: hydrotherapy, electrotherapy, aromatherapy (the use of concentrated plant extracts), pressure therapy, thalassotherapy (underwater massage), cyclo massage, and massage with jets of air or of water; baths of ozone, algae, steam, immersion in boiling or freezing water; sauna; "biological" remodeling; Scotch hose, "vibro-relaxing" drainage, paraffin treatments, breathing exercises, gymnastics, acupuncture, thermal and sun cures, reducing creams, friction gloves, homeopathic cures, water cures, sleep cures, hypnosis, dream recall, pep pills, diuretics, thyroid extracts, appetite-reducing biscuits and medications; immunological serums, ionizations (penetration of substances by electrical current); mini-piqures and multi-injections for local fat. Technology follows methodology: Here, salons devoted to the body beautiful are apt to bristle with numerous French electric machines and devices designed to roll, bathe, pressure, or shock into shape. Needless to say, much of this equipment as well as some of the methods cited above have not passed muster with the FDA for entry into this country and must be smuggled in. But such is the faith placed in mechanization by a certain kind of American woman that it would seem, after a glance at the services offered by many nationally known body shops, that the simple notions of diet and self-imposed exercise have still not crossed her mind.

Some of us are positively looped on self-help techniques. We have assimilated and even surpassed the Europeans in the ingenuity and complexity of our weight-loss technology. Every health club feels it must sport at least a hundred square yards of polished chrome machinery designed to buff, roll, and yank its users into sylphlike bliss.

Why is this happening in America? The sad answer is that here the wish for public acceptance is still strong, a distorted body image still common, the achievement of "ideal" beauty still desirable at all costs. Consequently, the single standard for bodies—perfection, in other words—reigns among the fashionable. The advertising culture has set up our ideals, making a whole nation of perfectly acceptable women feel that they are unglamorous if their measurements don't comply with the height-weight charts. Self-acceptance becomes a real achievement, to be won against the overwhelming odds of media brainwashing.

Even in these semiliberated times, few women in this country have bothered to observe the close connection between the two halves of that famous quote about being rich and thin. The fact is that the conditions are not only related but mutually dependent. It is no accident that superthin was a sixties' phenomenon. As the economy boomed, the old caste system in this country was beginning to crumble. Whereas in the past, dress was status, the mid-sixties thrust forward the thin body as the newest form of social Brahminism. "Class" was ceasing to operate on a clothes level, but had raised the beautiful body to new heights as a status symbol.

Underneath the cultivation of thinness were more generalized economic perquisites; it went without saying that one had to be rich in order to escape the fear of not having enough food—the fear most poor people are prey to. Weighing ninety-eight pounds meant one of two things—either you were very sick or you were very rich. If it happened to be the latter, you were accepted by a certain segment of society that recognized the code: Eating little meant you had plenty. Courting starvation was understood as a sort of subliminal defiance of the scarcity that existed elsewhere. It was perhaps even a manifestation of guilt for that scarcity. But above all, emaciation, in a reversal of all historical precedent, became Class. Of course the clothes designers were ecstatic, for clothes look better when bones show. The fashion complex was delighted: The editors of influential women's magazines, the photographers, models, and socialites who helped to sell clothes, were riding on what later looked like a decade of borrowed time.

chapter 4

the superthin
syndrome

How did the superthin syndrome come to pass? What was it about the 1960's that produced a mindless anomie in the American woman, a sort of anesthesia that led her to starve for the sake of fashion? True, fat is a health hazard. True, obesity makes us recoil in a fit of disgust. But all that aside, women were dying to pry themselves into a size eight at any cost. Why?

For one thing, women weren't quite yet themselves. We hadn't had time to think out to whom our bodies really belonged. We needed to be told how to look, which single way to present ourselves. In an era that standardized the possibilities, the decision had already been made for us. The primary deterrent to fat resided in the media message.

Thin, in body language, has always represented activity, speed, velocity. And by association, thin has become linked with success, which comes about through nothing less than untiring activity. Similarly, thinness is equated with youth, the look of adolescence. Perhaps it is this more than any other factor that accounts for the peculiarly American preoccupation with being built like a rail. Our high-speed mechanized society still lives very much by the Protestant ethic, rejecting indolence, despising the love of immobility. Our desire for slenderness is a sign—at least to ourselves—that we eschew laziness and desire success. There is a striking visual parallel as well, which links our ideal body type to the kind of architecture we are best known for—skyscrapers. It is our urban centers that are meccas for success-bound youth. Those skyscrapers are where the money is. New York has become, perhaps more than any other, the city most absolutely of our time. Its Machine Gothic architecture has a strenuous magic; its energy, its symbolism seem contained within our bodies. We aim to be linear, structured, engineered, clean-lined like our buildings.

The media supplies us with visual inducements to slenderness everywhere we look. The girl who gets her man in deodorant advertisements is a size seven to begin with. Magazine housewives, though they may cook up a storm for their families, appear to survive on celery. Our current movie queens are often ex-models: Ali MacGraw, Cybill Shepherd, Candice Bergen, and perhaps Margaux Hemingway, if her reviews improve. As for the recent past, there are always the films of Audrey Hepburn to provide inspiration for the dieter.

Jacqueline Kennedy Onassis' *crudité* luncheons at New York's *Grenouille* have passed into legend, and her own tall but bony frame has served so many terms as clotheshorse for the popular imagination that it must be permanently engraved on the retina of every magazine reader in the country.

From time to time, department stores that know their customers and want to score in the fashion world will use the direct hit method, as in this ad for designer Rena Rowan's clothes: "Her clients want the lithe, willowy look, that bony-model chic [heavy letter emphasis here], and they're willing to live on yogurt to get it." The calculation is obvious: If you don't live on yogurt or something equally noncaloric, you aren't entitled to an ounce of the moral superiority acquired by those who do. Nor are you eligible for that feeling of accelerated power, of exaltation even, which characterizes those who are thinner than their confreres. Quite simply, you are not in a position to lord it over other, unhappily fatter beings. The high moral tone of the diet industry is obviously something to be reckoned with in these days when other kinds of morality have been dispensed with. In some ways our obsession with slenderness resembles the eternal concern with being suitably costumed for an occasion. It was Herbert Spencer who wrote that "the consciousness of being perfectly dressed may bestow a peace such as religion cannot give." For many, the consciousness of being thin may do the same.

The absolute superstar of media manipulation has been without question the mannequin. Since the end of World War II it is she who has been most responsible for displaying the ideal body type for other women to follow. When she began her public career in the entourage of the famous French dress designer Paul Poiret, it was as a promotional gag. But Poiret's tour of Europe in the early 1900's with nine of his models beside him was a raging success. The girls were treated like celebrities in every capital, showered with roses and champagne on their arrival, and feted like the Duncans and Duses of the day. Modeling clothes began to seem like a combination of good business and glamorous opportunity. For the girl herself, free publicity was often enough to compensate for poor pay. In the dawn of the Age of the Media it was easier to get onto the runway than into the cinematic or theatrical spotlight. Today modeling might provide even more publicity; one has to pay to go to the movies or theater, but fashion showings are regularly covered by television, newspapers, and magazines.

The French couture, by following Poiret's example of using live models to show his clothes, powerfully influenced the way women wanted to look. In 1924, Jean Patou came to the United States and returned to Paris with six beautiful American mannequins. His preference for the athletic, boyish figure started a tremendous controversy abroad, where the feminine ideal was still more rounded and altogether more petite. But it is to Patou that credit must be given for launching the sports craze in France, and with it, as we have seen, the changes in body style on both continents. Such was the attention then paid to mannequins that Colette could write, "Among all the modernized aspects of the most luxurious of industries, the model, a vestige of voluptuous barbarianism, is like some plunder-laden prey. She is the object of unbridled regard, a living bait, the passive realization of an ideal . . . and her job is to excite covetousness."

In the twenties, the film industry was still in its infancy. It was not until the thirties and forties that movie stars usurped the field as goddesses and beauty queens to be emulated by women everywhere. There were, first and foremost, Garbo and Dietrich, who in their own way must rank with Brigitte Bardot and Marilyn Monroe as the all-time sex bombs of the screen. But in between appeared Ginger Rogers, Loretta Young, Joan Crawford and her ankle straps, Norma Shearer, Hedy Lamarr, Shirley Temple's curls, Bette Davis' voice, Katharine Hepburn's cheekbones. By the fifties we were again perusing fashion magazines for inspiration, and the face and figure most familiar to the fashion- and body-conscious woman of the time was that of Sunny Hartnett, followed by flame-haired Suzy Parker. The sixties saw the introduction of the socialite-as-model in the pages of commercial magazines not, as in *Town and Country*, to exemplify a certain life-style, but purely and simply to sell clothes. Then came Verushka, Jean Shrimpton, the eccentric Penelope Tree. Each had her own style and a certain peculiar individuality of face or body that made her imprint on the popular imagination all the more firm. The concept of the model as a personality was launched.

By the early sixties fashion magazines had begun to identify their mannequins by name. Young women who, a decade earlier, might have wanted to be in the movies, or failing that to be airline stewardesses, were now frantic to become models. They disembarked in New York City by the busload, only to return to their families in Ohio or Kansas, their money and their hopes equally drained. Fierce competition only made the profession more glamorous. For an era in which instant fame was possible, every young woman wanted to have a go at the media, that capricious maker and breaker of illusions. And the unacknowledged function of those who made it was to permit identification with that very fame—to extend an aura of attainability to all those out there who reacted to the come-on of money, publicity, and the Big Lights.

The film *Blow-Up* did nothing to demystify the profession. We were into an era that worshiped kinky behavior and far-out looks. The classically beautiful face no longer mattered; a Roman nose, an exaggerated mouth, a narrow skull all increased the appeal of extravagant layouts in exotic places for impossible clothes. What did matter was that the model's body be thin to the point of unreality. Verushka's six-foot frame led the field, but was soon surpassed in a torrent of Twiggymania.

Twiggy: that farouche boychild with the sad eyes, who told an interviewer at the height of her success that she didn't think she had a future. A common publicity puppet? A physical freak? But there was that extraordinarily vulnerable length of bone, the perfectly round skull with eyes drowning at the corners. What will she look like after thirty, her uncanny appeal to the young long past? Even in 1968, she said with her own grave candor, "I s'pose most of my fans are girls. I couldn't possibly be a sex symbol, could I, with a skinny figure like mine. . . ." Her wistful street intelligence remains essentially a phenomenon of extreme youth, all the youth of the sixties, when she was playchild of the Western world.

Prompted by Twiggymania, women began taking themselves back to the body shop for maintenance and repairs. The desire to be—and keep—thin has spawned a whole new segment of the beauty business. There are shops in every category: diet, cellulite, gymnastics, dance, old-fashioned exercise. Then there are the beauty spas that incorporate some or all of these. Finally, there are the most expensive body shops of all, those of the plastic surgeons.

The latest curiosity in the wake of the weight-reducing

mania is a condition first reported in medical journals in the 1920's, known as cellulite. Attributed by many to our chemical-laden diet, cellulite may be nothing more than a euphemism for localized fat. But it presents the disturbing appearance of permanent bulges at thigh tops, backs of knees, upper arms, and at the nape of the neck. The skin of these areas is dimpled like orange peel or like cottage cheese, and is by no means a disfigurement of the obese alone. Ironically, cellulite may show up on women who are otherwise very thin. It has been described as a sort of organized fat, encysted in little watertight compartments under the skin. Medically, it may involve problems of the connective tissues, and it does not seem to respond to ordinary diet and exercise. One of its most vocal spokesmen in this country is Dr. Robert Wallis, whose own practice is now predominantly devoted to treating cellulite. Dr. Wallis feels that the condition, being one very rarely found in men, is closely connected with the female's genital life. In his experience, 12 percent of the women whom he diagnoses as having cellulite acquire it at about the time of puberty, 19 percent when they begin to take the Pill, another 27 percent during or after pregnancy, 17 percent after menopause. For the remaining 25 percent, onset of cellulite, in his judgment, can be put down to hereditary diabetes, obesity, or various types of inflammation. Whenever it is acquired, it is usually accompanied by dysfunction of carbohydrate metabolism, and very often by edema, or collection of water in the tissues.

The controversy between French and American doctors on the subject of cellulite centers on whether or not it really differs from ordinary fatty tissue. U.S.-trained physicians say that cellulite is just plain fat. The dimpling effect may be caused by loss of skin elasticity, a normal—and irreversible—accompaniment of the aging process. Its treatment, they feel, is subject to the usual folderol that accompanies cosmetic problems that have no recognized basis in medicine. They look askance at French doctors who have pioneered the research on cellulite with a vengeance, no doubt making a fortune on treatments along the way. Needless to say, the French practitioners, headed by doctors Michel Pistor and Pierre Dukon, feel differently. They regard cellulite as a possible symptom of endocrine and metabolic imbalance. Many of the tests they have run show estrogen excess, and they have found that this must be corrected before the fatty deposits disappear. Paris physicians Léon Cariel and Jean-Paul Boutron have set up a clinic called Banville 19 for the treatment of cellulite. At capacity, the clinic takes 120 patients a day, giving each a half-hour treatment that costs about $20. Most women need about twenty sessions, some thirty, making this an expensive cure.

It can be painful to boot. The two methods most in use are ionization and multi-injections. Ionization involves application to the affected zones of plates wrapped in sponge soaked in a mix of enzymes, thyroid extract, or heparin. The plates are then wired to a medium-frequency generator whose electric current causes penetration of the medicines. The sensation is one of a slight muscle tic in the area under the plates. Multi-injections are done with short needles, seven to eighteen of them at a visit. Serums used depend on the individual case, but may comprise a mix of 2 percent procain, iodine, artichoke extract, or gonadotrophin. A maximum of about 40 cc of the cocktail is injected at one time. In addition to these two popular methods of treatment, there are others that can be administered without medical supervision. Hot seawater baths laced with algae are offered at the French spa-clinics of Quiberon and Trouville. Another method uses heat that is passed through plastic-wrapped paraffin by a timed ultrasonic machine. Other cures involve special massages with ivy extracts; substances bearing mysterious labels such as BL 191 or HCG; methods with names like oxydrothermalism; various pieces of equipment labelled "Diapulse" and "Theraffin"; or, simplest of all, diets eliminating salts, sweets, tobacco, and alcohol.

One of the most interesting and controversial partisans of the cellulite-as-disease cult in France is the eminent healer Maurice Messagué. He feels, as do most doctors treating the condition, that stress is a major factor contributing to the enormous increase in incidence of cellulite. Messagué, not surprisingly, singles out chemicals from the diet. He feels that proper breathing and elimination are also important in preventing the condition.

However virulent the disagreement between French and American doctors on the subject of cellulite, the condition may be a telling indicator—whether cosmetic or medical—of our bodies' response to the modern pace of life. No one is apt to dispute that, whatever its origins, appearance on the thighs of fatty "riding breeches" is unsightly, if not serious. But it is comforting to know that, whatever you choose to call it, a sagging body will generally respond to a healthful and practical regime that includes chemical-free diet, light exercise, proper massage, correct breathing and elimination habits, and relaxation. Professional cures are reportedly effective in some cases, but there is no question that they should be in the hands of a competent doctor. At the moment, books on do-it-yourself treatment are flooding the market. Cosmetic and pharmaceutical companies in Europe are making a financial killing on cellulite-related products, the majority of which are worthless. In all probability the American medical establishment will not recognize cellulite as a disease. But whether or not it is just "tension fat," it is a symptom of our times and one that can be alleviated, at the very least, by a healthier way of life.

There are many women, however, who seek shortcuts to weight loss, such as fasting and surgery. For those willing to go cold turkey, there are a number of farms catering to the starvation approach, notably Pawling Manor near New York City and establishments in Texas and Florida. Investigations have turned up occasional instances of malpractice and misrepresentation at the fasting farms, so one should make careful inquiry before enrolling. In any case, total starvation is a tricky undertaking which must be done under the most reliable medical supervision.

As for the surgeon's knife, it no longer occupies the position of last resort except in the case of the intestinal bypass operation for the very obese. Nonetheless, the plastic surgeon should not be considered a knife-wielding wizard, on hand to take in a seam here and a tuck there after a life of excess. Body sculpting is still being perfected and is not as developed an art as facial cosmetic surgery. The problem of scarring is major and must always be balanced against anticipated improvement in overall body aesthetics. Hospitalization for body surgery requires anywhere from one to three weeks; and the patient may be homebound or very restricted in activity for another few weeks, though sutures are generally removed within ten to twenty-one days. Finally, the cost of any major and extensive surgery is obviously high, running from about $2,000 to $5,000 for a simple procedure. A complete body overhaul could cost $30,000. If this is not enough to discourage the prospective fat fighter, there is the additional danger of general anesthesia, and the length of time needed to perform the operation, usually two to six hours.

What can the body surgeons do? There are basically three kinds of procedures: mammaplasty, to reduce or augment breast size; stomach reduction or lipectomy, performed when there is a sizable apron of fat left from weight loss or pregnancy; and arm or thigh reduction. Calves and ankles cannot be altered by surgery. The silicone injection route to bigger breasts has been discredited ever since it was found that silicone expands in heat and can cause cancer. Presently, a decrease in bust measurement is more often sought.

Fashions in bodies change as well as styles in the clothing we put on them. A Hollywood surgeon reports that legs were all important in the Betty Grable days, before anything much could be done to improve their contours. By the early 1950's, however, when plastic surgery had made rapid strides, the demand was for larger breasts. Today the trend is toward lifting whatever sags, wherever it can be done.

Who are the skillful men who perform these operations, and what are their clients like? In the United States, the general profile of a woman who wants plastic surgery is apt to include two factors: She is usually over thirty, and in many cases her husband's attention is beginning to wander. Unlike the candidate for face-lift, body surgery patients are not necessarily in the middle-aged category. Many just want to enjoy being in a bikini after losing a hundred or so pounds. Some, inevitably, are hung up on bodily perfection. They are the ones who are most extensively quizzed by the surgeon before he decides whether to operate, for the psychological element is overwhelming in such cases. They are also the chronic returnees to surgery. No matter how much their looks are improved, they are impossible to satisfy. A clever medical imagination will spot this anxiety at once, however, and prescribe help for the mind rather than for the physique.

Some surgeons have acquired a reputation as body sculptors to the jet set. Dr. Ivo Pitanguy is one of this elite, and the fact that his headquarters is in Rio de Janeiro causes no great problem for the world-traveler types who make the pilgrimage to seek him out. He is said to have performed his body-lifts on some of the world's most prominent socialites and a string of international film stars. Luciana Pignatelli Avedon, the jet set's newest entry in the competitive world of beauty reportage, is the only notable to admit to having had practically "everything" lifted or reshaped by Dr. P. But the surgeon has not restricted his practice to the Beautiful People: There is the example of some three hundred children left terribly scarred by a circus fire in Rio ten years ago. For them Dr. Pitanguy closed his luxurious clinic for three months and devoted himself to reconstructing their faces and burned bodies.

The Pitanguy Clinic takes only thirty-two patients at a time. The all-private facilities cost from $60 to $100 a day, a bargain when compared to most good American hospital rooms. There is always a flock of surgeons-in-training who are on site to observe Pitanguy; in addition, he teaches at the Catholic University in Rio. But his main contribution to the field may be in the techniques he uses to hide a thigh-lift. His incisions are made primarily under the buttocks, rather than vertically down the insides of the legs, thus permitting the patient the pleasure of bikini-wearing when the seams have healed.

Plastic surgery will never be popular as a solution for body problems; the pain and expense rule that out. For even the well heeled, the proverbial ounce of prevention is the only permanent way to cure an excess of pounds.

But as long as there are women of means, there will always be cures for the "higher-priced spread." Should the American way of eating result in Hostess Cupcake buttocks and Twinkie-shaped legs, should the temptation to watch television too often overcome the desire to exercise, the entire problem can be left to experts—at a price. A complete overhaul is the business of expensive body shops, those spas and health farms which are beginning to dot the greener and sunnier spaces on the American map.

The decision to do something about a body problem, whether an extra chin, riding breeches at the hips, or poor posture, invariably indicates the desire for a deeper sort of change as well. Most women know perfectly well that lack of exercise leads to flab as surely as eating nothing but fried food ruins the complexion. Those who spend a week at a spa don't go for basic instruction, therefore. They go for reinstruction, a repatterning of all the bad and seductive habits indulged in for too long. They are lured by premises in which no alcohol, cigarettes, or chocolates are allowed to appear. They go in order to reaffirm to themselves that living in a healthier manner can be a pleasure and does not always mean deprivation. Of course they also go to lose a few inches around the hips, or to tone up the skin, or simply to get away from the phone and relax a little. Basically they want to be taken under the wing of that stern schoolmistress who permits no cheating on the water exercises. And finally, they want the luxury of not having to make any but the most frivolous decisions, of relinquishing responsibility for others—husbands, children, friends, committees—so that their attention is free to devolve upon themselves alone.

It is temporary, that world in which one can afford to become a child again, fussed over by experts who, though paid, do care. All the breakfasts in bed, the scurrying to wake-up exercises in fluffy yellow bathrobes, all the attention to one's very own skin or figure problems, the companionable chatter around the tea table—all this must, inevitably, end when the stay is over. And that is the major drawback of the beauty farm: Lessons, though well learned, do not always survive the return to real life—especially in the case of the woman who treats the spa like a hospital in which meals simply arrive on a tray, thus removing most external cues to overeating. She is apt to be the yo-yo whose weight bounces up and down the scale depending upon her surroundings. Once she leaves the spa's hallowed premises, the battle with temptation resumes. Much better able to profit from the spa experience is the woman who admits to herself that she is going "on vacation," and expects to be pampered, to be freed from routine work, and is left only—as one is on a real vacation—with the freedom to focus on the physical and mental self. In this guise the spa resembles to a minor degree the psychiatrist's office.

Just what is the price of all this? And what sort of woman, of those able to afford it, chooses to spend her money this way? At Dallas' posh Greenhouse, the tab is a flat $1,000 a week plus 15 percent gratuities. The clientele is overwhelmingly business wives, and the money is, inevitably, their husbands'. Set down as if by mistake in a labyrinth of Texas-style freeways, the Greenhouse's calm structure seems all the more removed from twentieth-century realities. The living quarters for thirty-six guests are ranged around an enclosed pool framed by tall white southern-plantation-style colonnades. Fountains, courts, and gravel paths extend in every direction, stopping just short of the Dallas-Fort Worth expressway. But inside is a peach and mint-green fantasy; these *House and Garden* colors of eternal spring abound, from the drawing rooms with their antiqued elegance to expensive china services stacked in the stainless steel kitchen.

The Ginori porcelain dishes and what goes into them are the special province of Helen Corbitt, the Greenhouse's nutritionist, who must have originated more ways of serving up 850 calories than anyone in the business. Meals may be meager here, but they are undeniably attractive. Raw materials are of the finest quality. No additives are used in Mrs. Corbitt's kitchen; all vegetables are steamed or stir fried; all the melba toast and health breads are made right there. Guests breakfast on fresh fruit, a boiled egg, melba toast, coffee. At 10 A.M. there is an offering of potassium broth (said to work wonders for clearing the skin). The midday meal, eaten around the pool, may consist of a fresh artichoke filled with chicken, watercress salad, and orange and lemon sections for dessert. In the afternoon a fruit frappé is served: three ounces of fruit whizzed in a blender. Six thirty heralds "cocktails," which may be anything from raw vegetables to fresh caviar, accompanied by a beef bouillon. Dinner, always a formal meal done in full dress china and linen, laid in one of the drawing rooms, could be two ounces of meat, a vegetable soufflé, endive salad, and a dessert of poached pears or "sweetened wind" (another fruit-in-the-blender concoction). There is no way of knowing how many guests hide chocolate bars in their luggage, but at a tuition fee of $1,000 a week, one is not easily tempted to disobey school rules.

After dinner comes Culture. Lectures on music or painting, concerts or recitals, even small theater troupes make their appearance, while the audience sits like well-behaved children at an exclusive girls' school. There are fashion shows on the premises and a trip to Neiman-Marcus on Thursdays (the Greenhouse is run by the store in connection with the Great Southwest Corporation). Wednesdays end in "Quiet Night," with dinner served on a tray in one's room.

But the days are more arduous. At 7:30 A.M. a maid enters with breakfast. By 8:30 leotards are donned and everyone is at the pool for wake-up exercises. At nine o'clock, depending on one's individual program, one gets down to real business: massage, pedicure, hair or nails are done, or one can opt for another hour of gymnastics, this time to music. Then comes forty-five minutes of underwater exercise with giant beach-balls. After lunch, more activity; spot-reducing movements or rock-jazz. The time remaining until the evening meal is again spent in the whirlpool massage or under the hair dryer. Most women feel scheduled to the teeth, with no time to be bored. Some are downright exhausted by the end of the day. And there is always the misfit who is ready to emit a primal scream and climb over the walls at the first opportunity. Some returnees (and 66 percent of the women do return) form gossipy cliques that tend to exclude newcomers. Director Polly Williams is especially sensitive to this problem and does her utmost to spend time with those who, for reasons of background or shyness, feel neglected. But the ambience of the Greenhouse can have a way of alienating those who are not at ease to begin with. The decor is like that of a nouveau riche perfectionist re-creating a past she didn't fall heir to, and its intimidating hoaxiness is compensated for only by the extreme warmth of the staff. The personnel are, in addition, well trained in their specialties, and if a client remembers anything she has learned during her stay it will most likely be how to take care of her hair and face. The beauty department is run by Charles of the Ritz, and the emphasis here is on basic treatments rather than on off-to-the-party polish.

The Greenhouse is one of a handful of beauty farms for the superrich that draw an international clientele. Heading the field is still Elizabeth Arden's Maine Chance, the prototype after which the Greenhouse and a host of less expensive spas were modeled. It was here in the desert just outside Phoenix, Arizona, that the Arden staff developed the program of exercise, massage, and low-calorie meals that is now standard in every typical American spa.

In the over-a-thousand-dollars-a-week category is the Golden Door near Escondido, California. The emphasis here is occasionally as much on mind as on body. Recently, the Menninger Foundation has been running a periodic seminar at the Door, during which time the spa is open to couples. Additionally, for a ten-week span, men are admitted alone, a step that neither Maine Chance nor the Greenhouse has felt like venturing. The Door's specialties include hikes up a mountainside after a morning call at 6:20, and *then* breakfast in bed amidst the Japanese inn decor. The thirty guests are worked over by a staff of sixty, all proficient in the mysteries of facials, herbal baths of eucalyptus leaves, steam cabinets, and saunas—and in making the allotted 850 calories a day look like a sumptuous feast. Who checks in for the normal week's stay? Everyone from Maurice Stans, former Secretary of Commerce, while awaiting his Nixon campaign-contributions trial, to private-school headmasters, movie stars, captains of industry and their wives, and the Menninger psychiatrists.

Next in the ever-growing roster of U.S. spas are La Costa and Rancho de la Puerta in the San Diego area. Both are less programmed than their older models, but have available all the foregoing amenities and enough sports to rival the Club Méditérrannée: riding, golf, tennis, swimming, and hiking in the dry desert air. The Sanctuary outside Los Angeles concentrates on exercises developed by its founder, Anne-Marie Bennstrom, and has an annual membership that permits reentry whenever the need is felt. Men are included here, as at most of the younger establishments.

Florida boasts four major farms: Palm Springs, Murieta Hot Springs, Desert Hot Springs, and Palm-Aire. The latter is a good example of all-around facilities at about half the price of the superspas. Calorie allowances here are a mere six hundred, and guests are required to have a physical examination daily. Otherwise the routine is the familiar cacophony of exercises, steam cabinet, whirlpool bath, massage, body scrub, spot reducing, facial, herbal wrap, yoga—and whatever you are feeling up to, after all this, in the way of sports. Little Rock, Arkansas, has its Hillhigh, and the East has its Hambletonian. The latter, set in the greenery of Orange County, New York State, has an international staff and is run more along European lines.

The sheer amount of equipment at an American spa is apt to obscure the origin of the concept. People did, after all, visit Montecatini and Baden-Baden for their waters. Though up-to-date U.S. health farms provide baths of every kind from the tule root to paraffin wax, Europe still specializes in plain, honest mineral-laden H_2O. "Taking the waters" may no longer be the primary reason for a stay at Vichy or Quiberon, but the European resorts have remained much less programmed than ours. On the other hand, each is famous for something, whether water cures for specific ailments or cleansing diets, as at the Bircher-Benner Clinic near Zurich. Many are in hotels. The Grand Hôtel Beau-Rivage in the Swiss town of Interlaken now houses the new Schonheits und Fitness Center. Here the specialty is that revitalizing property called oxygen, which is pumped into a whirlpool so that a mix of water and oxygen swirls around you.

The Swiss have found that beauty farms are "in," drawing customers from all of Europe, but especially from France and West Germany. As in the case of the Beau Rivage, newly installed spas seem to be attracting clients back to the large sedate hotels which, around the turn of the century, were full of rich vacationers who never gave a thought to organized exercise. Newer sports stations like Verbier and Les Diablerets, as well as old towns like Locarno-Brione, are developing their own beauty centers.

In France, a corporation called Vitatop Fitness runs a nationwide chain of health clubs based more on the American model and including every inducement to the body beautiful, from Turkish baths to sculpture celebrating various artists' concepts of the human body. In England, on the other hand, the celebrated "milk farms" are without artistic pretension, relying on barely edible food combined with *lack* of activity, to coax the fat off. Often the cures are as austere as the appearance of these English establishments. Vegetarian meals, high colonics, hydrotherapy in unheated pools often await those who penetrate the elegant Georgian facades that bear names like Enton Hall and Forest Mere. Not all English health farms are haunts of the freaked-out or the frugal, but individual reputations do bear looking into.

The reaction to sixties superthin is not yet over. American women especially are still ambivalent about their bodies, about what shape is most in demand, about thin and fat. The media image has not altogether relaxed its hold on us. But although the past decade fostered thin as the new status symbol, there were, even then, unmistakable rumblings of a more comprehensive democratization of society than ever before. The economic boom had raised the standard of living across the board. As industry prospered, people of lower earning power were caught in the increasingly wider net of consumerism. In the business world the ideal of remote elegance had to be cast aside, consigned to an undesirable elitism. Fashion, beauty products, and all the props of the body beautiful had to be made available to Everywoman if the manufacturers were going to increase earnings. The sports enthusiast, the pretty woman in her thirties, the working mother, the modern mesomorph, replaced adolescence as the fashion ideal of the seventies. The girl in the street stepped onto the pedestal left vacant by Twiggy.

chapter 5

better fit than fat

After the tailspin of the previous decade, the seventies brought us down to earth with a thud. The recession began in earnest. Watergate taught us that we could survive even political psychosis. With the Viet Nam involvement at an end, our national aggressiveness seemed to turn inward, and the whole country went dance crazy and sports mad. Ballet became the new spectator passion. The Brazilian superstar Pélé reintroduced soccer and became a national hero. Everyone took up tennis or cross-country skiing or wilderness survival training. For those who needed more excitement, new danger sports were developed. One could always hang-glide, hot-dog, or deep-sea scuba dive to put an edge on things. We were finding the exhilaration of taking chances with our own bodies more fun than starving them. Sportswear, always an American specialty, became the backbone of the clothing business. Bonne Bell and other manufacturers of outdoor cosmetics boomed. Our idea of beauty was similarly changed, as were those familiar faces which represent beauty to the consumer: the models.

Now we have entered the era of Lauren Hutton, Margaux Hemingway, Beverly Johnson, Deborah Raffin—the Girl Next Door. First came Lauren Hutton, a model who is the consummate mirror of the times, an all-American contemporary woman without an ounce of hauteur, who laughs at her imperfections and wears jeans and workshirts off the job. The seventies brought in the look of "real" in bodies as well as faces. Hutton is past thirty and far from painfully thin. She is the clothing manufacturer's kind of client: older, active, refreshingly womanly in stature, a mesomorph incarnate. The public responds to her so strongly that in 1974 she signed an exclusive contract with Revlon to advertise their "Ultima I" line at a staggering fee, altogether an unprecedented event in the mannequin business. Since then, exclusives, or the identification of a model with a single product, are where the big money lies. A year after the Revlon contract, Margaux Hemingway (Ernest's granddaughter) signed on at Fabergé to advertise their new perfume "Babe," for a flat million a year. Modeling has become big industry in the last decade, with increased bookings and a doubling of rates to over $100 an hour for top girls. Out of this the agency itself claims an average 13½ percent. Other profits are incalculably high: One well-placed ad or editorial shot may sell a million dollars' worth of a single garment. Although a young model can make a lot of money, her career almost never lasts beyond six years or so. Physical aging aside, the public wants new faces. Agents are highly sensitive to the boomerang effects of saturation, though the line between comfortable familiarity with a face and overexposure is admittedly fine. During her five or six years before the public, however, a successful model has the chance to project a constant image of attitude, figure, or life style to be emulated. Hers is a business that hand-in-hand with the fashion magazine has always dealt in fantasy, and is just now beginning to adapt to the demand for realism. After decades of untouchable superstars in haute couture, we may have reached a stage at which the average woman is able to find herself in the pages of magazines, in the media, in the face of a popular model. The impossible dream is over, especially with regard to bodies.

No doubt the way was paved around the turn of the century by the uncorseted trend. Though the designer Poiret took credit for this innovation, it was certainly Isadora Duncan who publicized it. Duncan danced barefoot or in sandals, wearing only the briefest white adaptation of the Greek chiton. She eschewed tights. There was no question of her being strapped into any sort of constraining garment, and this preference for bodily freedom constituted a great part of her acclaim as a dancer. She even invented her own tunic bathing dress which rose above the knees, but most of her clothing innovations were regarded as the eccentricities of a much-envied madwoman, and the world would have to wait until the war years to follow Isadora's example. But the Duncan impulse was a healthy one and lay behind the later realization that firmness cannot be achieved by extraneous means, but only by diet and strenuous workouts.

Women began the trek to gyms and exercise studios, to the tennis courts and jogging tracks in earnest. It was not just that the seventies woman had more freedom; she had a new consciousness. She had survived the sexual revolution, accepted new facts about herself, and knew more about her mental and physical being. She announced that she too was changing and would, in turn, make alterations in her situation, her aspirations, her activities, and her body. The changes in her physical self came, as they usually do, before the others. They were inaugurated by the Pill.

The Pill, of course, meant sex without premeditation. The old male prerogative of sexual freedom was now woman's too. Released from the fear of pregnancy, she began to explore her own sexuality, and found it didn't square with many of the old myths. The ideal of feminine passivity and the vaginal orgasm, which sold so well in 1959 in the form of a book called *The Power of Sexual Surrender* by Dr. Marie Robinson, made way for Masters and Johnson in 1966. Now there was not only sexual equality, but equal responsibility for sexual failure.

Women themselves, not willing to rely on the authority of doctors, took on the job of educating themselves about their bodies. In the late sixties, groups like the Boston Women's Collective met to discuss common problems. Sometimes these were concerns about going back to work, or child care, or marriage; in the case of the Boston group it was a dissatisfaction with the kind of cursory gynecological treatment most had received. In talking together they realized the extent of their ignorance about their sexual selves, and assigned themselves the task of finding out more. The result was a book that spoke to an entire generation of women. It was called *Our Bodies, Ourselves.*

By the time their book came out in 1969, radical changes in sexual patterns had been evident for the best part of a decade. For one thing, the option *not* to have children had some confusing effects on the institution of marriage. As long as pregnancy had been woman's destiny, she found marriage comfortable. Indeed, for the majority of Americans of both sexes, the traditional family setup still seems to work best—on the surface. But almost inaudibly the gears were shifting here too. Wives announced that they were going back to work or school. Gerald Ford, while still Vice President, was photographed doing the dishes in one of *Vogue*'s editorial pages in 1974; men were being reintroduced to household tasks and were thought better of for their participation.

Had there been a sexual revolution? Some wouldn't go so far as to call it that. But the truth was that what started with the Pill and a little body knowledge became a liberating crusade. Jean-François Revel, the French social commentator, wrote that "the battle against sexual repression . . . is undoubtedly one of the surest signs of an *authentic* revolutionary struggle." Whichever way it rocked the boat, it changed women as they in turn changed themselves.

One of the first things women learned about their bodies was that they could do more, physically, than they expected. Body awareness comes, after all, only with movement. And women began to move. They got out of the house, went to work instead of to ladies' luncheons. They learned to do things like mountain climbing, canoeing, karate, and automobile mechanics. The old middle-class bias against women in competitive sports broke down. Exercise was beginning to be considered essential for emotions as well as bodies, good preventive medicine for the old bag of nervous disorders like headache, insomnia, and indigestion, better for you than aspirin, tranquilizers, and antacids. The whole notion of what was feminine and what was not was being turned upside down. Even the fashion magazines kept pace with the new activity. Today they are much less concerned with ivory tower life-styles than they used to be, more interested in telling the reader how to get the most done within a busy schedule, whether that involves a two-minute makeup routine or how to do isometrics in the office.

As the climate of women's liberation began to permeate the lives of most females—even those who were not at all active in the movement—there grew a sense of power and importance in being women. A tremendous release of energy—both sexual and work—was the result. "Lib" was being responded to on a personal level by hundreds of thousands, perhaps millions of women. Like most of the social upheavals in history, the results of the sixties were on the surface as well as underneath; women began to *look* different. Athletes, dancers, and models were taking the place of royalty (whether actual or Hollywood) as representatives of the physical ideal of the moment.

As for the actual change in woman's body shape, it happened in a remarkably short period of time. The Victorian female who was celebrated for her figure might measure 38-18-38. When shaken down, stays removed, her hourglass figure was not more than five feet four inches tall, and weighed about 140 pounds. Today the measurements of a typical modern mannequin may be 34-22-34; she is at least five feet eight inches in height, and may weigh 118 or so. Even more

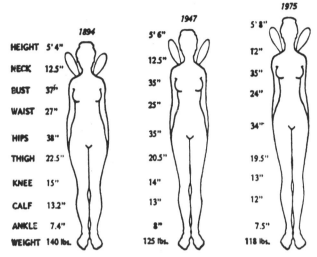

	1894	1947	1975
			5'8"
		5'6"	
HEIGHT	5'4"		
NECK	12.5"	12.5"	12"
BUST	37"	35"	35"
WAIST	27"	25"	24"
HIPS	38"	35"	34"
THIGH	22.5"	20.5"	19.5"
KNEE	15"	14"	13"
CALF	13.2"	13"	12"
ANKLE	7.4"	8"	7.5"
WEIGHT	140 lbs.	125 lbs.	118 lbs.

THE CHANGING SHAPE OF WOMAN. Psyche, the White Rock Girl, has
grown four inches and shed 22 pounds since her first appearance
in 1894. Though her measurements are closer to the ideal than the
average, her new image reflects a general change in female body
shape from endomorph (plump) to mesomorph (slender and
athletic). (Courtesy White Rock Products Corporation.)

astonishing is the speed with which body changes have taken place just since 1947. An example is the famous White Rock girl who kneels on the label of every beverage put out by the White Rock Company in Wisconsin. In 1894, when she was first dreamed up by the painter Paul Thumann, she was the perfect little Victorian endomorph. In 1947, when the label was redesigned, she underwent some alterations, growing taller by two inches and lighter by fifteen pounds. But in the years between 1947 and 1975, when she was again renovated, her progress was really spectacular. In a much shorter span of time she grew another two inches and lost all of seven pounds. Today she measures 35-24-34; not bad for a girl who started back in 1894 with 37-27-38, even if she existed only as a public relations fantasy. Nonetheless, she approximates the general height and shape profile of the female population. How did these changes occur within such a short time span? Better nutrition and participation in active sports and exercise, certainly—and, of course, sex.

As an object of men's devotions, the Victorian woman was still pursued for her potential bearing of children. The changeover from endomorph to mesomorph could come only when sexual mores were shifting. Idealization of the thin figure happens when a culture no longer needs more babies to insure its survival. Thus the final triumph of mesomorphic woman was not achieved until sex became irrevocably divorced from fertility in the mid-sixties. At that point, men were presented with a new phenomenon—the sexy but muscularly slender female. What about Mae West, Jayne Mansfield, Marilyn Monroe? They were aberrations of the pre-Pill era. Even in their own time their lead was not followed by fashionable members of their own gender, although their curves can still drum up a significant male following. When it comes time to size up the last half-century, it is the Modigliani-Giacometti representation of the slender woman that will survive as successor to the more opulent curves of Renoir's females or those by the sculptor Maillol.

In the United States, the transition from stocky to willowy figures was relatively sudden, taking place largely within one generational span. Elsewhere in the industrialized world a parallel trend has been evident, though more moderate. The Japanese are taller than ever before, and so are the youth of most European countries. But a look at the characteristic Frenchwoman does not reveal the same kind of abrupt growth pattern as in her American counterpart. Part of the explanation may lie in a cuisine that relies less heavily on meat proteins than ours; partly, too, it is that individual swings in weight are not as common among Frenchwomen as they are here. The French learn balanced nutrition early in life. Until fairly recently, children were not besieged by the thousands of varieties of junk foods that are such a staple of the American economy and way of eating. Moreover, the Frenchwoman was not so suddenly catapulted into free sex. She did not have to stage a sensual revolution; sex, like gastronomy and fashion, has always had high priority in French culture, where male-female equality on a basic level has always been taken for granted. We, however, are a nation of extremists, always in the market for a new look. Depending on what ideal is being flashed at us, we feed or starve ourselves into the current mold. The visual results are inescapable: nowhere else are to be found so many variations along the weight spectrum. Gradually, however, it dawned upon the seventies that there were two kinds of fat: the medically risky kind, and the kind the disappearance of which was promised by the vanity dieting of the sixties. Obesity is easy to recognize. But short of that, defining fat for oneself can be a tricky business. Whatever one concludes, the war against fat can be successfully waged by exercise.

Until the forties, programmed gymnastics were largely relegated to the football field or considered a rainy-day substitute for sports in schools. By the sixties exercise had become a way of life for many women, whether they went through their routine at home or in one of the new gyms and studios springing up all around the country's urban centers. The ladies who lunch were beginning to pass up the chocolate mousse for a whole new environment, one possessing a mystique as peculiar and almost as sweaty as that of the men's locker room. No doubt about it, the gym exerts a fascination all its own. One has the sense of being backstage at a performance that never takes place in public, a locale almost devoid of gossip, where the talk instead is about the longevity of leotards and the proper fit of tights. The bars, the bare floorboards, the mirrored walls may recall the decor of a nineteenth-century ballet hall, but there are no Degas ballerinas here, no tulle, no pink toe shoes and ingenuous smiles for the ballet master with his stick, no consumptive pianist. Here instead is a field of lively bodies warming up in second skins of pale blue, red, and violet, in shiny or tie-dyed tank tops, in winter leg warmers of maroon knit wool, in ballet slippers, jazz shoes or no shoes, in plastic overalls like those of astronauts, in Saran-wrapped thighs, in frivolous jumpsuits of the sort sold with Barbie dolls, or in the purposeful black of the classic Danskin leotard. And after class there is the cigarette, the talk of diets, the cup of coffee. Rarely does one know a great deal about one's

80 | BETTER FIT THAN FAT

classmates; discretion is honored, particularly in the most fashionable gyms. But there is, among the regulars at every sort of exercise place, an inevitable esprit de corps. Moreover, each gym or studio has its flavor, a spirit governed by the founder and head theoretician—in effect, by the twentieth-century version of Degas' dance master.

In New York City alone there are several distinct methods of exercise, each acclaimed by a band of ardent followers. One of the longest-established and most widely recognized gurus of physical fitness is the Russian-born gymnast Nicholas Kounovsky. The halls of his establishment on New York's 56th Street echo faintly with the padding of bare feet and the heavily accented directives called out by his East European instructors: "Hu*left*, ha-right, five, six," intones Ivo while the ladies groan discreetly. After the floorwork comes the litmus test of trapeze and rings. It is in the air that cowards are separated from those who have always harbored a secret desire to fly. Basic aeronautics include a backward rotation done ten feet above the mat, with Ivo in rapt attendance below. No one has ever had to be caught; still, the performance is apt to thrill only the bravest of acrobats. From initial headstand to the high-flown skills of the more practiced, Kounovsky's gymnastics look impressive, but can be learned by most in a few sessions. After an hour of them one feels "worked out," and that helps to keep most of his clients coming for years, greeting his handsome blond wife, Gally, at the desk, chatting with Shura, who makes the appointments, remembering instructors Ivo and Drago with Christmas gifts, and competing for the coveted magnum of champagne that Kounovsky himself bestows upon anyone who can tuck her toes under the uppermost bar on the rack, knees straight, ten times in a row.

Nick Kounovsky himself is a buoyant sexagenarian. Pink-cheeked and generally wreathed in smiles, he has been Russian Santa Claus to a horde of young instructors who, after having worked with him, venture out on their own to open almost equally famous gyms. But Kounovsky is far from relinquishing his title as philosopher-king of the physical-fitness movement. The exercises in his books are based on the careful planning of a trained engineer, which he was before leaving Russia. His notion of "sixometrics" (endurance, suppleness, equilibrium, strength, speed, coordination) provides a well-designed chronology of movement for beginner and expert alike. His writing also bristles with homilies and earthy anecdotes of the kind Khrushchev used to amuse reporters with. Relating the importance of appearance to how well one performs while exercising, Kounovsky recounts that one day he impulsively seized a pair of scissors and cut the bloomers of one of his female clients to well above the knee. Satisfied with the result, he treated the whole class to a similar abridgment of wearing apparel, to the great improvement of the ladies' freedom of action. Moreover, the following week, he reports, his enrollment had doubled.

The pursuit of a better body demands a rigorous faith. Like what used to be called the proverbial work of women, it is never finished. But unlike the training of a dancer or an athlete, exercise can become a nonprofessional pleasure, and some aficionados report that an hour once a week is more effective than a visit to the psychiatrist. And a whole lot cheaper. Kounovsky claims that mathematicians have worked out equations while suspended on the rings in midair. There is little doubt that when you seem to be concentrating on a complex backbend-and-roll, your mind is really somewhere else, presumably problem solving.

While gymnastics are Kounovsky's bailiwick, something closer to dance movement has found its exponent in Manya Kahn's technique. Like her Russian confrère, Mrs. Kahn's advocacy of muscle tone goes back to the early forties when she opened her first salon in Manhattan against all sensible advice from her friends. Figure-conscious women, few as they numbered, were accustomed to the perennial push-ups and knee bends designed more for the sports field than to fit one into the latest Mainbocher. Trying to change this age-old routine was thought to be folly. Mrs. Kahn managed to do so by a persuasive method combining what she had learned in her early years as a Russian-trained ballet dancer with her study of physical therapy. Her system of "body rhythms" is based on what she has observed in the instinctive stretches and positions of the human body from infancy through its natural stages of physical growth. Exercises begin with back flat on the floor and progress through sitting to standing movements. Throughout there is concentration on deep, controlled breathing. Like Kounovsky, Mrs. Kahn has written her own book of exercises wherein her attention to the body is total, encompassing excellent nutritional programs and sound advice on care of hair and skin. It goes without saying that both experts eschew machines entirely. Weighted belts, electrical machines, stationary bicycles, vibrating tables, and all such props are regarded as a waste of money, permitting the client the comfortable illusion that he or she is working, when in fact almost no effort is being expended.

Neither Kounovsky nor Kahn is primarily interested in

reducing as such; for them, weight control is a concomitant of good health, not something to be pursued for its own sake. Both put a high premium on relaxation. Indeed, one of the most seductive accompaniments to exercise in either gym or salon is the sense of restfulness it promises. Clients of both Spartan-fashionable gyms and posh salons are subject to an occasional sensation of returning to the womb. One is painstakingly and individually registered, along with all one's measurements, in a file with the other elect. The salons are apt to be carpeted in pink or grass-green. The atmosphere is hushed and calming, no more reminiscent of the outside world than is a greenhouse. Progress is recorded in one's file, which functions a bit like a report card. For some women, that hour of exercise may be the most disciplined part of their lives, a time when they are delighted to turn into little girls again, being called by their first names and following their instructor's directions to the letter. In those rooms given over to the betterment of the body by sweat (and sometimes by tears) many find themselves in ongoing competition with—themselves. Once the how-to is learned, there is the discovery that the unaided back bend or the high leg-extension has been part of one's native ability all along.

Jon Devlin is another New York exercise entrepreneur with a method. Throughout his set of programmed movements combining the virtues of both dance and exercise, he emphasizes the importance of mind over body—not in the *True Grit* sense, for none of his movements strains muscle—but because Devlin feels that one's attitude is the key factor in physical achievement. His recurrent phrase is "work weightless." Occasionally Devlin has his students close their eyes and pretend they are moving underwater. "Float *up*," he commands, and from a deep plié the arms magically rise as though buoyed by volumes of water. "Imagine what you want your body to do. Think where you want your arms to be. Attitude gives the position."

On the other hand, Devlin disapproves of storing away too much body knowledge. He feels that the old-fashioned ballet training, which included instruction in anatomy and musculature, is unnecessary—even harmful. "The mind can *place* the movement, but it is simply incapable of keeping track of what the body is doing. Do you realize how much is at work when your hand just reaches out to grasp something? If your intellect kept a record, you would end up like the centipede that, when questioned about how he managed to move all those legs, became instantly paralyzed!" Devlin has a good rule of thumb for how much exercise one should do. It's very simple: "As long as it feels good. When you have done ten tendus, you should still want to do the eleventh. Exercise is discipline, but it should never be boring. When you think you're not going to enjoy doing that eleventh tendu or knee bend, stop." And if one begins by not enjoying even the second? "Don't exercise that day. Get more sleep."

As for other ways to keep in shape, there is a veritable supermarket to choose from: jogging; aerobics (by the people who brought us the Air Force diet); Oriental imports such as Tai Chi Ch'uan, Kung Fu, karate, and judo. Yoga has quickly become the most popular antistress panacea in the United States, and it works, whether taken for body stretching alone or for the meditation technique it offers. There is even a manual on French street fighting for the more self-defensively inclined. In short, we have gone far beyond "one-two-three-touch-your-toes" in the search for shape, and in our recognition that modern life, while it happens fast, seems to be wreaking its particular havoc with more and more people who hold sedentary jobs. Work, we have discovered, is not action. Thus we resort to programmed exercise and we are better for it. Anything to get this country moving again!

chapter 6

the liberated body

By the early seventies, then, women had managed to bring themselves into better focus. The image of "thin" no longer hovered so obsessively within our truer outlines. We looked at ourselves in the mirror and liked better what we saw. So did others, including even the high fashion magazines. Their health and beauty editors began to run articles about the dangers of overdieting. The horrifying symptoms of anorexia nervosa were finally being aired in the popular press. In 1973 the style of the thirties made a big comeback, with all the attendant emphasis on glamour and bosomy film stars. The hippie cult of natural life-styles had surfaced as a major influence on how we looked.

What we were witnessing as a nation was the birth of a new sensibility rooted firmly in sensation—*physical* sensation. We had to find ways of coming to terms with velocity itself, both the physical speed of, say, airplanes, and the speed of images, as in the cinema. Our comprehension of velocity may have been fragmentary, but our experience with it was not. Expression of our new sensibility, a crowded, new world of intense physical motion, had to find a sort of audio-visual shorthand. We learned how to freeze-dry sensations for later examination. Much of the decade was spent developing our talent for that kind of shorthand and convincing ourselves that none of the old standards applied to what we now had to deal with. For women, the world was starting to turn bright colors again. They accepted new facts about themselves and knew more about their bodies. They were executives, jockeys, doctors, lawyers, writers. They were proving that they could express what was in this hard, physical new world as well as men could and sometimes better. By taking charge of their bodies they had in some way achieved an even more physical understanding of the new sensibility than had men. Moreover, women's lib was helping the cause by being out there announcing a new plurality of standards for female appearance.

The reaction to the superthin syndrome is still in progress. It is not a total recoil from slenderness, mark you, but it indicates a healthier course upon which women can embark, with the hearty approval of their men. Even the status-thins were beginning to feel the strain by the early seventies. Jet-set bodies are made the way everyone else's are, after all. Also, being skinny as a mark of caste was dying of overexposure in the fashion trade press such as *Women's Wear* and *W*. These very newspapers were starting to run stories in 1973 that poked fun at ex-idols like superthins Nan Kempner, Gloria Vanderbilt Cooper, and Jackie O.

By the time we were well into the decade, moreover, we had absorbed one of the overwhelming lessons of the sixties: Prototypes for physical beauty are essentially culture-bound—ours as much as any. Consequently, as the world shrinks and our exposure to different culture realms increases, our single standard must change. What we are getting used to now is the validation of a multiplicity of beauty ideals. Unusual is beautiful. Freaky is beautiful. The kids in their weird thrift-shop gear, a bit moth-eaten, would have frightened the fifties out of its wits, but it doesn't raise an eyebrow today. And certainly black has been officially recognized as beautiful for a while now. When Beverly Johnson makes the cover of *Vogue*, you know that fashion is telling us something. The days of hot racial struggle are over; the Girl Next Door is as apt to be black as caucasian.

We're part way to a new plurality, at last. Having accepted different ethnic notions of beauty and interesting, rather than conventional, faces; having given up an across-the-board insistence on Hollywood gloss and grooming; having relinquished the standardized nose or hair or expression or manner, we now have to learn to eliminate the standard body. We must start listening to specialists like Harvard's Dr. Jean Mayer, who says that correct weight has to be based on individual considerations like body frame, metabolism, and weight-distribution patterns that are inherited. We have to know what we cannot—and should not want to—change. The sooner plastic surgeons stop believing in their own omnipotent ability to alter everyone's appearance for the better, the sooner their patients will be forced to accept themselves as they are. (Part of the solution may be, as reported in a recent study, what some surgeons have long suspected: The patient hopes she will be turned away. That would indicate tacit approval of her looks on the part of the surgeon himself, which is what she so ardently wants in the first place.)

While the medical profession may be gaining insight into the superthin syndrome, the media people are still bent on exploiting it. As long as those designers who hate women can market their wares, as long as Madison Avenue can promote youth, as long as the diet industry is netting over $10 billion a year, thin will be in. But widespread revolution is just around the corner.

That spectacular release of sensual energy, so much a part of the sixties, may point the way. Superthin is, in the extreme, a denial of sexuality. We are now beginning to reject the angular old guard Anglo-Saxon build as the body-type supreme. Our democratic sensibilities are just as capable of picking Spanish-Americans or blacks as prototypes of beauty. And those girls have bosoms and hips. Although unisex will continue primarily as an attraction of the very young, who are not yet sexually defined, it is still nowhere near dropping out of sight as a fashion for more mature women, because of its emphasis on comfort. For women are through with letting designers put them into chic chastity belts. Having felt the advantages of ease in clothes, they are not likely to return to wasp waists or voluminous crinolines in the future.

As women—particularly American women—acquire confidence, they may even widen their acceptance of new standards to include the simple human fact of growing older. The fashion industry needs gray-haired women to model its clothes, even in an era that does not cater specifically to *Vogue*'s establishment prototype Mrs. Exeter. Perhaps our insistence on youth will linger even longer than our insistence on the standard body, but eventually it too will yield to the new plurality.

If we need proof that our rigidities have eased up a bit, we need only give a glance into that trustworthy mirror of ourselves, the "public eye." Witness such heavy talents as French film actress Andréa Ferréol or nightclub entrepreneur Régine. New York City has its very own restaurant and salon superstar Elaine; even the fashion world has Pat Ast (designer Halston's assistant) and the influential editor Rosemary Kent. Then there is the remarkable story of Barbara Cook, who needed to gain a hundred pounds before she felt good about her image as singer and actress. Throughout the fifties and sixties, she had been the perfect Broadway musical ingenue, 106 pounds of pertness. It took her seven years of professional seclusion before she felt that fat was right for her, but at her recital debut at New York's Carnegie Hall in January 1975, acclaim for the new Barbara Cook was overwhelming. Sick of being typecast in silly roles, she was for the first time her own person on stage. Voice and body were integrated. Both audience and critics responded with raves. Her lesson was clear: Being happy inside your own body is one way—perhaps the most basic one—of leading your public to love you.

Singers in particular notice that audiences are more apt to accept the fat person on stage than off. Perhaps it is part of the public need for Big Mama. Bette Midler, with her décolletage and bouncy hips, fulfills this image, as does Régine in more subtle fashion. Régine is one of those natural dynamos whose every move makes news. When she decided to lose weight, the whole French nation groaned. Fortunately, her efforts failed and she is reconciled to feeling *bien dans ma peau*—good in her own skin, as the phrase goes. Her legendary energy continues unthreatened. When asked whether men prefer heavier women, she replied with what has become a classic aphorism, *"Les hommes sortent avec les maigres et rentrent avec les rondes"*—Men go out with thin women, but they return [presumably to bed] with heavier ones.

One can only deplore the gap in female psychology between the rarefied, mysteriously seductive world of high fashion—into which one can presumably enter only through the eye of a needle—and a reality that is far more exquisite with possibilities than women seem to want to recognize. Most men are not couturiers. High fashion circles are not exclusively composed of wealth. It is not even true that most designers are homosexuals and hate women, although it is perfectly evident that some of the most influential are and do—and occasionally launch styles that could be more advantageously worn by adolescent boys. What *is* unbelievable is that some women still allow themselves to be enslaved by their own desire to participate in a magical, moneyed world called "Fashion," which in today's reality barely exists.

Régine, who loves clothes and wears them with tremendous éclat, has said that in this matter of dress women have a practical revolution to stage. What good is it to march in liberation parades, formulate slogans, meet in women's groups, if women cannot first accept their very own bodies, if they remain tied to an impotent standard of beauty, if they stay enslaved to a handful of designers who may or may not despise them (and may or may not know they do), but who in any case are using them for the ultimate profit of the dress industry? Régine's kind of revolution is not against the imposition of short or long hemlines; it is a head-on collision with the fashion fascists on the subject of image. The fascists who dictate style through the media must accept the differences in women's bodies too if they want to go on dressing them.

It does take an acute observer to disabuse the public of fashion's hermetic mysteries. Occasionally a sharp-eyed journalist will prick the bubble and announce that the clothes he is asked to review are unattractive. This is what *Elle*'s reporter, Gonzague Saint Bris, did at the 1974 Paris collections: Watch him. There he sits on one of the little gilt chairs, pen poised. But the clothes are ugly, and he finds himself more intrigued with the audience. Among the viewers, watching the deaf and dumb superbeautiful models parade against a background of airport-type music, sits Régine, *eblouie* in her crown of frank red hair. Of the guests, only she seems to be in motion; everyone else fades into the walls. Her very size gives her more authority than all the seasoned editors with their rapacious pens flicking like tongues over their notebooks. She is queenly. She gives notice of her presence in the same way as does that other monument to entrepreneurship on the other side of the Atlantic, Elaine of the great owl glasses and rumpled hair, 250 pounds of female restaurateur. One muses: Elaine at a fashion show—why not? It should give women something to think about. Certainly Gonzague's imagination is in full play.

He too agrees that if a woman's personality expresses itself in her physicality, in *grandes gestes*, in her sheer size, then she should remain heavy. Amplitude, generosity, depth, and that certain richness of character that comes of knowing how to laugh well, even in the very young, finds a natural home in statuesque measurements. Think of French film actress Andréa Ferréol, she of the buxom build and flaming bedroom hair. She was sensuality itself in *La Grande Bouffe*, that bizarre celebration of overeating. Remember that there are few female roles in opera that call for wispiness, *Bohème* aside. And Camilles are fortunately long out of fashion. This is not to say that fat makes for character or that heavy women automatically have it. More often than not, extra weight is just sloppy and transmits the reverse impression, lack of character. But there is a growing number of heavyweights who know how to dress to emphasize their solidity—women who feel good in their own skins, who possess that fierce pride of self. They are the only ones in our national parade of heavy women who have learned well the lessons of dress. Those barbaric jewels, massive torques, capes and caftans were made for them. Their hair should be splendid and wild, and never chic or geometrically lacquered. That's for Ms. Size Six who will be content to follow the Sassoon and Henri Bendel beat.

Emphasis is at the heart of all true style. A round face should be all blissful Boucher, long heads should appear narrow as Nevelson's, attenuated as an African amulet, modeled after Modigliani. Thin bodies must look incisive, move quickly, be bright. Heavy frames, on the other hand, have built-in presence and ought to use it. And what if one finds oneself in the middle, properly proportioned and weight-controlled according to the received ideal? Be glad, collect the kudos. But lest things get too boring, try some tricks of distortion, a little fantasy or sleight-of-hand. For it looks as though we are beginning to applaud individuality when we see it. With a Régine, a Ferréol, an Elaine, one can hardly miss.

They are, sometimes in spite of themselves, forcing a change, opening up a tolerance for opulence, what the French call pulpiness. There is plenty of room for these fringe prototypes to move onto center stage, and about time, too.

The assault on superthin is finally coming from another direction as well—the medical profession. Though physicians on the whole support the slender trend, there are more and more expert voices being raised against overdieting. Particularly against the yo-yo syndrome, in which one's weight bounces up and down the scale, creating trauma for the body and wrinkles for the face, not to speak of the psychological harm caused by turning oneself into a human accordion. Many weight doctors now believe that it is healthier for some people just to stay fat rather than to live from diet to diet, with the corresponding variations on the scales. "The time has come," said Dr. Paul Scholten, in a *New York Times* interview late in 1973, "to stop the war against fat and admit that people can be fat and healthy. We can allow ourselves to be plump and contented rather than neurotic over a few extra pounds."

Words to the wise. The new disposition has even been picked up by a few splinter groups in the fashion industry itself. Witness Estevez, who is now designing, with bodies like Eva Gabor's in mind, "for the 35 million of us with curves instead of angles." Then there is Régine's own line of dresses called Zoa. And listen to the noted fashion photographer Frank Horvat as he discusses his own approach to what constitutes feminine beauty: "Mannequins? *La Mode?*—I couldn't care less! It simply does not interest me to photograph those women whom all the world considers beautiful. The only thing which excites me is the notion of enlarging the idea of beauty. I have recently done some fashion layouts using fat girls. They pleased me no end, personally, but the real reason I did it was to show that they can be beautiful even though they are what others call overweight." Fashion photographs using heavier models like Halston's assistant, the 250-pound Pat Ast, have been gingerly tried out in the United States—without much success. In its April 1965 issue, *Harper's Bazaar* bravely included two photos of a rather fat childlike model with lush hair whom they christened the "New Botticelli Girl." A lace, pregnancy-style dress obscured her middle in one picture; striped knickers and a gigantic pandalike sweater performed the same function in the other. Nevertheless, her unconventional looks were lauded by the editors, who wrote, "We recognize and revere as many kinds of individual feminine beauty as there are forms in nature. Proportion, balance is everything, and that unself-conscious, carefree grace through which the spirit shines." The effect of this rather effusive audaciousness was, however, counteracted on the very next page by a major spread on Luna, the black model noted as much for her emaciated elongation as for her ability to dramatize a dress before the camera.

In France, experiments with heavier models have been well received. Bruno du Roselle, secretary general of the Salon du Prêt-à-Porter and a power to be reckoned with in the French clothing industry, says that even in his fashion-conscious country, not even 49 percent of women have anything resembling a good figure. The relatively new awareness of this, due to recently conducted polls, has plunged the industry into concern for providing smart clothing for the other 51 percent. And even in New York, center for the hard-boiled modeling profession, the cry for a heavier prototype has gone up. Both consultant Barbara Stone and Wilhelmina, who runs her own agency, observe that since the sixties, models have become taller, rounder, and more buxom. The Twiggy phenomenon—especially her measurements—had little effect on the profession; the followers of Twiggy were largely out there in greater America. Neither agency accepts skinny-minnies anymore. Good proportions count more than size; skeletons who nonetheless show promise are invited back only after they have gained some weight. On the other hand, Wilhelmina, herself a famous face in the sixties, feels that Americans are absolutely incapable of identifying in a healthy way with roundness. "They are pathological about weight," she says. "In Europe we were all brought up with the notion that physical size was not so very important."

Such an attitude requires a modicum of character, in this case the refusal to be intimidated by the rage for angularity. Both the women's liberation movement and the emergence of natural life-styles have helped reinforce this refusal. Increased interest in health, in sports, in activity, emphasizes stamina and strength rather than the languid indolence of extreme thinness. The lack of artifice that has become almost a trademark of both movements represents a symbolic decision: Feminists expect to be taken as they are, no makeup, arms unshaven. There is a tacit refusal to be made into decorative dolls by the host of commercial renovators whose stock in trade, they feel, is the conversion of woman into object.

One need not go that far to feel liberation in the air. What it comes down to is, first, a climate of change in which our range of appreciation is opening up, and secondly, the inward search by which one is able to discover one's *own* way to look. The result is, of course, as many styles of beauty as there are women. Such proliferation is going to mean running the gamut from morphological slenderness to congenital fat. As long as neither extreme is a health risk, our eyes will become accustomed to seeing both as beautiful.

There are those who are not all that patient about general acceptance of this new plurality of standards. They have felt the injustices of the superthin syndrome to the hilt and have been determined to do something about it. They coined slogans like "Fat Lib" and "Fat Power." There is even a book called *Fat Pride*, by Marion Grosswirth, an official of the National Association to Aid Fat Americans. Part of the militancy of organizations like NAAFA may be traced to findings about the origins of fat by such research institutions as the Rockefeller University in New York City. Studies done there have shown that people who were overfed as babies actually form more than the usual number of fat cells, and that these do not disappear when weight is lost later in life. Even though the cells shrink, they are always ready, like sponges, to fill up again. Consequently, the task of maintaining a low weight is herculean for such a person. It can become an artificial—and extremely nerve-wracking—exercise in futility. Better, within medically approved bounds, to let nature take its course and concentrate on stabilization. But the fat-hating public, reason members of NAAFA, needs to have its prejudices forcibly brought into question.

And so do we, all of us. Especially women between the ages of twenty-five and forty, who are feeling the first pangs of aging. A poll done recently in France has shown that these are the women who adhere most fanatically to the mythic association between youth and dieting. They are the ones who most hurt their health, their equilibrium, and their skin. They are the superthin establishment, the aesthetic fascists who are giving the new plurality a hard time. But even they will be forced to give up the charade, as they discover that not youth, nor money, nor success, nor social distinction—not even health—is to be found in being thin. Nor, they will learn, does size bestow identity. Perhaps some of them will even begin to listen to their men. As for those who steadfastly refuse to heed either themselves or their men—the ones who cannot free themselves from the image enthroned for them by the media—they will simply end up with males who are its slaves as well. This is the kind of man who is seen with show-biz types he doesn't even fancy, who is so intent on his own image that his partner is merely a prop. That he evaluates his prowess by his ability to catch a female who looks right, an object who wears the official stamp of media approval, says so much about the ongoing preeminence of prestige in certain segments of society that simple human relations may be doomed never to rise above the cocktail party clatter.

It is depressing, but nevertheless true, that there *are* men who want images. Male eyes are subjected to more or less the same advertising as women's. Inevitably men are brainwashed, inevitably they find failings in females, inevitably they are forced to accept the somewhat faded replicas of the image that materialize as their very own wives, lovers, daughters, secretaries, companions. It is all very well, one might say, to rail against the media as a put-on, but the fact is that it is a thread in our lives—it shapes our vision and tastes. The only successful channel for revolt would seem to be the battle to ignore it, and to do—to look—as we please. That this is not so impossible was demonstrated by the midi crisis in 1970. In that memorable episode, the fashion people got their wires crossed and began shouting in discord. The message, instead of being the usual clear directive, contained overtones of authority in chaotic disagreement. What was the woman-in-the-street to do but decide that if the designers themselves couldn't get it straight about hemlines, she would either wear last year's or buy what she jolly well pleased. And she did.

The same independent judgment is beginning to apply to body style. Women's struggle between what they are and how they are phantasized by the media has just begun.

chapter 7

paint

For all of fashion's emphasis on the body, it is still the face in which, if we allow, we see our deepest selves—and by which we are recognized by others. Part expression, part artifice, our eyes, nose, mouth all conspire to transmit a different Morse code from that of the body. Perhaps that is why their adornment is assigned its own special shopping section.

In the cosmetics department of any large store one has the sense of being let loose in a riot of pure color, color as it jumps to the eye from the walls of a museum or in the showroom of an elegant fabric house. But better. Because, like finger painting for grown-up children, you can actually *try on* all the colors, sniff the scents. Indeed, this little island packed tight as a painter's palette with tubes, sprays, charts, smears, samples, and other paraphernalia of the beauty trade, is a sensual oasis frequented by more and more women. Particularly now, as the price of being well-dressed zooms, shoppers are abandoning the clothes racks for the cosmetics counter. What you can't afford for your back can be diverted at a mere fraction of the cost onto your face.

The cosmetics promoters, quick to note the trend, have been even quicker to capitalize on it. Having learned from the sixties that promotion of many prototypes of beauty could actually increase profits, the industry went absolutely bonkers. Floods of cosmetics for men, children, and blacks were unloosed onto the market. Cosmetics from the Orient and from Morocco. Literally a thousand manufacturers got into the act. Products proliferated faster than the eye or pocketbook could keep track of. Today, the merchandising of "hope in a bottle" adds up to over $7 billion a year. But the beauty boom's newest moneymaker isn't just paint. Makeup, in fact, represents only one sector of the business. The really big items are treatment products—the moisturizers, cleansers, suntan creams, and other basics that constitute the *batterie de cuisine* atop Everywoman's dressing table. And for skin care, apparently no price is too high. Estée Lauder's "Swiss Performing Extract" sells steadily at $16.50 for a tiny flacon. Charles of the Ritz' "Revenescence," which was, at its debut in 1934, one of the first moisturizers, is making a tremendous comeback at $8.50 per two-ounce bottle. "Revenescence" sales hopped 35 percent in one recent year, and a faithful clientele can now buy its mythic properties encapsulated in a gamut of other CR products, from face powders to masques.

Why the rush to preventive medicine for the skin? Part of the answer is that there are few really new technological breakthroughs in face creams. Of course the laboratories are busy refining, isolating, and mixing new "miracle" ingredients, and the packaging engineers are inventing new devices and mountings and applicators. The public relations departments, in fact, are hard-pressed to find names for all the various dollops of this and that that are passed off to the public as revolutionary. But sometimes, for beauty as for the rag trade, the only way forward is back—in this case back to basics: skin *care*.

Part of the reason is also to be found, as usual, in what the customer really wants. And today's cosmetics clientele is savvy. She knows that a thick swathe of foundation is no substitute for decent skin. She has been told repeatedly that surface embellishment can't hide an unhealthy epidermis. She may not be aware that it was John Davies of Hereford who wrote, in 1616, that "beauty's but skin deep," but she knows perfectly well that he was wrong. She has lived through the 1960's. Having done so, she has witnessed—even worked on—the liberation of her body, and she has felt it happen to her face as well.

She has watched while all the old shibboleths about beauty have come under question and fallen away, leaving the portraits of Garbo, Dietrich, Grace Kelly, Brigitte Bardot, Shrimpton, Twiggy suspended like icons in a pantheon of the past. In their place is only that ability, whatever it consists of, to turn heads. And what *does* it consist of? she asks. Speculations rarely give recipes. All she knows is that there are no rules; that what is left in the wake of the historical pinup parade is nothing but the mystery of multifaced beauty itself.

She is beginning to realize, as she undoubtedly was told by her own mother, that beauty comes from the inside. The only difference is that now the women's magazines are giving the spiritual lecture. Ironically, those magazines which carry the most cosmetics advertising are the very ones that are expounding to their feminine readership the relativity of beauty and teaching that being born with glorious bone structure is an advantage fraught with ambivalence. Somewhere along the line, too, Freud has scored his point with the beauty editors; the cry in *Vogue* today is for what is known to beauty copywriters as "the whole person."

For explanation, we search far beyond even Freud's discoveries; we must go back to ancient Greece. There, we find, beauty was a virtue, a kind of badge of merit which stamped a person who was all-of-a-piece. It was expected, in other words, that outer beauty hinted at inner worthiness. It was logical that gods and goddesses should be supremely beautiful, as we know from the statues of Praxiteles and the many versions of Venus. But the worship of this definition of beauty was soon uprooted by Christianity which, as Susan Sontag has written, "by limiting excellence to *moral* virtue only . . . set beauty adrift—as an alienated, arbitrary, superficial enchantment." As a result, mind and body were separated, like cream from milk, and while the head was thought to be ruler of the greatest accomplishments of our civilization, the body was considered a mere object for narcissistic cultivation, the proper concern of women (those of child-bearing age, at least), a powerful vessel fraught with dangers for men, a work tool, an embarrassment, a bother, a burden, and occasionally a medical hindrance—but above all something *separate* from the rest of the human being.

The sixties, though they hardly revolutionized sex, did

manage to teach us how estranged we had become from our bodies. We had been trained, subliminally through the years, to look at ourselves in parts, and to evaluate each part against the set standard: my nose as compared to Garbo's or Kelly's or Hepburn's. The shape of my face: where it fit those charts that appeared regularly in the fashion journals, delineating square, oval, round jawlines and what to do about each structural fault. But today, if a savvy reader knows anything about her face, it is how to exaggerate what used to be called the mistake of nature. Done successfully, she senses that "faults" will add to her individuality; at the very least, she has the sense to leave them alone.

Part of the pent-up defiance against the single standard of beauty derives from the fact that America *is* a melting pot of beauty types and we are beginning to see it that way. Today, when a Princess Elizabeth of Toro bursts onto the fashion scene from far-off Uganda, we are quick to recognize both her beauty and her differentness simultaneously. As we travel we learn about other societies, other historical eras. What we may have considered primitive concepts of attractiveness are often, we now realize, manifestations of highly advanced cultures. Artifice, we learn, is less modern than we thought. The first clothes were the decorations on painted or tattooed bodies. Designs cut and burned into the skin were the beauty marks of ancient tribes. The Assyrians considered ivory implants in the nose a sign of aesthetic nobility. The blackened teeth of Labrador, the African neck stretchers and lip plates, the Chinese bound feet, the widespread removal of body hair, and an endless list of even more inventive mutilations are proof that concepts of beauty have always existed in awesome variety.

Every culture has a norm, whether explicit or unexpressed. Ours is no exception, but in the past it has lacked amplitude. The British have their fabled eccentrics; in England, an Edith Sitwell is considered a fit subject for an essay on fashion, and her views on dress are taken quite seriously. The French have their *rondes*, their well-fleshed *pulpeuses*, *bien en chair*, so well documented by photographers like Cartier-Bresson. Americans, being newer and less confident, have relied on the faces in their fashion and movie magazines. Hence the preoccupation with perfection, with measuring up to a cherished norm, with the physical dismemberment involved in testing the nose, the cheekbones, the length of neck against the certified prototypes. Most sadly, as we have seen, our rigidities have produced a nation of women unhappy with their looks and willing to spend entire incomes in order to turn themselves into stereotypes.

Europeans have long been capitalizing on American insecurities in the realm of facial as well as figure beauty. Cosmeticians abroad are known as aestheticians. They understand the superficialities of dermatology. They know how to work an unbelievable variety of little machines that peel, exfoliate, dermabrase, and claim to dewrinkle and smooth facial skin. Sophisticated new instruments that freshen, spray, tone, and oxygenate via low-frequency waves or compressed air seem to emerge from the Continent almost monthly. Europe is crazy about beauty machines and is delighted to export its dermascopes, Vapodynes, Esthetrons, Lucas Pulverizers, and Carbatoms to the United States, where women are wowed by such scientific instruments for facial treatment. Indeed, America is regarded by European aestheticians as a potential gold mine for the trade—clean, virgin territory except for a few operators such as the Rumanian-born Christine Valmy, the Hungarian Vera Falvy, Ilona of Hungary, Madame Cordin, and the legendary Vienna-born Georgette Klinger. And of course the most famous of all the exotically named skin healers was Dr. Erno Laszlo from Transylvania, who turned himself into a corporation before he died, thereby ensuring enormous product-profits for his survivors.

If Eastern European origins seem to be a requirement for skin expertise, treatment names have to be either garden-variety French or very technical. At Valmy's salon in New York, "byogenic" care is practiced. The face is vaporized, vacuum-cleaned, almond-creamed, placenta-enriched, electric-masked, brushed, cool-compressed, and stimulated with Dermatron rollers. Is it all balderdash? Mostly, yes. And some of it, like chemical peeling or dermabrasion, can be dangerous. But the pseudo-scientific ring of it all masks one very important factor: Women, especially lonely women, love to be fussed over. Next to the hairdresser, the "aesthetician" has made himself indispensable in performing this service. The beauty cubicle as confessional—that's what it's all about.

But the United States is not all *that* naïve. Moreover, this is a two-hundred-year-old democracy, and that happy condition is beginning to be reflected in the fact that for this country, too, beauty is becoming less ideal, more accessible, and more individualized. Because of our respect for mobility, physical attractiveness must embody, for us, a sense of action. Today, beauty is as beauty *does*. Because lack of time is one of the conditions of our society, the woman who spends hours working on her makeup is by no means an object of veneration—quite the reverse. Self-oppression in any form, from elaborate hair styles to pointed shoes that deform the feet, is no longer regarded as a prerequisite for beauty, but rather as inane enslavement. Suffering for the sake of one's looks, in other words, is finished. Beauty is out there in the real world, moving with the times.

All well and good. But there are still millions of women who have not yet got the message, who are afraid to call themselves beautiful merely by looking like themselves. This is because beauty, at bottom, is so deeply voluntary and such an integral reflection of the entire personality. This idea is not new. The legendary Lola Montez, a flaming success with kings, regents, philosophers, musicians, reporters—in short, a string of men all over the world in her mid-nineteenth-century heyday—wrote a book on the "secrets of beauty" which she dedicated to women "of every land who are not afraid of themselves, who trust so much in their own souls that they dare to stand up in the might of their own individuality to meet the tidal currents of the world." The theme runs through our countercultured sixties and is, if possible, even more pronounced today. Listen to two voices speaking on the subject. The first is that of Virginia Castleton, who writes a column for the underground publication *East-West Journal*: "For me, the [desire to be beautiful] culminated during my mid-teens. But as time swept me along and I became generally more aware, I realized . . . that my personal concept of beauty was simply that: my own concept. The face exasperating me could be the object of someone else's adoration."

When asked the same question, the extraordinary young spiritual leader of a successful religious commune had this to say: "I think that for me beauty is that inner illumination that you see in people who are good. I don't mean you can arrange your face into a certain shape, because beauty does not depend on the shape or anything like that, it depends on the soul. It depends on being lighted from within—that's having a lot of energy on. . . . I think people *get* beautiful."

Such statements, however, are not destined to encourage the cosmetics establishment. Its response to the counterculture tendency to shun fancy packaging and chemical ingredients surfaced in the direction of organic cosmetics, and it became adept at coopting the large ecologically aware market that was fast opening up. As far back as 1961, natural-base creams were mentioned in French *Vogue*. In Europe, health-food preparations had always attracted a following. It took the popularity of the hippie movement in the United States to turn the natural cosmetics trend into a multimillion-dollar rip-off.

By the late sixties, department stores as well as health-food counters were crowded with avocado shampoos, grapefruit tonics, strawberry masques, skim milk lotions, vitamin-E lipsticks, honey-laden soaps, musk scents, apple colognes, and herbs in *everything*. There were perfumes called "Seashore" and "Ozone." Human beings smelled like vegetable patches. While the back-to-nature movement did spawn some imaginative ideas in product flavorings, it endeared itself to buyers for all the wrong reasons, the primary ones being purely psychological.

There were hidden dangers as well. No matter how ardently a manufacturer claimed that his product contained no preservatives, chemical agents had to be used to bind the ingredients together, to emulsify and suspend the lemons or strawberries or whatever was used in their base of oil or humectants. Otherwise, the shelves would be laden with fresh-picked and bottled products in various stages of decomposition, the only truly natural consequence of the entire trend. Risks were passed on to the consumer in the form of both the chemical agents used as preservatives and the fruit and vegetable essences themselves. Both could cause allergies just as readily as any of the more commercial preparations of Revlon, Arden, Rubinstein, or other cosmetics empires. Moreover, estrogen and other hormonal ingredients in some creams are still under scrutiny for safety. By any standard, hormones are drugs. They change the metabolism of live tissues, even when absorbed through the skin. Although no harmful results from estrogen creams have reached public notice, the positive "plumping" effects are not significant enough to warrant their use.

Real dangers lurk elsewhere. There were 594 cosmetic-induced injuries reported to the Consumer Product Safety Division Bureau of Epidemiology between July 1972 and July 1973. In 1974, 5,300 complaints were registered. This is par for the course, although some estimates run as high as 60,000 injuries a year. A weighty percentage of these derive from allergy to dyes, acids, waxes, oils, and chemicals. Deodorants are particularly noxious offenders, as are depilatories. There is no question that all cosmetics, like drugs and pesticides, should be adequately covered by federal regulations. But labeling laws have been resisted by many sectors of the industry, ostensibly on the grounds that extra lettering would destroy the aesthetics of their packaging. In spite of casualties ranging all the way from sensitive rashes to death, the customer with identifiable allergies usually has no way of knowing what she is buying, even in the hypoallergenic lines. And the very promise of purity that lured the public to natural products has been the cause of an inestimable number of dermatological problems.

Though the back-to-nature movement flourished in the sixties, it didn't necessarily begin, nor end, there. As early as the 1950's folk remedies, hormones, royal jellies, vitamin creams, ancient pastes, exotic enhancements for eyes and hair were dug up from historical accounts, from travel to far-off lands, from ancestors' recipe books. Whereas in the West, rouge and powder were the only cosmetics commonly in use for centuries, women in the sixties suddenly began to treat their hair with rasoul, redden it with henna from North Africa, and ring their eyes with Moroccan kohl. Rice was revived as an ingredient in face powder, clay from France and mud from Arizona became the newest discoveries for removing impurities from the skin. Powdered akkar in earthenware cones was sold with directions for staining the palms in the decorative fashion of Muslim women. Books on how to make your own creams and powders began to proliferate on the paperback racks. Directions for glycerine and rosewater lotion, recipes for compounds of lemon juice, white wine vinegar, and brandy offered to make any woman into a cosmetic chemist.

The beauty-care moguls were not to be outdone, however. Cleopatra's secrets could be just as easily updated by chemists in white coats as by housewives in aprons. Green malachite and black sulfide were still good eyelid enhancers—with a little help from the packaging and PR people. Since there is evidence that women began wearing mascara at least as far back as 5000 B.C., all the industry people had to do was to devise that little magic wand with which to apply it most efficiently. This simple notion revolutionized the eye makeup industry in the 1950's; a decade later came brushes that, when removed from the mascara tube, applied tiny fibers to the lashes, making them appear thicker. The lab wizards had come a long way from Egyptian remedies. But they didn't stop with ancient history. If the milk bath was popular in the Paris of

1840, perhaps it could provide even more solace for the face of today's anxious women. The year 1971 marked the onset of competition between the milk-based lines of two gigantic manufacturers. Revlon was the first on the pages of *Women's Wear Daily* with its "Skim Milk Natural/Organic Skincare." Three months later, Estée Lauder announced her discovery of Pure Whole Milk, employed in everything from face wash to moisturizer, and packaged in frosted glass. At 1971 prices, the miracle ingredient in Mrs. Lauder's product could be computed at a cost of $21 a quart.

Cosmetics empires like Revlon, Lauder, and Rubinstein are not making millions by chance. When it became apparent that many women were developing allergies from creams or lipsticks, they hired dermatologists and chemists to purify their ingredients. Many started hypoallergenic lines. Although there is no such thing as 100 percent nonallergenic cosmetics, major manufacturers have taken great care to insure minimum instance of allergic reaction by the scrupulousness of their production methods, by elimination of harmful or questionable ingredients, and by extensive testing. The oldest hypoallergenic lines are, like Allercreme and Almay, offshoots of pharmaceutical companies. Clinique and Etherea, divisions of Estée Lauder and Revlon respectively, made their debuts in the late sixties. Their boom relies heavily on the "ecologically pure" connotations that wafted over from the counterculture at about this time, but the survival of all hypoallergenic lines relies ultimately upon their use by women whose skin does react to such standby cosmetic ingredients as shellac, orris root, hexachlorophene, formaldehyde, and certain oils and vegetable dyes.

Another reason why the empires are doing billions of dollars' worth of business is that they started to pay attention when reports came in about the dangers of sun-tanning for the skin. Although many cosmetics companies had marketed tanning lotions, almost from their inception, it was soon clear that mere protection from burning of the sun's rays was not enough to insure health. In fact, it rapidly became apparent that sun was a prime factor in premature aging, drying, and wrinkling, and the major cause of skin cancer. What may begin at twenty with a year-round tan can, in just a couple of decades of constant sun, make a person look like sixty. Meanwhile, the leathery buildup of top layers of skin hardened by exposure fails to provide protection from cancer-producing rays, and the dreaded disease may result. Thus, not only has heavy tanning become less fashionable within the last few years, but the cosmetics people, to their credit, have responded with alacrity. The empires got busy and developed, with proper professional know-how, a gamut of sun-exposure products that enable the buyer to roast to a dark brown with relative safety, or to remain completely white. Artificial bronzers, chemicals that tan the skin without sun, sun screens, and total sun blocks now provide the option of being out of doors without running the risks either of burning or of sun-produced skin cancer.

Still another explanation for the cosmetics boom has to do with a very simple human attribute—vanity. The instinct for appearing at one's best, putting one's prettiest face forward, has survived all the plain-Jane onslaughts of women's liberation, the no-makeup-back-to-nature movement, and an economic recession. Indeed, the instinct seems to thrive, like the things most basically human, in spite of adversity. Oh, there are switches within buying patterns all right: Johnson & Johnson Baby Oil at 99 cents may suddenly sell better than

Arden's Bath Beads at four times the price, but that can be explained in a different context. In general, yes, business is up.

What about the Johnson & Johnson phenomenon? Why have some women started to buy their cosmetics at drug counters instead of department stores? One of the big switches in the industry has been to basics. Recent books by noted dermatologists such as Bedford Shelmire, Jr., and Irving Lubowe announced that expensive face preparations are nonsense. Lubowe wrote that all cleansers have a similar chemical composition, differing only in fragrance and packaging. Shelmire extolled the benefits of ordinary soaps like Ivory. Both doctors agreed that no moisturizers really penetrate the skin, no matter how much they cost. All work alike: By depositing a film on the skin's surface, they merely prevent moisture loss. Substances like Vaseline or vegetable oils—even Crisco—perform this task exactly as well as a $20 cream. And paying a premium for royal jelly, hormones, placenta extract, vitamins, proteins, milk, honey, and all the other "magic new" ingredients in commercial creams is just a waste of money. Did these pronunciamentos crush the cosmetic house giants? Hardly. Charles of the Ritz is owned by Squibb, which produces plenty of mineral oil. Though you don't see CR pushing it in simple little bottles on its counters, the corner drugstore is doing a land-rush business with the stuff. The dual effect of department-store and drug-counter sales is what helps to keep the high-cost cosmetics business on its feet nowadays. (Charles of the Ritz, incidentally, is only one example of perhaps half a dozen corporate takeovers of cosmetic houses by pharmaceutical firms in recent years.)

But even before the Shelmire-Lubowe revelations in 1973, the treatment-product market had come close to overextending itself. How did a customer know whether she should use a skin toner or a masque? How was she to know whether she had oily, normal, or dry skin, or which parts of her face harbored what degree of dryness? The industry's answer was that good old American reliable fixit, systems analysis. The hypoaller-genic companies came out with complicated charts. Orlane introduced an electronic machine with as many dials as an airplane control cockpit, called a skin-scanner. Magnified photographs of the skin's surface are projected onto a screen and analyzed by Orlane saleswomen. The experience is like that of watching the moon's crust being investigated by astronauts. Questionnaires are handed out to be filled in by prospective customers. The scientific hustle and bustle around the department store beauty counters was becoming even more frenetic than back at the terra firma of the laboratories.

Some women—mostly those with time and money to spend—liked the whole idea, the exactitude, the search for the *right* product. But the young didn't buy it at all. They had somehow arrived at the conclusion, even before the Shelmire-Lubowe salvos, that such excessive proliferation of products was nonsense. And so they headed for the corner drugstore and bought the oldies but goodies: Noxzema, Pond's, petro-leum jelly, baby shampoo, Chap Stick. And they continue to do so today. The results are visible on the stock-market listings: Chesebrough-Ponds, Avon, International Flavors and Fragrances, are right up there on top with Revlon. For young women between the ages of sixteen and thirty-five, such basics buying has a symbolic dimension as well. Many of them are actively involved in sports. Most have jobs and little more than five minutes each morning to care for their faces. Many travel, and whether it amounts to dashing round the city or around the world, they travel light. Creams have to do more than one thing for a face, and so cleanser-cum-moisturizers were invented. What active sportswear has become to the tennis freak, baby oil is to the youthful consumer. She is as indifferent to frills and promises as she is, temporarily at least, immune to psychological pricing. Hope, for her, does not reside in a jar. To be sure, young women are still spending a lot on cosmetics: $652,000,000, according to *Seventeen* magazine's report in April 1975. That's 20 percent of all women's beauty expenditures in the United States. But younger women are buying different products for different reasons than the forty-ish matrons with advanced cases of wrinkle-fright.

What is this young realist's attitude toward paint? She loves it, of course. But she is not the customer for Norell's $7.50 lipstick which may, like most lip colorings, have cost about 50 cents to produce. She knows instead where to find Elizabeth Arden's formula under another name, at Woolworth's, for a third of the normal retail price. And she is the prime customer for a new concept in makeup marketing: gigantic displays in which samples of the colors are out there next to each other in little pots, to be gazed at, dipped into, and tried on. It is the Baskin-Robbins idea, with lots more than thirty-one flavors on view to tempt the eye and mouth. And, in fact, credit for the Face Factory, the first of such retail operations, goes avowedly to the ice-cream people.

The Factory has proved a great success in New York City, with the first four branches opening in a little over a year. Part of the appeal may be for impulse buying, to which cosmetics lend themselves with remarkable ease. Self-selection, in addition, eliminates the overhead of sales personnel and much of the formidable advertising cost that is usually built into the introduction of a product in department and chain stores. The customer who can forget about prestige and packaging reaps the benefit; all Face Factory products sell for about $2 each. The possibilities for suburban franchises of this type are, theoretically at least, limitless—*if* women can surmount the deep-seated notion that, in some magical way, paying more can make one more beautiful.

Paris, not surprisingly, developed its own version of the cosmetics supermarket in 1973. It is called Sephora, and comprises a multitude of little boutiques selling beauty products and perfumes by brand name. There is a salon de coiffure, and a health-food bar, a bookshop filled with literature on diet, a men's toiletries section, and even a bureau listing baby-sitters and physicians for each area of the city. The merchandising notion is slightly different from anything in the United States. It is the boutique concept transferred to beauty products and housed separately, with each manufacturer remaining in his space allotment, as at a Mideastern bazaar. Rather than attempting to cut costs to the consumer, Sephora fosters violent competition. The fact that the Sephora concept can coexist with low-overhead merchandising in today's internationalized cosmetics industry may tell us more about the varieties of female taste than about successful sales formulas.

However and wherever cosmetics are sold, it remains an axiom in the trade that they are recession-proof. The current economic slump may provide the industry with its greatest test to date. So far the optimism rampant at most levels of the beauty business does not look like a cover-up. In addition to the $7 billion spent annually on the products themselves, another $5½ to $6 billion is paid out at beauty and barber shops. It would seem that the American public spends most of its time washing, cleansing, moisturizing, shaving, deodorizing, brushing, manicuring, shampooing, polishing, sunbathing, and making up its face. What have the giant cosmetics industries done to create the rage for all this care and, particularly, color? Who needs the visual glut of twenty brands of pink, each shade only slightly different from its neighbor on the chart, and each bearing the sort of improbable name that more than likely represents a desperate last-ditch effort of some manufacturer's "creative" division to come up with an original adjective? How many colors can there be? How many names can there be? How many can *sell?* Is there no such thing as market saturation in the lipstick and nail polish field?

The answer is a resounding no. Lipstick is the target of more impulse buying than any other beauty product. As long as women go on having impulses, it will prove worthwhile to keep the counters stocked with a virtually inexhaustible supply of tubes. In the old days, when there were fewer colors, a woman bought a lipstick to go with something. Now that there are sixty shades of mauve, she is more apt to fall for the name. A shaft of "Milano Mauve" cannot put you on a plane to Italy, but there's little harm in accepting it as a substitute. As for the numbers of colors, Revlon's seven lines make a grand total of 535 separate lipstick shades, counting the frosts, the glosses, the creams, the crayons, and the little translucent pots. Move over, Baskin-Robbins! Like the famous ice-cream chain's flavors, new shades are introduced every couple of months; old ones that don't complement current fashion colors or just don't sell are periodically withdrawn. At Lanvin–Charles of the Ritz, a much smaller house whose list nonetheless numbers 1,400 items and 300 lipstick colors, about six new shades are introduced each season, while another six are phased out.

At the Lanvin–Charles of the Ritz factory in Holmdel, New Jersey, there is a special lipstick room. Production of that little tube of color requires seven separate operations: weighing the ingredients, pouring, stirring, mixing, molding, cooling, and unmolding. The primary materials may include natural vegetable, mineral, or animal waxes; suspensions (usually either sesame or castor oils); antioxidants that stabilize the mix; perfume; and chemical dyes. As many as twenty separate pigments may be used to make up one color. Generally, the more subtle and refined the shade, the more pigments are used, and this does account for some of the price differential in lipsticks. Up to fifty thousand filled tubes come out of the assembly line at Holmdel each day. Local women in blue uniforms do the handiwork, and there is a good deal of it to do; machines are still incapable of making cosmetics all by themselves. Although the liquid substance is mixed, heated, and poured automatically, the unmolding is done manually, each bright, solid little cone placed on an ice table to cool. Then every cone is scraped at the mold seams, and inserted into its metal case. Labeling and boxing are also done individually. All products are coded by year and day (7523 means the 23d day of 1975) so that if there are returns they can be traced.

The creams are even more fun to watch in production. The cream room is like a basement kitchen in the castle of a giant king. One must climb ladders in order to peer into cauldrons where the oils and waxes are rotated by long pipes with propellers attached to their ends. As many as six hundred pounds of face cream may be mixed at one time. The alcohol is then pumped from its underground storage vault through color-coded pipes into the suspension, and the churning continues until the creams are ready to be run off into jars. As in the kitchen of a scrupulous cook, the kettles must then be cleaned before the next batch; here it is done by lowering a man into the vessel from above.

Each type of product is assigned its separate kingdom. The room where powders are made looks like the Sahara in a pink windstorm—one must wear a mask to view the procedures. At the end of the day the storm subsides, leaving drifts of pale dust along the floors and in the corners. By the time "Camellia" or "Pink Geranium" reaches the customer in boxed and stable form, it has already had a tumultuous life of its own.

In still another section of the plant are the labs and the "weather area." It is here that the environmental testing is done. Extremes of heat and cold, dampness and sunlight, can be reproduced artificially. Shelf life depends on the elements, and the skin safety of products is ultimately due to the correctness of evaluations made in this department. Quality control is the last important phase of a company's regulations. This step insures that whatever exits from the factory is uniform with the company's standards, no matter where the product is to be shipped and no matter what the climate of its destination.

Most major cosmetics companies based in the United States have an international division. Revlon's is probably the largest, with sales in Europe, Africa, Asia, Australia, and Latin America adding up to over $186 million in 1974. (Revlon's total volume including the United States was nearly $606 million that year.) Plants in eighty-five countries throughout the world employ fifteen thousand workers. Although Avon, which sells on a house-to-house basis, is the largest cosmetics firm in this country, Revlon with its 3,500 products is second to none in stores. We tend to think of the United States as the single world market for cosmetics; it may come as a surprise that Japan is right on our heels.

It is advertising, of course, that makes a market. You must have lyrics to romance a product. You have to know about that one moment in her life when a secretary will pay $15 for a night cream. You have to know about the throes of impulse purchasing, about the lure of freebies even among the very rich, about what youth wants and what age will buy, about changing life-styles and every fad of the fashion industry. Are colors going to be Mexican or Moroccan for summer? Peruvian or Siberian for winter? Are we going to have alpine greens? Indian pinks? Which part of the world is currently flashing its ethnic electricity? What famous person's charisma is being beamed across the media waves with particular appeal this year? Are American women dreaming of county cottages and patchwork or of imperial gardens in Peking?

You have to do something brilliant every season with those two thousand raw materials you have on hand in the cosmetics lab. The oils, fats, herbs, dyes, synthetics, acids, drugs, eggs, milk, lanolin, fish-liver oil, wheat-germ oil, iodine, salt, tomatoes, orchid pollen, coal tars, silicones, minerals are waiting to be injected into rabbits, rats, and guinea pigs. The women out there are lining up to be cleansed, stimulated, conditioned, healed, protected, and made young forever by your product. Beauty editors' pens are poised over paragraphs on how to combat rough skin, unclear eyes, wrinkles, and lackluster hair. It is up to cosmetics to rush into the vacuum—the answer may be in the very next jar, the very latest development. One is never too old to start being youthful, as any convincing merchant of euphoria will tell you. It was the head of Revlon, Charles Revson himself, who said, "It is never too late to turn your life around. Cosmetics are just a means to that end."

He should know: Your face is his company's fortune. Revlon was begun in 1932, in the midst of the great depression, with a bottle of nail lacquer. Women hadn't much more than pink, old rose, and red to choose from before that, and those women who did the choosing were more than likely either ladies of the theater or ladies of the evening. The rest of the female population was loath to dip into the wicked stuff; paint had been associated with harlotry even before Shakespeare wrote "God hath given you one face and you make yourself another." As far as Everywoman was concerned, Charles Revson sounded the death knell of the Victorian age in the thirties. The glittering world of fashion was available to anyone for pennies a tube or a bottle. Pink and red were replaced by "Bravo" and "Fire and Ice." The connection between romance, *la dolce vita,* and a woman's fantasies had been made—by nail polish and lip color. The method? Double-page ads in magazines. With the help of fashion journalism, cosmetics advertising centered on that most private realm, the dream life of total narcissism—all made permissible by the fact that it lay in the public domain, was paid for by real money, and sold real products. The gestalt was made by the woman herself: No romance was *guaranteed* by the manufacturer. But the public relations people had done their homework. They studied film and fashion idols. They knew the meaning of glamour in concrete terms. And by offering the public penciled eyebrows in the thirties, fire-engine-red lips in the forties, lacquered hair in the fifties, and Italian eyes in the sixties, the PR departments both followed style and created it.

Yes, beauty products are recession-proof. Women will always want to be *à deux* on desert islands or in ravishing organdy at exclusive garden parties. Since there is something sexy about being very, very rich, the mannequin with hunting dogs at bootside, standing in cobbled courtyard, will attract some imaginations, just as others will be seduced by drawing room settings. Where the locale provides fantasy life, an ad can be effective even in black and white. This explains the success of Estée Lauder's invitations to visit the quiet luxury of a rooftop greenhouse or to dine tête-à-tête in black lace like house model Karen Graham.

But it is inevitably the Revlon two-page spreads that grab the eye with their zingy color, their glossy retouched perfection, be it for the Rich Girl Reds, the Vampy Mankiller Darks, the Frankly Foxy Firecolors, or regression to the nursery in tones of Powder Pink. The embarrassment level of such ads is low, but if a girl wants to be rich or voluptuous it need be a secret between only herself and her lipstick. From the "Fire and Ice" lady in silver sequins and Fu Manchu fingernails to today's Charlie girl, Revlon and its competitors have womanhood down pat. We are still buying images, and they are nowhere less expensively for sale than at the cosmetics counters.

chapter 8

the sweet smell of success

Another factor in the cosmetic industry's boom is undeniably the fact that success *smells* sweet. We live in an age that longs for sensuality. Bound by four office walls, hemmed in by metal desks, we are aware that part of us, at least, is still animal, magnetized by earth, drawn by our senses to that which is primeval in the world outside our windows and in other human beings. Ever since sex was rediscovered in the last decade, since the upsurge in body awareness, we have been conscious that the sense of smell is our most primitive endowment—and also the one most obscured by modern industrial life. Perfume used to be expensive, a status indicator like immaculate grooming and haute couture. Today it is the body cosmetic par excellence, well within the budgets of the youth culture which forms its prime consumer target. Scent has, in the 1970's, lost its snobbery and gained back its sex appeal. There can be no true boom in the modern marketplace without its trail of sociological sleuths determined to sniff out primary causes. The fad for wearing body oils has been explained as an attempt to entice the opposite sex in the same way that the male musk ox or civet attracts the female. Advertising of these oils (which must be chemically approximated, as real musk is rare) fails to take into account that human beings are not on record as being sexually partial to oxen or civet cats. Musk is, in fact, a fixative used in very expensive perfumes; by itself, the name evokes an aura, but not much else. On the other hand, human body odors are sexually provoking. In 1974 Atlanta medical researchers managed to isolate aromatic chemicals from the vaginal secretions of young women. These substances, called pheremones, stimulate males and have been known to exist in almost all animals, but had never before been verified in human females. It is ironic that in the American woman's anxiety about genital odors she effectively douches away most of her hidden cache of automatically produced attraction.

Once launched into natural fragrances, manufacturers were not willing to stop at musk. We seem to have gone full circle to Shakespeare's day, when a character in *King Lear* pleaded, "Give me an ounce of civet, good apothecary, to sweeten my imagination." Today patchouli, grasses, herbs, spices, and even green apples as well as civet are being bottled for the youth market. More and more scents are being created for every taste and price level; in 1974, $83 million was spent on fragrance—more than on toothpaste or shampoo. Old brands and bottles are being revived too. The venerable houses of Coty and Lanvin have lived to see the day when the original packaging and formulas of some of their products are enjoying a new vogue.

Like lipstick or nail polish, perfume is still cheaper than couture. It is well known that Madame Chanel's famous "No. 5" kept her design firm financially afloat for many a season, and that the same is true today at nearly all the couturiers. In fact, the prestige of a fine bottle of perfume is more enticing now than ever. There are a number of dress houses in France whose scent division is so economically sound that this part of the business would survive no matter what happened to haute couture. One of these is Parfums Lanvin, set up by Madame Jeanne Lanvin in 1925, and now managed by her nephew's son Bernard.

The mystique surrounding the formulation, manufacture, and advertising of "My Sin" and "Arpège" still recalls the glitter of the 1920's, when these perfumes were created. Like other fashion leaders of humble background but enormous flair, Jeanne Lanvin had been drawn to the stylized and slightly Turkish decor of the time. She commissioned the illustrator Paul Iribe to design a logo for her perfumes, and he produced the gold-lined drawing of herself and her daughter that still identifies all Lanvin products. The black ball that contains "Arpège" is as much of a classic as Chanel's celebrated bottle for "No. 5," and both products indicate the extent to which visual enhancement can contribute to the success of a perfume.

Unlike most couture houses producing their own line of toiletries, Lanvin is very much a family operation. Because

Madame's daughter, Marie-Blanche, was childless, Yves Lanvin, a nephew, continues as titular head of the company while his wife, Madame Yves, is chairwoman of the fashion house. In 1963 their son Bernard became general manager, and has expanded both men's wear and toiletries.

The most important figure in this retinue is, however, M. André Fraysse, *"le nez"* of Parfums Lanvin. Like a family retainer, M. Fraysse has worked for the firm for more than fifty years. It is he who created "My Sin" in 1925 and "Arpège" two years later, as well as the handful of other scents like "Scandal," "Rumeur," and "Prétexte," which are retired or revived according to current fashion. M. Fraysse, now in his upper seventies, is a man in love with his work. Like any fine "nose," he is a rarity. His olfactory senses are so acute that if they could be packaged in any way they would amount to a national treasure. He calculates that he maintains in his head and distinguishes between about sixty separate fragrance "notes" simultaneously. To this repertoire he has added over the years a multitude of different tonalities. When he talks about scent, it is often in musical rather than chemical terminology, though his laboratory at Nanterre, just outside Paris, is as modern as anything in a science-fiction novel, and the formulas he concocts there are just as top secret.

Winemaking, however, provides the vocabulary for M. Fraysse's descriptions of the manufacture of his perfumes. Jasmine is cultivated on the slopes of Grasse, in southern France, and must be picked between four in the morning and noon, when its petals are open. The extraction of essence is usually by *enfleurage*, a process by which the flower is pressed into a layer of oily matter which then retains the scent. Drained like squeezed grapes, the petals are discarded. The scent is distilled into a basic oil which is strained in huge tanks, then drawn off from a spigot, and stocked in smaller aluminum kegs, corked like wine. Eight hundred pounds of jasmine are needed to produce a single pound of basic oil, and that pound is worth a fortune. When combined with the sixty-odd different essences that go into a bottle of "Arpège," it is obvious why fine perfume is costly. Unlike a cosmetic preparation, the major expenses are not packaging and advertising, but the essential oils, the alcohol, and the blending. In a $35-an-ounce perfume, these costs may run the manufacturer upwards of $4.50, with promotion coming to much less than $4 a bottle, depending on the prestige of the house. (The more established the house, the less it has to advertise.) Some perfumers are able to put less than 10 percent of the wholesale price into bottling and packaging; conversely, their expenses for ingredients are skyrocketing to as much as $3,000 a pound for the very best French jasmine. Because of labor limitations, raw material shortages, and other effects of the economic recession, many are cutting corners by buying inferior Italian jasmine at half the price of the French, or by using more synthetics. The irony of all this is that expensive perfume, once considered pure luxury, is more in demand than ever. At $85 an ounce, Jean Patou's "Joy" is selling impressively. Between 1969 and 1973, general perfume sales rose 20 percent, from $68 to $83 million annually. Companies both here and abroad are having difficulty keeping the store counters stocked.

At the Lanvin factories near Bordeaux, eight thousand bottles of perfume spray and double that quantity of toilet water can be made up each day, but transportation costs must be added, for all those bottles come back to Nanterre to be shipped. Thus the Lanvin method of production goes full circle, winding back to the simple 1914 concrete building that houses M. Fraysse's sunny lab in one corner and a fleet of black Lanvin trucks in another. On certain days in the autumn, "Monsieur le Nez," as he is known, will call his dog, put his hands in his pockets, and stroll out of doors into the sunlight, leaving the tester strips to dry out and the Bunsen burners and beakers to gurgle on by themselves like something from *The Sorcerer's Apprentice*. On those special days, M. Fraysse heads for the woods, his pinched nostrils twitching like those of the dog, but his mission is neither hunting nor pleasure. It will be perhaps the thousandth time he will have tried to stamp his sensual memory with the aroma of mushroom or a mélange of oak moss. He has not quite resigned himself to the improbability of reproducing with exactitude the moods of substances he finds in nature, their scent at certain times of day, in fog or sunlight, in the spring or autumn he loves. That inquisitive nose for nature is a quality so removed from but so essential to the rest of Lanvin's operation, that the terrain of Monsieur le Nez is regarded as a preserve, a sanctuary. Even the truckdrivers greet him with friendly awe.

Unfortunately, M. Fraysse will probably have no successor. His son, though he has inherited his father's talents, is more interested in philosophy. Aside from the venerable house of Guerlain, no other perfume manufacturer in France has a resident "nose." When the skilled specialists go, all the experimental work will be farmed out to the large companies that hire chemists to create new formulas. When it comes to developing a fragrance for a couture house such as St. Laurent, the final decision on the exact scent to be put into production will be made in a board room, by vote. The head of the couture house has a veto to be sure, but his power is apt to be bureaucratic rather than personal.

An increasingly important part of even a family-run operation like Parfums Lanvin has come to be the market research division. Lanvin employs a public relations firm which runs surveys and does depth interviewing every two to three years in order to test the continuing validity of the Lanvin image. Panels of psychologists, experts on everything from human and animal sex behavior to the sensual significance of wine, food, and tobacco are hired for discussion of such issues as the role of perfume in the disguise of human sexual odors, the importance of the social acceptability of scent, and the new findings on territoriality and the significance of odor in intrusion on male power-holdings.

It is claimed that these brainstorming sessions influence Lanvin's future research and development activities, but in actuality, experience in the business seems to hold sway when major new decisions are made. For example, it is well known that a Frenchwoman will not change her perfume if her man doesn't care for it, although she is hesitant to adopt a radically new hairdo without his consent. (Interestingly, however, a Frenchman will change his cologne if *she* registers disapproval.) Perfume is an intimate part of self, and it plays an identity role with numerous inflections. In the United States, the popularity of the women's movement gave tremendous commercial "hype" to a perfume called "Charlie," which grossed $10 million in its first year. In France "Charlie"'s success is limited to a self-consciously liberated few. Lanvin's 1971 perfume "Via Lanvin" arrived on these shores with no special message for American women, and has failed to do well here. Similarly, in France where perfume is considered so much a part of one's self-expression, a man does not offer a woman a new scent; that would amount to subtle disapproval. Rather, he affirms her as he knows her by buying more of the same. Thus the continuing popularity of "Arpège," "Chanel No. 5," "Femme," and the other five or six classic perfumes. In the States, however, the feminist movement, combined with the new economic independence of women who work, has led to a pronounced trend toward women buying perfume for themselves.

The psychology of scent is even more a factor in the sale of men's toiletries than of women's. American men prefer heavy "notes" that transmit overt masculinity. Whereas the largest market for Lanvin men's products has always been Italy and to some extent England, in the United States Lanvin is still far behind Revlon's "Aramis" line, far and away the American best seller. Yves St. Laurent's toiletries have made a dent here, but the American male is still bent on buying domestic. Whereas some light, dry colognes of Guerlain or Roger & Gallet have a limited appeal in this country, the very European Eau Lanvin is not even marketed in the U.S.

Bernard Lanvin feels that this will change as tastes evolve; right now, however, perfumers are concentrating on still another phenomenon, the unisex cologne. When "Canoe" was first advertised as a scent for both men and women, it took off slowly. But as the unisex trend acquired momentum, "Canoe" 's precedent became an established advertising trick. Fresh "bright" scents with an ambiguous undertone, neither too floral nor too woodsy, do well today. In addition, new perfumes have been launched specifically for the sporty woman, notably Hermès' "Amazone" and Estée Lauder's "Aliage."

The latter has undergone a saturation advertising campaign that features a typical modern mesomorph engaging in all sorts of activities ranging from Ping-Pong to mountain climbing. The perfume itself is green and packaged in a no-nonsense bottle. Obviously, the perfume people, like their cosmetics counterparts, have figured out who today's woman is, even if she hasn't quite allowed herself the benefit of a clear identity yet.

chapter 9

streetshow

By 1970, the modern mesomorph was growing up. She had emerged from the Merry Widows and schoolgirl cinch belts of the fifties. The sixties stripteased her out of brassieres and girdles. Thus exposed, she learned about her body, inside and out. How was she going to clothe all this knowledge?

For a decade she played "try on" in front of the mirror. Shirtdress and chemise were relegated to the back of the closet as the costume changes took place. First she was a beatnik with long black stockings, then Jacqueline Kennedy in a pillbox hat. Successively she came on as a Poor Boy in tight sweaters, a gypsy, a Rich Hippie. She wore Op Art, paper dresses, silver-mesh legs; her hair was converted by elaborate switches and hairpieces into an accessory. She progressed through plastic madness, kitsch, the twenties, thirties, forties, and fifties. She went from low vamp to Haute Rétro, with a long pause at pants, work clothes, and the natural look. By the end of the sixties, she was weary of the great fashion circus. Fortunately at that moment the decade had the good grace to turn the corner.

But there was little rest in sight for the woman who kept up with fashion. As the seventies got under way, being à la mode was beginning to produce a noticeable strain, and responsible journalism was quick to record the fact. *Women's Wear Daily* drew a new readership to a section called "Eye," its on-the-spot reportage of *WWD*'s roving photographers. Instead of Jackie O leaving the Frog Pond (chicster name for the "in" restaurant, La Grenouille), they began to snap the kids at Bethesda Fountain. Their cinéma vérité photos made it plain that *Vogue*'s "last word" was falling on deaf ears. What women were really wearing was something else. *Vogue*'s high priestess, Diana Vreeland, to the contrary, there was no difference between fashion and what was popular.

Photographers like Bill Cunningham got interested in what Seventh Avenue mannequins actually wore to work. He took shots of them arriving in Woolworth tennis hats, turtlenecks, jeans of course, and perhaps a 59-cent scarf from Azuma. Such clothes were almost a ritual, he found—a trade talisman, an antidote to spending the day in a Galanos chiffon or a $2,000 de la Renta. With magazine models it was the same: "Lauren Hutton—just chosen the million-dollar-a-year girl for Revlon's "Ultima II" line of rich-lady cosmetics and destined to spend part of her future being photographed in stately home settings—this new idol of the seventies avowed with glee that her own wardrobe was "minimal denim."

But it took a devastating article by Gloria Emerson of *The New York Times* to produce the kind of ready response that every status designer has learned to dread. In snapshot and diatribe, Emerson enumerated all the silly mistakes of the current clothes scene. Not having to sell anything made her job as reporter easier, but the piece was also a spectacular departure from the *Times*'s usual comfortable glance around the world of family, food, fashions, and furniture. Suddenly, through Emerson's eyes, readers saw that the fashionable woman looked very much like a dupe of the latest profit gimmick. We have seen her so often: overaccessorized from outsized sunglasses to Gucci loafers; weighed down by gold chains, Ultrasuede skirts, and every letter of the alphabet from Adolpho to Valentino; her extremities decked out by the mindless and expensive vulgarisms of Vuitton and Pucci. She looked pathetic; she looked unreal. She seemed so very far from the way women really lived and felt, in fact, that it actually became démodé—right then on October 5, 1973—to wear the latest thing.

Furthermore, fashion, in spite of such foibles, actually admitted to a sense of something to which it is usually immune: guilt. Gloria Emerson's article was part of the attack that brought with it an agonizing awareness that neither the Cartier tank watch nor an Hermès scarf automatically confers nirvana on its owner but is, in fact, just another watch and another silk scarf. This realization brought on what was an occasionally embarrassing public outburst of envy from women who had everything. What they coveted, it seemed, was other people's *simplicity*—the "sophistication of the baby blacks" that had made New York socialites sit up and take notice at the Bernsteins' rad-chic Panther party in the late sixties.

Guilt took the social-consciousness route in the form of Bedford-Stuyvesant Bakuba fabrics conceived in that part of Brooklyn where racial clashes had been hottest in the sixties. The fabrics were used, however, in the collections of the likes of Seventh Avenue's Pauline Trigère and Bieff-Herrera. Even Bloomingdale's got into the act and produced an African-inspired housewares pattern created by disadvantaged ghetto students. Nor was the irony of chic lost on the little Manhattan boutique called Serendipity. In April 1974 it reported tote bags marked "Goochy" and "Weetonn" selling fast—but to the kind of customer whose closets no doubt already contained the original Guccis and Vuittons. Status in reverse is amusing only to those who can afford the joke in the first place, and the occasional sniggers of satire only seemed to point out how ridiculous things had really become. But at least the seventies swept in with a sense of humor—and a highly critical eye.

Gloria Emerson's last laugh had replaced *Vogue*'s "last word." That made it easy, at first, for everyone to relax a little. But before the party was over, the fashion fascists made a climactic mistake: the midi crisis threw the garment industry into a gigantic slump. After years of looking like coltish teeny-boppers, women weren't ready to put their legs in uniform again, and the mid-calf skirt length was a resounding disaster. As the curtain was rung down on Seventh Avenue, women heaved a sigh and turned back to slacks. Confusion reigned in the fashion forests; had the publicists like John Fairchild and his influential *Women's Wear Daily* gone too far? Why were *Vogue* and *Harper's Bazaar* following suit? A lot of money was riding on the midi. What were buyers supposed to order? How were stores going to get rid of all those long lengths? And what, in God's name, were manufacturers going to push for next season? Better to play safe and make pantsuits? Take a flier on hot pants? Try dresses again?

As it happened, the notion of a return to the classics moved in to occupy the burnt-out fashion imagination. No flights of fancy were taking off from designers' drawing boards in the 1971/72 season. The word came from Paris that Yves St. Laurent considered any woman well dressed who owned pants, a cashmere sweater, and a tailored raincoat. Meanwhile, women were having second thoughts about the whole runaround. After all, classics were never destined to turn anyone on. They are fine if your wardrobe has been decimated in a fire and you need new clothes. But so far as the industry is concerned, classics do not contain enough ideas to keep it afloat for even one season.

Then women themselves jumped into the breach. They had some ideas of their own about what to put on their backs. It seemed a good moment for them to get off on a new tack entirely: themselves. And what followed was a phenomenon known as antifashion. As the seventies opened, antifashion just seemed to will itself into existence. It was the solution for everything. There was not going to be any look. Women would not be taking dictation from the fashion magazines and publicists. Designers' clothes would be bought if they were desirable, not because they were in. It suddenly became evident that one need not buy an envelope bag and wedgies this season and discard them the next. There was no fashion hit parade. In addition to knowing her body, the modern mesomorph was beginning to acquire her own sense of style. And if "style is the dress of thought," she was, for perhaps the first time ever, clothing herself.

Not surprisingly, there were immediate visual consequences. At no period in fashion history have women looked so unlike one another. The seventies are a sweet street scene in which chronologies overlap: down-home dude to spaceship elegance, mini to maxi, flea market to silver screen—the woman watchers have never had it better. It's all out there on the street, where events have become the substance of our lives. Event-dressing began with early sixties' "happenings," and became a feature of the 1968 university riots, when what you wore to the barricades was picked up by every newspaper in the world. It continued the next year at Woodstock, and has become a permanently flickering newsflash, a public address system for "the way we are." Throughout all the political upheaval of succeeding years, event-dressing tuned us in to changing life-styles. Marriage and living together. Unisex and homosex. Nuclear families and communes. The urban circus and the suburbs. Work and play.

Take the latter. As patterns of living began to sort themselves out even more determinedly into job and leisure, the casual and sportswear sector of the clothing industry boomed. By day, women continue to wear functional separates and pantsuits (from what used to be called career sections of junior dress departments) for errands or office. But perhaps as a gesture against the tedium of technological day work, play clothes are enjoying an explosion of color and individuality. Underneath is the pervasive sense that people's most valued existence takes place on weekends and after work, in their homes or those of friends. At the same time, our public life is staged on the streets. Streets are the setting for strikes, parades, boycotts, demonstrations, rallies, riots, block parties, and celebrations of everything from politicians' victories to the rites of spring. Even if we live in the country, mob scenes choke our television screens nightly. In New York City, more and more sidewalk cafes are being licensed. At lunchtime, after five, on Saturdays and Sundays, in bars, parks, restaurants, galleries, museums, theaters, stores, resorts, and public plazas, the main occupation of everyone who is not actually working seems to be people watching. More and more we are experiencing what the French call *une foule de monde*, the great unraveling of the life of crowds. It provides a close-at-hand course in current events. There is enormous pleasure in it, a contrast to what is for many a drab work life. Like the Greek agora of long ago, like the medieval market fairs or the royal courts, or the salons and boulevards of nineteenth-century Paris, street life breaks our isolation and returns us to humanity. Most of all it gives us a chance to use our bodies and our clothes as a form of social language.

The crowd scene gives antifashion its time and place; in addition to all the other forms of communication, it provides the opportunity for either self-disguise or self-announcement. We know that dress, makeup, body style are intensely expressive of self. Looked at collectively, they measure society's barometric pressure. They are, that is to say, *political acts*.

That clothes have been useful as protest, for example, has always been true. Youth has always chosen to flaunt feelings of ill will toward parents, the establishment, middle-class morality, or whatever, by dressing in a way calculated to produce angst in society at large. And youth has always used the uniformity of its dress as a badge, a sign, a greeting of like minds, a triumph of its own solidarity. But what makes antifashion today so potent is the fact that it is rooted in a period when youth, for the very first time in history, is in a position to call the numbers all by itself. Thus the post-World War II *rats des caves* of Paris' Left Bank, the dark humor and anticorrectness of Juliette Greco's black sweaters and long hair, the negativism of Sartre and the cultivated slovenliness of America's beatniks were the real beginning of an antifashion attitude that may be around for a long time.

If we define ourselves by everything we put on (and by everything we take off), women today express where they stand on the liberation movement, on jobs, husband, children. By his tie or turtleneck, a man discloses his views on the stock market, careers—and women. The temperature of society at large is similarly revealed—increasing democratization; pollution; economic recession; distractions of information overload and media bombardment; the possibilities of travel; extended interests and activities; chronic lack of time. The sheer complexity of modern life: It is all there to be examined in what we wear.

If what fashion has always really been about is how people live, then antifashion can tell us even more. In a sense, it is fashion in lower case. But it matters little whether fashion is granted a capital "F" or prefaced with "anti": in either case it gets the message across faster than any sociologist, if we only know how to read it.

So let us grant the seventies its claim to antifashion, for the freedom to wear what you want, where and when you want, is finally here. With antifashion, clothes become street art. Through what they wear, people are now affirming their allegiance to groups rather than to backgrounds. It is no longer who you are, how much you earn, but whether you are a Mets fan, folk music freak, ballet enthusiast, Francophile, or university student. This explains the T-shirt, which announces your interests—and therefore yourself—to an ever-widening audience of curious people-watchers. Below the "T" is that other symbol of antifashion, the uniform of the clothes revolution itself, that tough blue fabric from Levi Strauss, the street scene's own indigenous, ingenious, inimitable, and probably irreplaceable jean.

If antifashion was invented partly to lend us a hand with identifying ourselves in the crowd, jeans certainly provide one of the best backdrops ever dreamed up by man. When they are, coupled with the billboard possibilities of a T-shirt, self-advertisement can have a heyday. By the mid-sixties, contemporary folk art was blossoming in psychedelic profusion on the rumps, cuffs, and legs of jeans everywhere in America. Embroidered peace symbols, sayings, astrological charts, landscapes, talismans of people's inner lives, mandalas rich with beading, omens, flags, designs borrowed from the Hopi Indians or from Tibet, animals, clouds, butterflies, rainbows, studs, buttons, patches, beads, tooled leather, patchwork, shells, old lace, dress labels, fur, feathers, braid—the profusion of stitched, stuffed, and sewn fantasies that flowered on denim in the jeans heyday was, and still is, a measure of our hunger to sign our *own* name to what we wear.

There is a deeper hunger too. We are a relatively new nation, with voluminous energy in manufacturing but all-too-short roots in crafts. As a nation we somehow envy the San Blas Islanders who appliqué what they see into their fabric vests, or the Eskimo or Lapp women spending long evenings embroidering their lives into the artifacts of daily use.

IN JAPAN THE COAT IS KEPT SIMPLE. Example of an almost patternless garment cut so as to waste no fabric. This is an early 20th-century man's coat that shows the indigo blue and white material to good advantage. (From *Are Clothes Modern?* by Bernard Rudofsky, Paul Theobald, Chicago, 1947)

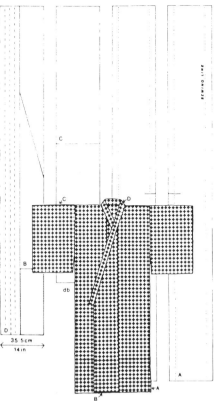

EVEN IN WESTERN DRESS of not so long ago, simplicity was possible. This is a basic garment cut from only three widths of fabric. It was made in the mid-19th century in northern Greece, but its influence is still felt in some Balkan clothes. (From *Cut My Cote,* by Dorothy K. Burnham, Royal Ontario Museum, 1973, reproduced by permission.)

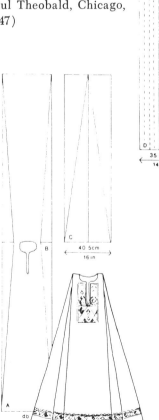

Americans have always woven their own histories into quilts and samplers, but, compared with the needlework of other peoples, ours is a curtailed tradition, though one both indigenous and strong. The satisfaction of making what we wear was aborted when the first Sears catalog came out in the mid-1890's.

It was not until the sixties that the counterculture broke through with a revival of handicrafts. Too busy hacking out a new lodging or life-style, too broke or self-involved to add significantly to the mainstream of the arts in this country, the counterculture has nonetheless given the craft movement new life. In the last decade, crafts made a significant impact on the fashion scene. Macramé, knitting, crochet, embroidery, and sewing all lent themselves to that expression of individuality that seemed to be lurking in each of us, ready to jump out and bark at the mass manufacturers whose imaginative capacity for anything but dress detailing was almost nonexistent. Implicit, too, in the whole do-it-yourself movement was a gesture against shoddy workmanship, uninspired design, lack of fit, and all the other by-products of a clothes consumption gone mad. We were all pioneer hipsters, up to our desert boots in the environment, recycling, nutritional ecology, and the whole six-pack of this nation's neoromantic Friends of the Earth stage. It was a mass, middle-class preoccupation, and everybody joined in, at least with the refrain.

Making things continues to help people feel good. We want to recapture the sense of personal effort made tangible in wearable folk art. Denim is so durable that it can be worn almost a lifetime. It holds a needle well and is easy to stitch. Even after the backing has worn away, a piece of all-over embroidery can be removed, recycled, handed on. During the sixties, people began stitching their life histories into their pants. And with the birth of the mass-produced T-shirt as the last capitalist caper, one could increase identity impact by literally wearing one's heart on one's sleeve. We were costuming ourselves for the street.

The sixties showed us that we needed popular craft roots, and we found them. Before home-decorated denim had run its course it had given rise to a tremendous revival in crocheting, tatting, appliqué, macramé, bargello, needlepoint, and quilting. Magazines for young women, in addition to those directed at the matron trade, began running sections on how to cut bikinis from dishcloths and jazz up T-shirts with studs. Books called *Hassle-Free Sewing* and *Clothing Liberation* appeared on the shelves with directions for turning old clothes into wearables—out of the closet and into the streets. The results are still with us, and the needles go on clicking.

But manufacturers were burning to supply us with their own parody of the down-home look—in multiples. After all, Fruit of the Loom and Levi Strauss didn't make a fortune by watching little old ladies and liberated hippies take over the sewing industry. They geared themselves up for a killing. Several million dollars later, the world found itself short on natural cotton and almost out of denim. In 1964 Americans bought about a million pairs of jeans. Net sales at Levi Strauss amounted to $111,500,000. Nearly a decade later, volume had multiplied six times over—$653 million in profits in company pockets, and 400 million pairs of jeans on American backsides. Moreover, a rage for denim was coloring everything blue: wallpaper, upholstery, luggage, bed sheets, linings for mink coats, watchbands, nail polish. There was even a denim-covered Bible. The air itself smelled of denim, thanks to colognes that bore the name and a brand of French cigarettes called La Vie en Blue Jeans. For the 1973/74 season, American Motors offered denim car seats in their Hornet and Gremlin models. The greening of America was turning blue.

The Bavarian immigrant named Levi Strauss could hardly have foreseen, in 1850, what would happen to his product. By now everyone knows how the fabric got its name: Strauss needed a tough cloth to make pants for gold rush miners; having run out of the sailcloth he originally brought with him, he sent to France for *serge de Nîmes*, used by Genoese sailors for their trousers. On these shores "de Nîmes" soon became "denim" and "Genes," the French word for Genoa, was anglicized to "jeans." At 22 cents a pair, these tough-wearing garments got around. Cowboys, lumberjacks, farmers, and railroad men as well as miners bought them. Back at the plant in San Francisco, they were being perfected—double-top-stitched for strength, reinforced at the pockets to prevent tearing.

When women began to work in factories during World War II, jeans, popularized by Rosie the Riveter, proved to be the most practical garment by far. Later they were made for children. As kids grew up they kept on wearing jeans, right into the James Dean-Marlon Brando era, when denim topped with a leather jacket spelled "tough." By the end of the fifties, Levi's stood for another kind of nonconformity—they became "beat" and signaled a rejection of middle-class decorum—until *Vogue* and Yves St. Laurent picked them up and made *le jean* the last word in chic. Today *le jean*'s popularity has settled somewhere in between; it has become the great international mid-cult classic.

In microcosm, the jeans story provides a look at how fashion actually operates today. The usual process of filtering down from the elite to the masses has been stood on its head. What is new about this is not just the reversal of procedure; it is the role of youth as entrepreneur and catalyst in the system. Style now starts from the street (or soil) and works its way up, generally through adoption by young people quick to grab new trends, until it kicks off some designer's imagination and emerges in the expensive guise of haute couture. The metamorphosis of denim into a costly commodity reached its apogee in the year the furrier Jacques Kaplan did mink coats dyed the exact color of blue jeans. But perhaps the final irony in the denim story is the importing of French jeans into this country at prices sometimes reaching $75 a pair. This about-face provided the Madison Avenue chic with their kicks, demonstrating that anything from the other side of the fence has to be better. It was in much the same spirit that American blues became objects of veneration to Soviet youth, who will still do what they can to plead or plunder a pair right off the visitor's unwary frame. In St. Moritz boutiques, high boots inlaid with denim patchwork were all the rage in 1974, while lace-appliquéd jean skirts and embroidered Westerns were still going strong at rarefied prices in St. Tropez. Denim has since gone through a gamut of phases: washed out, sharp new indigo, secondhand, studded with nailheads, frayed, creased, legs ripped off into shorts, sides pieced together into skirts, farmers' overalls, low-rise, high-rise, tie-dyed, *Easy Rider* style, U.S. Navy style, bell-bottomed like the original sailor's version. With all this to choose from, Americans are up to their eyeballs in the blue stuff though France is only slightly less jeans-crazy than we—38 million sold in 1973, and by now, who knows?

The irony of the jeans story is that denim has proved to be in the social sense truly democratic, but not only for the reasons one might think. This is not a case of the same pair of farmer's jeans being bought and worn in the fields, while being simultaneously purchased in boutiques to be paraded down Fifth Avenue. This is happening too, and it's true that, wherever they're bought, the difference in price is slight. But the kind of social leavening we're talking about concerns a more subtle clash of values. Moreover, the values in question are strictly urban. One might call it Madison Avenue versus SoHo. The ladies on Madison are fashion-conscious. They are first with the trends, they have money. They are the ones photographed at Orsini's having lunch with Halston. They— and their numberless followers—shop at Veneziano and Yves St. Laurent's Rive Gauche. They are first at the couture-copy showings each season; in the sixties they popularized Kenneth Jay Lane's snail-shell earrings, they bought Courrèges. They bought the clothes with designers' initials. When the decade turned, they bought jeans.

Meanwhile, the inhabitants of SoHo, New York's newest Bohemia after the demise of Greenwich Village, profess no interest in clothes. Though SoHo began as a few square blocks of old cast-iron warehouses and small leather-goods manufacturers, it is now chock full of artists, carpenters, journalists, mathematicians. First discovered by painters and sculptors who needed space, the area is now overrun with art groupies who live on the fringe of SoHo life. The reason for jeans used to be obvious: They're good work clothes if you paint. But now antifashion has made its mark in a curious way in SoHo.

Everybody there wears jeans. And while disdaining the Madison Avenue art dealers and their denimed wives who come slumming in SoHo on Saturdays, residents of the area can often trace their new affluence to those very same uptownies. Of course, SoHo citizens do not trade in their jeans the moment they can pay the rent. But it does cause a conflict: uptown and downtown, both in the damned blue stuff. Insofar as democracy can result in uniformity, New York City certainly has both.

There is one variation on the Madison Avenue-SoHo battle worth mentioning. SoHo's brand of antifashion is to seem not to care. Though many really don't, one does notice that people look at one another. In its way SoHo offers the liveliest street life in the city. The best-dressed girls are the ones who are in the most basic sense of the word self-conscious, as opposed to clothes-conscious. They already know their style and put themselves together like mobile works of art. A far cry from the Madison Avenue scene, where what one first notes is the abundance of gold jewelry, all of it heavy. The clanking can be heard for blocks, like the shrill consumerism, the rapaciousness for whatever's new. SoHo may exude an insinuating reverse chic, but the idiosyncrasies of its women are far preferable to the lacquered mummies of uptown. The secret is perhaps that SoHo is where a lot of street fashion is originating. It's the very center of antifashion—the kind that grows up around the arts and draws on them for inspiration. Poiret at the turn of the century hired Dufy, de Segonzac, and Maillol to work with him; Schiaparelli in the thirties cultivated Cocteau and Dali, whose influence lent her designs a whole new scope. For some reason, many people think that fashion today is created on Seventh Avenue; Seventh Avenue creates mummy cases. SoHo, with its medley of Orientals, Italians, Spanish, transplanted French, blacks, and college dropouts, is its own melting pot, its own hippiedom. No Louis Vuitton pocketbooks down there except on a visit; but uptown will soon be seeing Ethiopian string bags. SoHo is where you can hate fashion and have it too.

Does Denim bring freedom to its wearers? Or is there a denim dictatorship? The battle of capitalist versus SoHo blue jeans goes on. But it is only part of the antifashion picture. The rest is up top in the shape of the T-shirt. Like denim, T-shirts are French in origin and plebeian enough to please any fashion democrat. They began as cotton underwear, discovered during World War I by American doughboys and preferred by them to their own itchy wool union suits. In the 1940's they reemerged as "tee" shirts for golfing and other active sports. It wasn't until the sixties that they became part of the scene, an everyday occurrence. Today, it is the T-shirt that has put ego into clothes; has underlined the "I" in fashion. Whereas denim, whether uptown or downtown, bespeaks conformity, the T-shirt acts as a tabula rasa for personality. Its social anatomy is a lot less subtle than that of blue jeans. T-shirts are bought not for convoluted antifashion reasons, but to allow their wearers to announce—to amplify as with rock mikes— the screaming-meemies of self-hood. A T can project availability (*Voulez-vous coucher avec moi ce soir?*), nationality (*Je suis Americaine*), affiliation (Boys' Town), aspiration (Superman), education (Rutgers, CCNY), partisanship (New York Mets), parody (New York Bets), rock-star preferences (The Rolling Stones), or subtle forms of commercial advertising with which the self is identified, like wearing a *New York* magazine sweatshirt or one printed with a Zabar's logo. The first says "I am into the scene and read a groovy magazine"; the second indicates allegiance to the Upper West Side of Manhattan and affection for its local delicatessen and gathering place for lovers of lox. Like graffiti artists, T-shirt owners can disclose their identities outright, by names, initials, telephone numbers, or even blown-up photographs of themselves transferred onto the cotton. The effectiveness of this route to selfhood is reflected in sales, which have reached nearly fifty million printed T-shirts a year.

There is street humor in T-shirts too: in-jokes, harmless swipes at racial groups, a celebration of pop culture from Chicken America to Bungalow Bars. The messages are all there, easy to read as flash cards. The more sophisticated versions are often unlettered, however. They bear the latest in decor, proceeding from tie-dye to ombre, through kitsch (silk-screened palm trees) to plain pretty (embroidered Mexican flowers). Whether or not they bear a wearer's ego on their chest, the T coupled with a pair of jeans is the one street uniform that carries another built-in significance of superimportance for the seventies: It is unisex.

chapter 10

from bralessness to unisex

At a time when the "in" life-style is bisexual, it is not surprising that dress should be unisex. Remember the bra burnings of the sixties? Even the French cried, *"La poitrine en liberté!"* If the moment of birth for a new trend can be documented, it was then that unisex was born. We have seen how physical liberation proceeds along with the peeling off of clothes; total body lib in the literal sense is, after all, nudity. The sixties had allowed women to step out of their corsets, girdles, waist nippers, crinolines, and all the other paraphernalia of Dior's long-lived but much outmoded New Look. Leotards, bodystockings, and pantyhose took over. The brassiere was deboned and the stuffing removed until it resembled nothing more than a deflated blowfish. The no-bra created by Rudi Gernreich was an updated version of what used to be called a bandeau, worn only by those women who felt they needed its support. As for the rest, bosom visibility was nearly 100 percent. When seen through the perspective of a T-shirt, the braless trend provided some compensation to those men who missed the miniskirt.

The underwear business went into a coma, however. If women were going to wear as little underneath as men, where was any money to be made? The survival of a company became a matter of how quickly it could diversify. Partly in order to satisfy and partly in order to create a demand for "at home" wear, the lingerie people turned their attention to the sort of clothing of indeterminate classification that looks as though it could move from bedroom to poolside with ease. Suddenly women found themselves in long skirts or palazzo pants. It was chic to stage little dinner parties on patios, in greenhouses, around swimming pools, and even in bedrooms. The lingerie industry itself had opened the latest salvo on lingerie, switched from inner to outerwear, and survived.

Not only did the industry circumvent extinction; it prospered. In addition to the at home alternative, there were variations on the sportswear theme to be tried out. The best-known bra company of all, Maidenform, was already manufacturing bathing suits by 1970 or so. As bikinis gained their slow acceptance on American beaches, adventurous women were no longer forced to pay import prices for French or German merchandise; U.S. firms went into the bikini business for themselves. Once Rudi Gernreich put the topless bathing suit into the news, if not actually on the sand, swimwear became a most profitable sector of the trade, often forcing a merger of lingerie with sports manufacturers. The cry for topless yielded first to the Brazilian string, a reduction of the bikini that joined the crucial patches by the thinnest of threads. Then, in 1974, Gernreich was back on the scene with the thong, a one-piece bathing outfit that approached bottom-lessness, being cut high of thigh and low of back. After topless, backless, and bottomless—now what? The only certainty is that familiarity breeds contempt in the clothing business. And that the male eye becomes rapidly accustomed to finding sex where least expected.

Nudity? Never. Or probably never. The mind's eye craves mystery too. In spite of the predictions of writers like Gerald Heard and early psychoanalysts of clothing trends like Flügel, total uncover will probably not become a common public sight. Apart from the need for protection against the elements, everyone knows that partial clothing is far more erotic than the totally bared body. Meanwhile, nudity as a political wedge remains useful. People *do* want to swim from time to time unencumbered by social convention. But once local laws prohibiting nude bathing are repealed, swimsuits, having been reduced to mere symbols, may cover up again.

No, the only modern phenomenon that would put the lingerie people out of business would be a preponderance of female streakers. Barring that possibility, loungewear, as it is called in the trade, will be around for a long time to come. Particularly as the lingerie unions demand less pay for their members—under half the amount set by the coat and dress unions. According to the logic of Seventh Avenue, therefore, we will be seeing more and more variations of casual dress on the market, as manufacturers exploit the low pay rates of the lingerie makers. One new twist is for dress establishments to cash in on the financial bonus offered by the dissimilar rules of the unions. Stephen Burrows and John Kloss, for example, both have casual wear divisions for which they design, leaving production to be farmed out to lingerie sewers. This accounts for the big difference in price between, say, the more formal Stephen Burrows evening pants, and a "Stevie" (Burrows) lounging suit—both of which could be worn to the same party.

The latest sector to get into the body business is that of the dance apparel firms such as Capezio and Danskin. When many women started wearing their leotards to work so as to avoid changing for the lunch-hour gym lesson, it was apparent that leotards were fast becoming the modern mesomorph's underwear. The styling was so simple that leotards were quickly popped into service as both streetwear (with jeans or wraparounds) and evening dress (with a long skirt). The evidence was plain: All that sixties body consciousness produced enough good figures to make leotards as classic as blue jeans. If our decade has any article of underwear to call its own, it is certainly the leotard—in twenty different colors.

The final irony of the underclothes revolution was the popularity, in 1974 and 1975, of old-fashioned Sears, Roebuck woolies as outergarments. Home-dyed, threaded with ribbons and appliquéd with lace, the winter bodice of yesteryear and the hated Carter's undershirt of one's prepuberty days made their debut as evening chemises or hot-weather tops.

In spite of everything, however, it is safe to say that maximum exposure has not yet run its course. Bare breasts, naked navels, strapless tubes, backless backs, fig leaf fragments—what it comes down to is something more than the mere hullabaloo of skin-deep liberation. There is a far more profound emancipation at stake. After all, women bared their breasts in Minoan Crete, in the Renaissance, in the courts of Burgundy, and in the aftermath of the French Revolution. There is plenty of precedent for such partial nudity, especially in culturally and socially adventurous periods of history. Why again now? Because we too are living in exciting times. And uncovering those areas of the body commonly accepted as erotic brings with it an exhilaration, a new-found freedom from, of all things, the very fear of nakedness. When asked for comments on the "new wave of nudity on public beaches," a lay psychologist was thus quoted in *The New York Times*: "Having exposed yourself, you no longer have to fear that someone else may expose you. You have made yourself completely open to the world, but you have picked the conditions." Just so: Modesty is Out. Do-it-yourself is In.

If near-nudity is exhilarating, its opposite, the clothing of constraint, affords its own kind of erotic stimulation. The veil of sexual fantasy runs a gamut from the body-clinging pleats of ancient Greece to the corsets of yesterday and the perennial reappearance of those old dependables, black stockings and garters. Given our modern concern for comfort, we have come to call any garment that restricts movement punitive. But for many women, and men too, such restraint upon muscular— and emotional—activity tends, as Havelock Ellis remarked in 1942, "to heighten the state of sexual excitement." Pain is the logical result of tight bodices, chokers, corsets, belts, and shoes. And discomfort can intensify body awareness in a way that is sometimes pleasurable to the wearer—as it can be, apparently, to the onlooker. That our most sophisticated fashion magazines are aware of the appeal of punitive clothing has been pictorially evident since the sixties. A 1967 issue of *Vogue* featured Twiggy in leather handstraps and headband.

In 1970, armbands, laced belts, and thongs made a multiappearance on another mannequin. It is not necessary to go as far as the heroine in *The Story of O* for physical restraint to be mildly pleasurable. Think of the cinch belts of the fifties.

To a certain extent, the seventies' equivalent of what psychologists call skin eroticism is the body dress. Made of a clingy synthetic or real silk jersey, its appeal lies more in the realm of touch than in constraint. Like fur, velvet, and satin, the material itself can act as an erotic stimulus. Relieved of the linings and interfacings of the architectural school of clothing design, we are left with a collapsible silken tent, a body covering that communicates a truly seventies sensuality. Its effect might be best described as the intensification of physicality by means of dress.

Clothes can be sexy to the ear as well, as Robert Herrick's famous lines amply illustrate:

> Whenas in silks my Julia goes,
> Then, then, methinks, how sweetly flows
> The liquefaction of her clothes.

But above all, dress is visual stimulation. As such, dress must be in a state of flux if it is to play a role in attracting the male and keeping his interest. Most men need to *see* sex appeal in order to feel it; therefore, the focus on erogenous parts of the body shifts constantly. In the late sixties, legs bared by miniskirts headed the list of female attractions. Even as late as 1971 Gloria Guinness reported in *Harper's Bazaar* the following statistics from London: A radio opinion poll reported that 90 percent of the men noticed a woman's legs before anything else. Eight percent thought breasts were sexier, and all of 2 percent looked at a woman's face before making up their minds as to her appeal. With the simultaneous advent of bralessness and the T-shirt, masculine preoccupation has moved upward. Whether it will ever actually focus on the face for the majority of males is a moot question, but this seems unlikely.

One thing is certain: Clothes are and probably always have been a metaphor of sexual subtleties. In the eternal tension between revealing the body and concealing it, in the urge to exhibit—whether it be a glimpse of ankle or stark nudity—in the play of motion versus the excitement of restraint pulses the very ambivalence of erotic encounter. Refusal, assertion. Leading the other person on, running away. Yes, no. Clothes can be the continuation of sex by other means. We clothe ourselves, we say, to attract. But sometimes our aim is to protect as well. Whole societies may lean one way or the other. Compare the Victorian age with our own or even with the freedoms of France's Directoire years.

The sexual significance of clothes relates not only to the wearer and her audience but to the designer as well. Take the matter of homosexuality, for instance. It has always been assumed that most dress designers are gay. Dr. Edmund Bergler, a psychiatrist whose study of the question was published in 1953, agrees with this assessment. Having analyzed over a hundred homosexuals connected with the fashion field, his findings are undeniably accurate. But the stereotype of the designer with a neurotic mother-fixation and a built-in hatred of women is out of date. There may be a few classic cases around, but even they are not uniformly bent on either making females ugly or transforming them into little boys.

Occasionally, but less often than one would expect, a flagrantly unrepressed comment surfaces in Bergler's inquiry.

Once, in the midst of treatment, a patient burst out with a diatribe against "fashion-crazy women [who will] accept any style, even if they have to be pressed between two steamrollers before they can fit into it. . . . Let them wear corsets so tight that they can't eat at all. Who cares?" Part of the coming-of-age of women in the seventies has to do with their refusal to accept this sort of sadism, even in milder versions. The old exclamation "I don't care if it hurts—I want to be beautiful!" hasn't been uttered (audibly, at least) since pointed-toe shoes went out of fashion. The "Big Look" of 1974/75 signaled an extreme move away from punitive clothes.

As for female homosexuality, that too has been taken into account by the fashion press. Some of the more sophisticated women's magazines began to exhibit a covert lesbian appeal in the late sixties. Since the artfully laid-out fashion photographs of models in the altogether coincided with increased nudity in theater, film, and the arts in general (remember Charlotte Morman's topless cello concerts?), it is hard to say whether *Vogue* and *Bazaar* intended a new openness that would inevitably attract a lesbian readership, or whether those magazines were simply following the trend. In any case, their glossy pages graced with Verushkas and Marisa Berensons in the buff sent out a message of almost strained modernity and with-it-ness that was bound to be interpreted as a sexual come-on by some fashionable voyeuses. Those naked bodies were not, after all, in there to sell clothes. As lesbianism continues to come out of the closet, new publications appear that address themselves even more directly to such female preferences.

Meanwhile, the sensual innuendoes of the expensive fashion publications have reverted to an almost self-conscious heterosexuality. Witness the May 1975 issue of *Vogue*, whose editorial focus is intimacy. Shot in the St. Tropez villa of Elsa Martinelli, the first photo has a male model unclasping (or perhaps struggling to hook) the front of a mannequin's bikini top. Neither of the two wears anything else. The result is a strangely glassy-eyed look at the possibilities of haute porn. But when the small print is examined, the real sales pitch is revealed: Revlon perfumes. The scent theme continues with provocative close-ups of a man biting a woman's ear lobe, a modern version of the dabbing-on of perfume behind the ear. A dog sniffs a girl. There are looks, whispers. A female onlooker pops up from behind the shrubbery to watch a couple kiss. A model sits with her legs apart. What might seem like deliberate titillation was actually very carefully planned so as to avoid total nudity and to demonstrate, in the words of publisher Alexander Liberman, "respect for the artist, respect for the reader." It was done at a cost of $10,000. No expense was spared, perhaps on the premise that the result might thus be rendered good for the soul.

Such is the price of modernity. But *Vogue* is not, after all, *Town and Country*. Just so there would be something for every reader, the same issue included a series of all-female photographs taken by Deborah Turbeville at a public swimming pool. Though the models were clad in bathing suits, there was an unsettling feel of lesbian lethargy about the way they shot looks at each other that just avoided eye contact. Readers found the Turbeville pictures even more offensive than the sexy villa shots, perhaps because—content aside—they were more atmospheric, more connected to unconscious meandering.

Turbeville's method leaves a lot to the imagination. No one

objects to the *garçonne*, the woman dressed in man's top hat or tie and tails—a mode in which both Dietrich and Twiggy have often been photographed. The woman-as-man is an explicit joke in tangible black and white, a sophisticated exaggeration which, it is claimed, only helps to enhance a woman's femininity. But a moody, steam-filled locker room at a public pool, with women looking mysteriously past each other, is something else. Such photographs feed fantasies, and fantasy is what both sex and fashion thrive on.

The fact that gays and lesbians are beginning to be recognized as people has brought to the fore a few essential conflicts we experience as a society. In the past, a continuing, subconscious fear of regression to homosexuality has certainly been the strongest force behind sharp sex differentiation in clothes. If a man exaggerates his virility with codpiece, sword, helmet, top hat, high collar, or whatever emblem the tailors of his era provide him, it is in part to affirm his sexual definition to himself. Similarly, the pinched waist, low décolletage, and sweeping skirts of feminine dress. Bobbed hair, short skirts and cigarettes were, at the outset of the twenties, felt to be irreconcilable with womanliness. But with that uncertainty past, and the fear of sexual ambivalence reduced by our knowing that we are *all* "a little bit of both," clothes no longer have to perform the duty of differentiation and can relax into being just clothes.

With the final onslaught of women's emancipation in the sixties, plus the arrival of the Pill, the roles of the sexes vis-à-vis each other received a violent shaking up. The resulting social confusion was expressed in dress with the advent of unisex. Long hair, male peacock clothes, and all the attributes of a return to Edwardian dandyism for both sexes served only to muddle an older generation that wore itself out muttering about how impossible it was becoming to tell boys from girls. In its own many-feathered multimedia way, the fashion industry promoted unisex as the perfect expression of our psychological ambivalence. And so it is. As long as the confusion lasts, so will unisex. For any fashion that correctly represents altered attitudes between men and women is bound to be around for a while.

Mid-seventies, the chicest way to swing is ambisexually. Rediscovery of bisexuality was destined for the spotlight from the very beginning, it being the avowed preference of such luminaries as Mick Jagger and his wife, Bianca, the social von Fürstenbergs, and film star Maria Schneider of *Last Tango* fame. Not that the AC-DC mode is anything novel: its roots are entwined with those of even preclassical civilization.

Another sidelight of the fashion business, as of literary and artistic circles throughout history, are those women—not necessarily of lesbian leanings—who have provided *inspiration créatrice* for male homosexual designers and artists. In an enthusiastic espousal of sensual sophistication, publicists now like to call these women "fag hags." But in the fashion demimonde they perform a valuable service. Many, such as self-styled "fag moll" Loulou de la Falaise and Picasso's daughter Paloma, work as creative assistants to designers like St. Laurent. Others, like model and socialite Marisa Berenson, give visibility to the clothes made by friends such as Halston. In return they are squired around to various parties by these designers who pose no romantic threat while providing intelligent and sensitive company. The interplay of varied sexual modes cannot be omitted as a source of ideas in any art. But in fashion, sex is just beneath the surface, and its ambivalences are there to be drawn on directly.

It should be no news by now that body consciousness itself is a form of sensuality strongly ingrained in the world of fashion. For a while in the mid-sixties, we were so carried away as to make it seem that the cult of the body had replaced love as an ultimate ideal. Certainly body consciousness acted as a shoring-up against the kind of social anesthesia that produced Herman Kahn's unthinkable predictions and the Dr. Strangelove terrors of an automated society in the midst of cold war. The body became our protection against loss of feeling. But the sixties gave us the body with a difference: Through its touch lay the route to the "inner person." And although being naked was hardly new, it was the means to an end, unlike the nudist colony where *only* the body is so chastely exposed. For the sixties bequeathed us Esalen and Big Sur and innumerable weekend retreats all over the country— "wild game preserves" in which the "encounter of souls" supplies the element of eroticism. The cult of touch, the catechism of the body, had taken up the war against one of the commonplaces of everyday life—alienation.

And it worked. For whatever reason, we began to feel more comfortable first with sex pure and simple, then with homosexuality, and now with androgyny. Some day we shall no doubt be able to take ordinary sexual confusion in our stride, though our preoccupation with male-female roles is still at a stage that precludes this further step. Meanwhile, unisex in dress provides a reconciliation of sorts, and a tangible proof that our sexual tensions have relaxed a bit. At least, freed from exaggerated differentiation in dress, men and women are no longer constrained to behave toward each other in certain prescribed ways because of the way they are clothed. A frill-shirted dandy can be straight, while pinstripes can disguise the most perverted longings. The man carrying a shoulder bag is more than likely not in the least effeminate, while the one in the mock-macho zoot suit may be. Especially in Nescafé society do the varieties of sex mingle. No matter how much we reprove the Beautiful People for their antics in the realm of sexual tolerance, they provide a lesson for us all. Plurality of mores is what it's all about. Notions of what is sexy can be changed as often as the one-night-stand dress, which is returned to Ungaro's or Valentino's in the morning. Learning not to be astonished is part of the game. One's petticoated dinner partner with the Bardot décolletage might be a follower of Betty Friedan, a playgirl, a pop singer, a garden-variety lesbian, a transvestite, or even an ordinary BP. In sex as in social status, clothes are not being asked to do the job anymore. The outer, safe rigidities are gone, and the burden of one's erotic preferences in the seventies is squarely on one's inner self.

chapter 11

when "vogue" is out of style

In the seventies, style has become one of our minor obsessions. Perhaps this is because it has taken on an entirely new meaning in our vocabulary. When we talk about fashion today we can be referring, as often as not, to life-styles as to body shape and ways of dressing it. A far cry from what fashion's proper concern used to be: the achievement of elegance and good taste.

Style, elegance and taste had always been inextricably linked. Combined, they created a rarefied atmosphere, an aura apart from real life, a world to be aspired to. For one thing, they involved the acquisition of valuable objects: real pearls, real chinchilla, real Chanels. These possessions embodied style.

The word was also used to connote the things one did. There was the high style of high steppin' at the Stork Club, living the high life swank of the thirties, letting the good times roll. Style was the audible, visible measure of pleasure, the *way* you spent your money or your lost weekends. F. Scott Fitzgerald had the right kind of obligatory sense of fun. Josephine Baker purveyed it. The stylish consumed it.

Style could be place: Hollywood, Harlem, Southampton, Biarritz, Monte Carlo. Style was definitely manner. It might be spirit, too, but it was always spirit made manifest by things. For decor, style was the enhancement of a room by beautiful objects. In clothes, style resided in choice of ornament, in the detail of a seam, the correct fall of a bias cut. One worked at style the way one worked in classic ballet—one practiced technique until it appeared effortless. But whether it was clothes or nightclubs or houses one discussed, style was above all evaluated in terms of the diehard standard of good taste.

Today, the old definition no longer works. Now we know that taste has always been an arbitrary matter, a means of presenting the unadventurous consumer with a convenient measurement for choice, and a pat on the back for reassurance. Good taste is apt to be the last resort of people who are afraid of being reckless with a sense of who they are. One even begins to suspect that tastefulness may be the all-too-familiar middle-class repression of baroque instincts. If that is so, honest vulgarity points the way to one of our truest pleasures, a humane preference for what is generous and full of vitality against that which is inhibited and static.

Whatever became of elegance and taste as the epitome of style? The seventies have forgotten elegance; deep down we even despise it. Although 1973 heard a great deal of talk about smoking jackets, formal dinner parties, supper clubs, and feminine glamour, it all had a false ring, being an exclusive product of fashion journalist mentality. The only real style around that year was the cool of black and Puerto Rican dandyism in the streets of New York.

For us in the seventies, ornament is a trivial part of style. Interior decoration has almost ceased to exist. The Billy Baldwin clutter of objects has yielded to built-in furniture or pillows on the floor. Flower arrangements have been replaced by weed pots and vegetables as centerpieces on dinner tables. As for the high life, it now survives most notably as a brand name for beer. To speak of high style in clothes nowadays is to talk in purest camp dialect, akin to using the word "classy" to describe an outfit.

No, style today is none of these. Instead, it comprises the way we live, which is to say that whatever way we live becomes what fashion is. Or seen from another viewpoint, style may be considered that manner in which it is possible to give some personal flair to living.

But we have only recently begun to come to terms with this new concept of style. If we look back to the early seventies, it is evident that what was meant by it then was really *stylization*—that amusing flamboyance, that special use of the conscious artifice of decay that occurs in the sensibility of a culture that has exhausted its innovative élan and is waiting for the lights to go down. During the time lag between the ebb of creativity and the blaze of new ideas, many artistic gifts abandoned themselves to stylization, to perfecting and "doing a number" on what was already old hat.

Perhaps it was a reaction to the kaleidoscopic ferment of the sixties. We found ourselves at a creative stalemate, and the natural stance in such a situation is to look back, to pick and choose from the ragbag of history those eras that provide us with a ready-made image. The late twenties to the forties provided such an image, and we expended much of our creative energy on nostalgia for their imagined virtues. By the early seventies we were wallowing in *la nostalgie* to the brim, from flea-market fashion to Art Deco ashtrays to kitsch, until we had nearly managed to forget who we were. What were once thought of as popular vulgarities, like Coke bottles or saloon advertisements, were elevated to levels of hermetic interest that automatically made them objects for connoisseurs. In such ways we cherished the twenties, the lost innocence of our prewar past.

Designers of clothes, furniture, and utensils, like their counterparts of fifty years ago, found themselves preoccupied with style as an issue in its own right, something that rarely happens when true innovations are taking place. Of course there were exceptions. Andy Warhol, who combines in his person and in his work that sweet-tough mix of child artist let loose in a roomful of the toys of supercontemporary industrialization (scraps, broken machines, plastic radio parts, wires, telephones, viscous recording tape, and acrid-smelling film reels in their metal casing), is the archetypal all-around manufacturer of what might be called "artifactory" concepts. Warhol is the best designer we have in the new sense of style because he infuses these playthings with his own city-child appreciation—an appreciation born of innocence and of necessity. His toys are the things that surround us all and animate our lives. We are all space children, by turns subdued, entranced, frightened, instructed, connected to the world by objects like these. As grass and cows recede into the unreality of storybook scenery or are visited like aging relatives in the country, the actual props of our lives emerge from fantasy, like Superman swooping out from the television screen. How does a designer create objects for clients to whom Mother Goose is a kind of salami and Monty Python and Marcus Welby are real people? The only solution has been to retrace the origins of such modern fantasies to when they first began to dominate the media, and the media had just begun its assault on us. That time was the late twenties and the early thirties.

So back they went, those designers, to put their questions of style to another era. And soon we were wearing their answers: the floss and dross of *la mode Rétro*, as the French christened its determined tackiness. Rétro became for some a sophisticated sign of ambivalence toward Warhol's industrialized playthings on one hand, and at the other extreme, rejection of the whole "artifactory" of urbanized and mechanized living. Mostly, however, Rétro was just another form of escapism by dressing up.

While a return to the twenties and thirties seemed a bizarre state of affairs for those who had actually lived through them once, no such problems were posed for the very young, who espoused Rétro with enthusiasm. For them, it was a playback in time, dressing up to the sounds of Tommy Dorsey, decade-tripping backward to eras they thought were luxuriously troublefree and worldly as a child's image of adulthood. Smoking with a six-inch holder suddenly seemed as daring as making up in public for the first time or lighting up an illicit cigar. All that innocence was before the war and the Bomb changed everything forever. We needed to recapture just a smidgen of what shock may have meant before the world became permanently shock-proof. But in the flea-market psychology of youth in the early seventies, there was disdain threaded through all the fascination: the square-shouldered suits of the forties were grotesque, the Bakelite clocks supported by yellowed nudes gave off a deadly whiff of incipient over-consumption. Plastic meant mass production in its infancy: how amusing yet disconcerting to discover the first hexagonal earrings in the exact shade of clotted blood, the first pop-up Chen-Yu lipstick case, the first automatic coffeepot in the shape of a Deco dog. Objects were sought after with a slightly superior smile—and perhaps barely disguised annoyance—for Today was what it all led to.

Today began with the postwar fifties and the wind-up American dream that didn't work, then proceeded to the cynicism of the sixties when all hell broke loose in the form of happenings, art that self-destructed, strontium 90 in our milk, sodium nitrate added to our soup. The whole catastrophe of hysterical over-consumption began—and worse, much worse, was to follow. So we have had to put up with it all, but at least early seventies fashion afforded us the option of dressing like fugitives. You could go down to the flea market and pick any century you wanted to belong to.

In the course of their rummaging in the not-so-distant past, designers unearthed an idol who serves now—as he did then—as a summary of stylization. He is a gentleman still very much alive and active at over eighty, and his name is Erté. As fashion illustrator to the twenties, Erté fixed in the elite imagination all the excitement of life as an extravaganza, but one rooted in an exacting and crystalline elegance that had even then outworn itself and worn out its creators. Though highly innovative, Erté's avant-gardisms were confined to the realm of clever earrings that merged into a pendant, or bracelets snaking up the arm like huge sleeves of jade beading.

Erté's witticisms and elaborate conceits seem at first glance too theatrical, too fussy for the seventies. But the affinity for nostalgia is potent: One can't help but be seduced by the logic of a slotted ascot, the slyness of a sable cape wrapped like a conch around the pearly silk cone of its underslip. Erté's women possess lethal eyes and preserved hair; there is an almost conscious cruelty in many of his drawings, such as that of the figure suavely garbed in silk chiffon trimmed in fur, and rammed, legs apart, onto a wooden hatstand. There is menace in that cuff consuming the hand of its wearer like a predatory plant; in the medieval cowls, the padlocked belts, the jewelry devised like an intricate harness; just as there is madness in his masks, his woven ribbons, his hatpins of invincible grandeur, suitable for a Borgia.

In contrast, what sweetness in the man himself! Who else was there, in the twenties, to take so much trouble over pockets, pleats, folds, tassels, trinkets? Erté is still an artisan of the imagination. In his costumes and sets for the Casino de Paris spectacle of 1972 he is as much *il miglior fabbro,* the best of "makers," as he was in the early drawings of 1911. But he has confined himself to his own kingdom like one of his small jeweled beasts! His black and lemon satins are not for today. Nor, unfortunately, are his maids' uniforms with their farcical Feydean aprons, nor the tasseled togas, the arrogant aigrettes, the hornet-shaped helmets made for mythical heroines of the decade's fast set. Perhaps Erté should have costumed *The Story of O.* That would have given scope to his erotic finesse, the sashes tendriled like wasps, the hair bindings, the feathered face masks, chin straps, tassels, furs, and fans. Instead he merely recorded his own fantasies, and it is with kindly amusement that he has watched women come to resemble his stylized versions of them. As a working observer of the fashion scene, he continues to present us with a view of what we are, and he has just finished designing a set of unisex tunics for the sort of people we will probably become.

His achievements have not gone unnoticed by the keen eye of Yves St. Laurent, who brought Erté's legacy with him into the trade like a fabulous inheritance. In 1972, one of St. Laurent's rare visits to this country coincided with Erté's eightieth birthday party, which was being celebrated simultaneously in Paris, London, and Manhattan with exhibits, posters, publication parties, and other commercial fireworks. At a reception held by his American editors and packed with fashion groupies, Erté was greeted by St. Laurent as "Maître." The shy younger man spent nearly all his time at the party in reverent horn-rimmed examination of the folders containing his idol's India ink sketches, magazine covers, and costume designs. Like Erté, St. Laurent has designed for ballet and theater. But the resemblance ends there. Erté is an illustrator who happened to turn his hand to fashion. He gave his audience what was then the range of the possible, showing women how to dress like works of art—if they cared. As it happened, they mostly did not care. Yves St. Laurent, along with others of his ilk, offers what he thinks his prototype woman *wants* to be seen in. By doing so, he reflects precisely one of the differences between the aware taste of our times and that of the twenties. Erté drew in detail what resided in his imagination, but he did not see women. St. Laurent, on the other hand, must clearly envision his kind of client, the kind who will buy and wear his clothes. That he has in mind prototypes and not individuals is merely a shortcoming of our own times brought about by the demands of production and of the ready-to-wear industry.

Erté may represent the formalities of style past, but a Puerto Rican illustrator named Antonio is probably more in touch with style future than anyone else in the fashion business nowadays. It is no accident that he grew up as a New York City street kid; his vision of what lies in store for fashion is tough and metallic. The melting-pot technique of his art ranges from Léger to pop. There is ferocity in his women, and a merciless macho in his sketches of real people dressed as they are, looking as they actually do. No fantasy, no prettifying touches up his portraits of Paloma Picasso or Pat Cleveland. Though he is barely past thirty, his work has appeared extensively abroad and he is just beginning to be known to magazines here. Perhaps Americans are not quite ready for the absolute truth of rippled thighs and furrowed foreheads in our jet set idols. Nor are we willing to accept frump in our clothes. For us, photorealism is still a school of painting, to be bought off the wall of a SoHo loft and not off the rack at Sears.

As for style present, perhaps St. Laurent more than any other designer has widened its meaning to include the whole way a woman lives—while having been, at the same time, one of those artists most interested in rediscovering the twenties and thirties and most attuned to what they had to offer. His collections show progression from a mannerist's insistence on the exquisite end of style (his tramp dresses of 1971, which so upset the journalists) through the sort of awareness of the absurdities of industrial civilization that brought on the disenchantments of *la mode Rétro*. In 1968, St. Laurent was the only designer on record to go down to the barricades at

Saint-Germain-des-Prés to see the new definition of style in action. After that, the word "elegance" all but disappeared from his vocabulary, and though he still draws on past decades for inspiration, his concept of dress has done a radical about-face.

Today, St. Laurent will not talk about clothes and style in the same breath. He believes that style is a manner of living: *"C'est un façon de passer dans le monde—de vivre."* It has little to do with how you dress, and is not to be found in objects. What he does feel is that women should build up a simple tailored wardrobe, like that of a man—one that can be renewed season by season by whimsical accessories, cheapies, throwaway fads, and occasionally some solid additions. Like the great American dressmaker Norman Norell, St. Laurent feels that women are given too many looks, too much bad gimmickry from which to choose. To have "more and more practical, fewer and fewer things" as Norell once said, would put the burden of selection squarely on the client instead of on the designer, as in the past.

One of the great attractions of Rétro was that it demanded exactly that sort of individuality of imagination. One had, quite literally, to put oneself together from finds, oddments, bits and pieces. To look conventional was an impossibility. Before the swing to Rétro, one might have fallen irrevocably in love with an impractical dress that reminded one of childhood or country vacations, only to have the voice of reason pipe up with "But where would you *wear* it?" And it would remain in shop or closet while all the sensible little Courrèges-like dresses were trotted out for everyday. But now, now one could don one's fantasies daily. And fantasy was fashion enough for a while.

In the evening, Paris cafes were awash with secretaries in pre-Raphaelite hair and floating chiffons, prewar wedgies and rayon dinner suits, or slimpsy gathered dresses with a paper carnation in the bosom. The dreamy, make-believe undercurrent of life was being plugged into once again, and the dated decors of Julien and Bofinger's, the Pompeian red columns and echoing spaces of La Cupole resounded with late diners. "Trashy" carried a new cachet: it was the look coveted by gays and straight alike. A borrowed elegance ruled Parisian nightlife, and though it lacked its Boris Vians and Juliette Grecos, though its old-fashioned stylishness was self-conscious and a bit warmed-over, it was nonetheless nice to behold. St. Laurent's wardrobe is all very well for daylight and the economic logic behind it is faultless, especially in a recession, but it will never do for evening when dreams float to the surface of street life. For those times, the maverick and amusing couturier Louis Féraud has his definition of style— and notice that though he uses the word "elegant" it is in an entirely eccentric new way. To be elegant, says Féraud, is to be a little crazy—on the condition that it hardly appears evident (*Etre élégant c'est être insolite à condition que cela n'apparaisse presque pas*). *Insolite* is a very French word which has no real equivalent in English. Perhaps the closest our language comes is "unusual," or "unprecedented." That has to be the modern definition of elegance if the word is to survive at all. And it applies nowhere so well as to the vagaries of flea-market finds.

Although not so well-endowed with such markets as the French, American women do have thrift shops and attics. One admirable facet of Rétro was that it opened up so many possibilities to anyone whose choice of clothes was not passive. Caprices could be satisfied by serendipitous finds at hospital charity shops and school bazaars, by digging into the proverbial grandmother's trunk. Some of the finds were lovely, gauzy Gatsby frocks made like handkerchiefs, or high-collared "waists" of the nineties, monobosoms filled in with handmade lace. But less attractive items showed up too: yellowed straw boaters; crushed and dusty velvet flower trimmings; the glassy-eyed fox muffler, jaws clamped on its own tail, which did nothing to warm the shoulders of her who wore it. Then there was the inevitable, funereal geometry of Art Deco: the silver diamond spangles on knitted vests, the machine-carved double belt buckles, the endless metal clips for hats and necklines.

What was underneath the fascination of Rétro? Why the welcome granted almost anything from another decade? It was nothing so simple as not being able to face our own times, as some have suggested. It was not just that a whole generation of young women was being unnerved by future shock. It was not even our inability to invent design forms to suit the world we live in. Perhaps, when we thought about it, the future *did* frighten us a bit, for we seemed totally unable to imagine the clothes for it. Even the futuristic *Clockwork Orange* had its characters in jumpsuits, which had been worn on the streets for some time. Or perhaps we had a need for distance, for perspective, for calling a screeching halt to progress, to the telescoping of time, to velocity. By looking back, we may have thought we could see more clearly where we actually were. But social inadaptation was only part of the answer. The fact remains that in the absence of an avant-garde, a leadership, you quite simply have Rétro: if you aren't going forward, you gotta go back. At least it provides society with some sense of motion.

And then there was the plain fact that those who had the nostalgia habit, being too young to have known anything but the sixties, and perhaps the fifties, were at liberty to re-create the less immediate past any way they saw fit. Rétro was a past made by almost-children, colored in by the old films they were crazy about, personified by Garbo's off-the-shoulder silks in *Camille*, by Dietrich and Hayworth in strapless satin, by the pristine perfectionism of patent leather and faultless makeup, by fabulous furs and cashmere dressing gowns and white interiors. What escape it all offered: the idea of sitting solo, somewhere in a dark cafe, slouch-hatted and oh so sophisticated, having a Dubonnet! It was a mood that even an occasional fad for glitter snoods or turquoise toreadors failed to undermine.

There were solid economic reasons for Rétro as well. Where else but in secondhand shops, at reject prices, could one find fabric with the slimpsy feel of silk and crepe? Where else to buy a dress of early rayon, its surface tart to the touch like the insides of an unripe melon? Where else to unearth garments made with so much attention to detail and ornament and seaming, for a few dollars at most? The young were sick of sportswear, the country-club look of it all; they no longer wanted to look "trig," as *Vogue* liked to call the shipshape products of its favorite tailored designs. The sixties were barely over when kids were beginning to stage another romantic rebellion in the realm of clothes, but now it was fur boas, maroon nail polish, and Carmen Miranda platform shoes. It was, that is to say, antifashion in yet another guise.

This time around, unconventional dress didn't include the sullen retort of stringy hair and filthy jeans. Instead, it was firmly based on two tenets without which antifashion could not exist: the personalization of clothes and the refusal to buy from mass producers. The Frenchwoman has always been mistress and guardian of the first; Americans have occasionally led the field in the second. Even a Parisian schoolgirl will not hesitate to remove the collar from a ready-to-wear dress bought for her by her mother, or to add fringe, change a belt, pin on a flower at the very least. With the emergence of Rétro, she was in her glory, at last able to track down a dress that could be hers alone, one of a kind, without having to take out her sewing machine.

In the United States, impatience with the shoddiness of mass-manufactured clothes was given an outlet in thrift-shopping. There has been increased grumpiness about paying—not just a lot of money, but any money at all—for polyester cheapies that don't fit, that open at the seams at first wearing, that are hot and uncomfortable. The same anticonsumption impulse took hold abroad, in France particularly, although European ready-to-wear, even in the early seventies, was nowhere near as gargantuan an industry as our own.

The sequel to the Rétro story is a familiar one in a society as industrialized as ours. Soon the racks at Macy's and the pages of French and American magazines such as *Elle* and *Glamour* were full of ready-to-wear versions of the 1930's geometric print rayon dress, complete with gathered shoulders and big plastic buttons. As with jeans, manufacturers were quick to copy what they saw on the streets. The now-defunct London firm of Biba was one of the first to capitalize on the Edwardian look in the sixties. It is significant that Biba did well enough by

1974 to open its own department store, which offered the trendy customer every period from pre-Raphaelite to fifties in Biba's famous muddy colors. Stores everywhere began to stock contemporary camp fashions. Fake fur boas appeared, as did the famous platform sandals, the halters and tubes of the forties, the little European dirndl-skirted sundress which was actually worn on beaches in the fifties and was really quite pretty in flower-printed cotton.

True romantics, meanwhile, have been ransacking history all over again for other ways to dress. The neoclassicism of the early 1800's may be next on the horizon. And it must be said that there are some specifically practical advantages to being able to pack one's entire wardrobe in a single bag, or to pull a chiffon dress through a wedding band, the supreme test of chic in Empress Josephine's age. Much of Directoire dressing we can easily appreciate. Was it not Mademoiselle Tallien who attracted Talleyrand's attention at an Opéra ball when she appeared wearing a simple white silk tunic, no underwear, and only sandals and rings for ornament? Such *negligé* clothes are much like our own body dressing. Indeed, one contemporary designer, John Kloss, is famous for his nightgowns delicious enough to wear to parties.

When all is said and done, Rétro bore with it an eventual sadness. Perhaps it was the creepiness of wearing another person's clothes, which seemed unnatural, like living someone else's life. Rétro in the end was nothing more than a disguise, though it was a colorful one, demonstrating, as it did, so many ways to decorate one's personality.

The death of Rétro coupled with the worldwide recession of the mid-seventies has produced another curious flowering of antifashion. In a 1973 copy of the fashion newspaper *W*, designer Michael Taylor had this to say: "We're moving away from the lush, pretentious period look toward the 'poor look.' It's always been in great taste to be poor." There you have it complete with the comfort of taste certification. It's okay to be poor. It's even chic. But you can be sure that what a designer calls poor will cost you a lot of money. Like Sonia Rykiel's Poor Boy sweaters or Chanel's little working girl jerseys, which made her famous.

While playing poor is a sign of devotion to fashion among some, poverty is a fact to be taken seriously for a lot of American women. They are putting their money where it counts, "on food, education, and travel," said Eleanor McMillen, director of the powerful industry-related Fashion Group, in 1974. And she should know. "These things are more important to her than what she puts on her back. We in the fashion business must change our thinking." But that same autumn brought the following report from Françoise Giroud, France's newly appointed secretary of state for the condition of women. When asked how the female population had responded to her appeal to economize on clothes in accord with the economic austerity program, Madame Giroud had to reply: "The reaction has been quite simply awful." There are some sacrifices that Frenchwomen are not ready to make, even for the good of their country.

In France, as among the imaginative elite everywhere who were still relatively unaffected by rising prices, the cult of poverty took hold nonetheless. But its evidence was in the look of things, not in what they cost: fashionable indigence doesn't come cheap. *La mode pénurie*, as the French tagged it, was not brought about by necessity so much as by a retreat from all the fin-de-siècle decadence that fashion had just been through.

This reaction was what prompted all the talk about a return to simplicity, recycling garments, and what I shall call thinglessness, or the wish not to acquire, to own very little.

As with other types of antifashion, the street served as laboratory for the new reality clothes. The hallmark of reality dressing is wearing what you already own. Like the proverbial lady from Boston who never went out and bought hats but quite simply "had" them, too much concern about clothes has become passé. It is as though we suddenly realized that indulgence in Rétro, in camp, in fostering an eye for objects, is an art borne upon affluence. It represents, like Michael Taylor's kind of poor look, a fashionableness that demands that we be consumers, though consumers with a highly inflected ideal and a rationalized selectivity. It is an old story, this effort at not buying, which turns us into purchasers nonetheless. The surest way to avoid the entire problem is, inevitably, thinglessness.

Using what you have may be a permanent psychological legacy of the ecological sixties; it may be dictated in many cases by a real need to save money; and it is most certainly a reaction to the high prices, overstandardization, and poor quality of Seventh Avenue's products, but, for whatever reasons, the tenor of the mid-seventies is certainly anticlothes. Signs of this were sporadically evident in the glossy magazines as far back as 1972 or so. Whereas *Vogue* used to tell you to sling last season's fur-collared cashmere into the nearest trash can, it began developing a new conscience about ditching such articles of clothing. Instead, you were told to tuck it in for spring. That little touch could make all the difference. Fashion magazines may yet have a future as specialists in the little touch, which has become their brand of recycling. Designers have their own conservation methods. St. Laurent, for one, is on the right track when he talks about a wardrobe of basics that can be worn forever and not thought about twice.

At a lower price range than St. Laurent, a young designer named Bernard Carasso has staked out territory in the old Les Halles district of Paris and opened a shop called La Porte Bleue. Here he sells nothing less than dresses made from recycled flannel. He expects the women who purchase his clothes to remake, lend, or give them away once their fashion lives are over. But *never*, he says, should they be destroyed. Originally bought from an old man in Cambrai, a small town in the north, this flannel was three francs a meter, all of it a rather unattractive color which the French call goose shit (*merde d'oie*). Carasso (a Ph.D. and formerly a sociologist at the Ministry of Education), now buys surplus goods wherever he can find them and redyes his fabrics to vegetable hues of violet, green, and blue. His purchasing price has been forced up to six francs a meter, but the principle remains the same. It is *la mode pénurie* at its purest—just one step removed from not buying anything at all. How does Carasso account for the success of his *flanelle de santé?* It is, he says, the triumph of "the supersimple, superaustere, natural, ecological, and the cheap."

The direct origin of this impulse can be traced back to the great midi crisis of 1969/70, after which, as everyone is tired of hearing, womankind kicked the habit of fashion slavery and struck out on her own. Normally, tracking down fashion changes is a risky business at best, but 1970 presented women with a foul-up of such magnitude that buying nothing at all amounted to taking a political stand on the midi issue. A confluence of factors both ideological (like women's lib) and practical (what Seventh Avenue was telling the magazine editors to print) added up to the kind of watershed in fashion history that turns everything upside-down once every—oh, perhaps thirty or fifty years. From the confusion, women themselves emerged the victors, industry the loser. Manufacturers were in despair. Unemployment was rampant. The authority of commercial tastemakers dwindled to near zero. Among them was John Fairchild of *Women's Wear Daily*, along with all the rag-trade publications that had, in a doomed joint effort, pushed the midi over the brink.

Short of a specific industrial goof like this one, the vacillations of fashion are elusive to say the least. Pinpointing some of the factors of change can, however, show a good deal about the kind of social climate that dominates a period. For example, only during the era just past, when haute couture reigned and designers were kings, could you have had the explanation of the engineering of change given in this quote from Christian Dior's *Memoirs*: "One fashion comes as a reaction to the preceding one, and changing it is a delicate business, practically a matter of conscience. The most successful ones are those which develop the slowest, and I always try to distinguish between what one no longer likes and what one still likes and what one is about to like." That sort of assertion is exactly what 1970 overthrew.

What else changes fashion? War, of course, is the absolute arbiter. Technological improvements may alter methods of production and fabrics themselves. A place—such as St. Tropez—may spawn fads like the bias-cut swirl skirt or the basket shoulder bag. Personalities, intellectual movements like nineteenth-century romanticism, a rise or fall in standards of living, mass education, events: a play, a party, a film, an exhibit, a political victory, a pop song. In 1909, when Diaghilev brought his Ballet Russe to Paris, women responded with a frenzy of esteem for everything Eastern and faintly barbaric. Colette describes some of the effects: "Ever since the appearance of the Russian ballet my friend Valentine has worn, in a stiff manner, fashionable clothes which might just be tolerable on someone with the smoothest Oriental grace. She uses rose and jasmine scents, swears by Teheran and Ispahan, and she doesn't hesitate—while wearing a Byzantine dress brightened by a Marie-Antoinette fichu, a Cossack cap and American shoes shaped like sabots—to exclaim: 'How can one not be Persian?' "

People outside fashion tend to speculate on the action-reaction theory. Clothes are tight for a decade and then extravagantly loose. Hair was chopped in the twenties, waist-length in the sixties. Both, say the sociologists, meant the same thing—rebellion. The visual results were exact opposites only by chance, due to the times just preceding them. Before the twenties, ladies of proper demeanor wore their hair in a bun; the fifties, on the other hand, were a haircutter's dream. And so fashion is pushed along by the mere need for change, whether politically charged or the result of market saturation or sheer inertia. In the past, the impulse sometimes has been created by necessity. From China and Persia came the infamous *chopines* of seventeenth-century Venice, for example. These were shoe platforms that raised women as much as twenty inches from the ground. Their original purpose was to keep the owner's feet well above street filth, but soon they became signs of elevated social status as well. Today's platform soles are more a matter of caprice. They are throwbacks to the forties, when wedgies were the rage, and thus part of our

Rétro mood. They also have acquired another significance during what is now close to a generation of wear. When higher heels took the place of the beatnik ballet shoes and "flatties" of the fifties, there was nowhere to go but up. They were a boon to petite women who wanted to look tall and slender, and to females who were no longer content to be shorter than men.

Costume historians favor Laver's law of change, which is that "a dress is indecent ten years before its time, daring a year before its time, chic at its time, and dowdy two years after." James Laver, the well-known British expert on fashion, was no doubt correct in principle, though the speed at which society changes may have thrown off the time calculations a bit. Another favorite theory of Laver's was the "shifting erogenous zone." According to this notion, changes in dress occur as the focus of interest moves from ankle to breast to thigh and back again.

But none of this explains how all the major design houses in Paris happen to be filled with chinoiserie one season and Russian motifs the next. In the winter of 1974 everyone wore cossack skirts, frog closings, Orthodox crosses, and high boots. Two years later it was the mandarin influence. Is there a couture Mafia? Do designers discuss their collection plans at cocktail parties? Do the fabrics manufacturers sell every house the same bill of goods? Although the conspiracy theory of change has won a lot of converts among women who believe that the industry is bent on putting their personal wardrobes out of commission, it appears that any consensus of designers on, say, hemlines, is purely accidental. What happens in fact is that designers themselves are prey to the law of action-and-reaction. If skirts have been short for so long that the eye is bored, hemlines simply drop. And that's all there is to it. Within the trade it's called the jungle-drum factor, which is to say that communication is almost never direct but by invisible airwaves. Carmel Snow, the wise editor of *Harper's Bazaar*, described it best. She said that "to be in fashion one must be very aware of the weather." To *create* fashion thus takes even more delicately attuned antennae. It's all a question of atmosphere.

In today's postmidi crisis, without the old fashion machine that shrieked like a nanny if you didn't run out and buy *Vogue*'s own list of the top twelve key looks of the season, women have nothing to rely on but themselves. And it has worked. Even the security blanket of investment clothes—the classics—has diminished in importance. You have to develop a forked nose about fashion. We have distanced ourselves from where we used to be. Those charts of what to wear with what in the glossy magazines are amusing relics of a past in which women wanted to be pushed around. Similarly, the do-and-don't lists: "DON'T settle for a shirt out of the past. The shirt you're looking for now is as soft as a blouse—not a blouse-y blouse with lots of fabric, but sensuous-soft, thin as the thinnest silk handkerchief, with an unbanded collar that falls back like a sigh, or no collar. . . . DO own—even if you have to learn to sew and make it yourself—the shirt that's a blouse in a small, classic print—a foulard, a dot, a flower." All the what's-in, what's-out compendia, the editorial fashion lectures of yore, simply make us laugh. As far as the future goes, industry forecasts, whether by computer or via consultants, trend spotters, or bulletins like "Fashion International," record what's happening but don't go out on any limbs. Such newsletters are for store buyers, and they can't afford any more large-scale mistakes. More often than not, they are hesitant enough about the next season, let alone five years from now.

Even the computers have given up, since none of their predictions about style changes has turned out to be correct. Promostyl, a syndicate for the promotion and distribution of French fashion, has tried to program trends and cycles on their IBMs, but the results have been thrown off time and time again by everything from the October 1973 oil crisis to the unexpected tenacity of jeans as a look no one tires of. The computers don't know why tennis sweaters were a flop in 1973. They have no answer as to why pedal pushers didn't make a comeback in a given season. Was it because the particular models on the market proved unwearable except by giraffes? Or was it because, in August 1973, *le culte de la nostalgie* was confined to romance and ignored sportswear? Will seamed stockings remain the disaster they were that summer? Or will they, perhaps, return as the ultimate camp item in some frowsy future?

The great fascination of fashion is, of course, that no one knows how to predict with any measure of accuracy. The speed at which society moves, the complexity with which it operates on different levels simultaneously, its sheer velocity make a mockery of past attempts to nail down the significance of trends. The efforts of sociologists and costume historians to do so seem strained today. Demonstrations of how rising or falling hemlines correspond with ups and downs in the stock market appear just plain ridiculous. James Laver's attempts to correlate periods of liberation with increased nudity and periods of social repression with covered-up clothing may be accurate generalizations for the past, but even Laver was confused by the sixties and hesitated to play the oracle about things to come.

That trends are becoming harder and harder to read there is no doubt. But there is still comfort in the fact that clothes, of all the things we own, are easiest to change in and out of. And thereby, we create our own trends. That alone is enough to satisfy the personal yearning for a new skin, a sense of awareness of oneself set off by something different. For sometimes we need to shed our layers like onions. Psychologically, one feels more alive wearing a just-acquired dress to a party. Doing so banishes that residual fear that one might back right into one's familiar and perhaps disagreeable shell if one wears the same dress too many times. Once clothes seem old, we tend not to be aware of them, they become invisible, and we feel unnoticed in them. To renew ourselves, we need change. However, the trap that we must not fall into is the expectation that they will ever really change us.

Style today has thus taken on a new breadth of meaning. Whereas in the past it reflected outer decorum, surface, exterior embellishment, nowadays it is inseparable from the way we are inside. Appearance has become our manner of being. As Cocteau wrote: "Style is the soul, and . . . with us the soul assumes the form of the body." "Life-style" is the word that captures this for us and puts distance between ourselves and the stylization of the past.

But new definitions present new difficulties. Evolution in life-styles tends to be a seamless web. We no longer have access to a sensible progression of tendencies, a ticker tape that can be read off to show what we were like at convenient breaks in historical time. Styles no longer succeed one another as in the past. Rather, stylistic changes occur almost simultaneously, giving their audience no chance to assimilate one before the next variation—or reversal—comes along. It takes time to accustom the eye to change, but modern society has no patience for repetition. Thus the exasperation when the voluminous Big Look of one season is almost instantly dated by a return to skinny tube dressing. Thus the consternation when everyone, having just stocked up on below-the-knee skirts, is regaled by Halston's skimp, which rises to the thigh. And thus the inevitable break with fashion altogether, after which a woman can settle down to her own pace.

Or she may forget fashion, preferring to put her expressive energies into her house or her job or her children. In that case she will either resemble the lady from Boston or, at most, settle for reality clothes, a clumsy term used by copywriters, but one that nevertheless expresses an antifashion whose content is not purely negative. Reality clothes include everything from St. Laurent's wardrobe to active sportsgear now worn in the city. It is army surplus, work clothes, uniforms, and recycled flannel. But the term excludes the tough and expensive chic that used to be rendered obsolete by the merest word from manufacturers, magazines, and newspaper reports of the Paris collections. Does reality dressing mean giving up all the lovely whims and ephemera that make fashion fun? Certainly not, for presenting oneself always has to do with qualities such as beauty of fabric, with touch and rustle and scent, and the charm distilled from their particular mix. Even being in fashion still means something, but how different are its sources today! The woman who wants to follow what's being worn must keep her eyes focused on the streets. For the first time within memory, the fashion fascists are irrevocably—and perhaps permanently—out of style.

chapter 12

the lowdown on high fashion

While more and more women are turning to the streets—or to themselves—for their own style examples, there are still a few who want *la mode de luxe*. And those women will always find a handful of designers specializing in superlative workmanship, especially in France.

Many of the great couture houses of Paris are strung along the Faubourg St.-Honoré. On the opposite side of that elegant crescent stands the Elysée Palace, seat of French government and for many years residence of its president. Nearby is le Matignon, where the premier has his offices. Thus, ambassadors, heads of state, distinguished visitors, daily pass display windows filled with those objects of luxury in silk, cashmere, leather, those perfumes and *robes de soir* that have given France its reputation for artistry abroad and are an unshakable mainstay of the French self-image at home. No less important —and here is where the couture's centripetal proximity to the government is significant—has been the splendid effect of couture on France's balance of payments.

Has been, and still is, though in dwindling measure, for France is no longer quite the fashion leader it used to be. Its authority, however, was irresistible from the year 1858 when the house of Charles Frederick Worth opened its doors, right down to 1940, when Europe was cut off by the war, and American designers were thrown back upon their own resources. By that time, high fashion was part of the French mystique, which France dispensed along with its gifts of language, painting, music—*la culture*, in short—to the rest of the world.

Following Worth, Paul Poiret, beginning about 1907, contributed mightily to the legend, his own as well as that of his country. He was the first to put on fashion shows, little demonstrations of the fabulous wonders he created for the women of Parisian society. Poiret's Oriental balls were part of the image of opulence he generated, and his "Thousand and One Nights" extravaganzas were followed eagerly by the press. His business sense, though it failed him toward the end of his career, which spanned nearly a half century, was unflagging at the beginning. The Poiret empire branched out into the allied fields of perfume, accessories, fabric design, and interior decoration, thus providing groundwork for the financial mainstays of today's couture houses.

Haute couture and publicity have always been so mutually

dependent that on those occasions when one fails the other, the whole precarious structure is endangered. From the beginning, the fashion industry in France was shored up by artists and by photographers. Many of the latter, such as Atget, Baron de Meyer, Munkacsi, Hoyningen-Huené, had enormous distinction. Some, like Steichen, Cartier-Bresson, and Man Ray, later became famous. The fashion magazines, of course, played a part by publishing their photographs and by sending journalists to the showings. Almost from the beginning there were copyists, too—firms that existed more or less illegally in order to reproduce, at lower cost, what the couture made every woman shamelessly desire. Sketchers were sent to the collections to draw detailed facsimiles of what they saw and to buy the models they couldn't get down quickly enough on paper. Occasionally a private customer of one of the couture houses would lend a copyist her dress to be knocked off cheaply. Finally, a Chambre Syndicale de la Couture Parisienne had to be formed to protect against such piracy. In recent years it has been customary to demand "caution money" as a sort of entrance fee to the showings. Though these sums run in the thousands, they are put up against the purchase of actual models, or *toiles*, and their donors are carefully screened.

One of the reasons for the immense popular interest in couture has always been its intensely visual quality. From conception to the final file down the runway, the production of a *robe de style* has always lent itself to whatever media treatment has been available, and today dressmaking has become a kind of performing art. When moving pictures came into wide use, films were taken of Balenciaga fitting models who stood almost motionless, like patients being examined by a physician. Balenciaga himself wore a white coat slung with scissors and pincushions, and was surrounded by young assistants. The sound track was almost silent, reverential. Models did not smile, their faces stony as Nefertiti. Before the presentation itself, a little burst of music, the sprays of flowers sent in, the rows of tiny gilt chairs. The showroom was inhabited at last, but never gay. Fashion was serious business, a matter of breeding, of ladylike touches, white gloves and hats, perfect seams. The mannequins were well past thirty, or at the very least looked distinguished. Elegant was never sexy; the clothes were like architecture, costly and permanent.

And the fabrics! Matelasse, zibelline, ciré, silk gazar, chenille, pongee, organza, silk broché. The words have almost gone out of our vocabulary. The paillettes, point d'esprit, bugle beads, the pure spectacle of strass and boa, of ermine, satin, and chiffon. No wonder Dior once said that, for inspiration, he "just felt fabrics." Contrary to most assumptions, a collection always begins with the cloth rather than with an idea. There remains a handful of fabric houses in Europe that do not merely supply designers with the "makings," but have by tradition been highly influential in their own right. Moreover, their role has made them rich. Just after World War II, it was Boussac, the textile emperor, who launched Dior in a conscious effort to reestablish France as fashion center of the world. In return, Dior's famous New Look of 1947 gathered as much fabric as possible into its ballerina skirts. Today, although more than thirty kinds of synthetics are on the market, fine dressmakers still insist on fabrics from the old houses such as Abraham, Bianchini, Ducharne, and Rodier. These firms keep a sharp eye on style trends, since goods have to be ordered a year in advance and there is an increasingly large margin of risk inolved in sales. Sometimes specifications are made by the designer himself; more often, a salesman from the fabric manufacturer comes to the maison de la couture to show his wares. Nine times out of ten the couturier's choice of fabrics actually governs both color and cut of his collection, thus determining the whole look of next season's clothes.

Buoyed by a flourishing fabrics industry, a rich clientele, and general postwar prosperity, French couture kept afloat until the mid-sixties. Edited by a flotilla of women who all seemed to be nicknamed Deedee or Babs, the glossy fashion magazines induced a hypnotic trance on their public. It was a world of fantasy, of almost ceremonial clothes which elicited for their wearers a feeling of security and respect. This was particularly true in America, as we had never had the tradition of custom-designed clothes for the private customer. In the early part of the century, if one was rich enough, one went to France to be clothed. In the twenties French designs were imported by firms like Valentina, Elizabeth Hawes, and some specialty shops. Hattie Carnegie had her own exclusive models. During World War II we developed our sportswear manufacture and the great innovators like Claire McCardell and Norman Norell got their start designing for American women. But the moment the war was over, France exerted the old magic.

No one could mistake American design, interesting as it was, for haute couture. Among other things, the French couturier performed a secondary but distinctive service. He was his client's artistic director, relied on for advice about every insecurity from how to tie a scarf to the proper length for her hair. The total image was apt to belong not so much to the woman herself as to the man who fitted her clothes. To many Americans as well as Europeans this was a psychological boon for which it was impossible to pay too much. Since artistic direction was not part of the American designer's tradition, clients again went abroad. For it must be remembered that, at the height of French couture's influence, from the mid-forties to the mid-sixties, rich women were still both decorative objects and consumers. Buying things to decorate oneself, to perfect one's image, was one of the functions of privilege. The periodic rhythm of the collections themselves helped to stimulate the desire for change and thus for buying.

But something else was brewing underneath the glamour boom of those years, and by 1963 or so it was too obvious not to notice: a worldwide ready-to-wear industry was flooding the market with cheap copies of couture clothes. Even in France, from 1949, the mass manufacturers were tooling up for what they knew was going to be a tremendous postwar sell to young people. Although the techniques for rapid production were not perfected until the early sixties, the gears shifted just in time for the youth explosion that detonated in a blaze of boutiques, Beatles, chicerinos in hipskirts, Mary Quant pantyhose, and all-out underground funk. Before then the pattern had seemed practically unshakable: At the time of Charles Worth, couture was valued for its ability to distinguish itself from what were then the beginnings of assembly-line clothing. As long as high-priced dressmaking could maintain a distance from the commonness of "factory made," it was coveted, cherished, and paid for dearly. No small part of this price was the cost of time. The pace of couture was slow, every detail being fitted directly on the customer. When her dress or suit was ready she found she had purchased a carapace, a second skin to last a lifetime.

What there was of novelty in such clothing drifted down to the masses with equal slowness, descending into the department stores in modified form at least a year after it had first been worn and publicized by its fashionable owner. The exclusivism, the veritable hothouse atmosphere of couture, was maintained like some exquisite helium balloon floating above Paris, its manners established, its cliques formed, its language a dialogue within. It was a spiral of self-consciously interacting circles both envied and detested from below.

Meanwhile, youth went about its own business, blowing up barricades by day and dancing the monkey by night. The fashion journalists were attracted to the action and moved quickly onto the scene. Before 1962 had changed into 1963, American *Vogue* had acquired a new queen bee, Diana Vreeland, ex-fashion editor of *Bazaar*, whose outrageous energy and eye for flamboyance changed *Vogue* almost overnight from haute elegance to mod. Its pages were crammed with real people instead of masks. Julie Christie, Françoise Hardy, Baby Jane Holzer, Benedetta Barzini, Barbra Streisand were the new youthquakers. "What's happening" became the prime editorial criterion, and "pizzaz" was the Vreeland word for it.

Right from the beginning, Diana Vreeland was a legend. Her instinct, her "forked nose" for fashion, was total. Under her tutelage, readers were told that health is the basis of beauty, to which clothes add only the finishing touch. The physicality of youthful styles was manifest in her editorial supervision. She upheld the vigorous sportsclothes of Courrèges. She instigated some of the first nude photographs to appear in this previously un-hip publication. Her magazine appeared to be "with it," but the paradox of *Vogue* in those years was that underneath the mod veneer, the extravagant rhetoric, and the daring space-age photographs of Hiro, Avedon, and Saul Leiter, there remained the same old symbiotic dependence on the couture houses. Magazines are made to sell things, after all. And Vreeland's appreciation of French haute couture went deep. For her, it was and is a way of life.

Today, in her crimson-walled office in New York's Metropolitan Museum, where she is consultant to their Costume Institute, she disclaims any rumors about the death of couture. You know her answer before you ask the question. For she is wearing an arrestingly simple Halston, severe as her own figure, and obviously fitted to it exactly. She is, her bearing implies, nobody's double. Everything about her demeanor is thought out, from the lacquered black hair to the measured walk, feet placed just so, like little birds. She holds forth in her red-walled box like a precious emaciated Chinese buddha, declaring the splendors of Vionnet's bias drapes of the twenties ("The genius of the idea! The ingenuity of rescuing crêpe de chine from linings and making dresses from it instead!"), pronouncing on couture ("There will always be women like me who know exactly what they want and are hard to fit off the rack." Here she pauses. "And will pay extra for it."). She flips open a malachite box with her red-tipped fingernails and inserts a cigarette between her teeth without a break in discussion. "Fashion, you know, is a very special thing. It is not just for anybody. Fashion is like breakfast in bed. If you can have it, why not?" She readjusts her spine vigorously, lips pursed. A moment later she uncrosses her legs, sprints across the room, and fishes a pair of violet-tinted glasses from the depths of her pocketbook. Thus shielded, she bravely fires the first volley in what has become a touchy issue. "You must understand that what is fashion and that which is popular are two different things. What you see on the street is not fashion. I like elegance. I like my clothes well-pressed. I like to look soignée." Since this is evident, the dialogue ends prematurely. But, as she seems certain that couture will survive, what about the future of ready-to-wear? Isn't it giving custom-made clothes a run for their money? How does she explain the mass appeal of blue jeans, for instance? Her answer is astute; it also circumvents the relationship between couture and assembly-line clothing: "The great leveler is availability." And with that the subject is closed.

There are others who feel that, even before the mid-sixties, elegance was becoming estranged from fashion. The moment when being a slave to clothes lost its chic, fashion dropped its capital "F" as well as its identification with couture. Fashion, lower-case, became what was bought, what was popular, what was worn in the streets. And that is what fashion remains today. It is not surprising that Diana Vreeland feels as she does, given her position of responsibility toward an industry that her magazine—and her way of life—supports. But if the same question is asked of quite another personality, a Frenchwoman whose career as *directrice* at the couture house of Nina Ricci has given her even more firsthand experience with custom dressmaking, we get an entirely different answer.

Geneviève Antoine Dariaux, couture manager now turned novelist, feels that high fashion in the sense of custom-made clothing is at the end of the line. The reasons are simple: two few clients with enough money, general lack of interest, and less time to spend on the two or three mandatory fittings. Furthermore, the ready-to-wear industry (called *prêt-à-porter* throughout Europe) outdates the couture collections almost before they are on the showroom runways. Dressing is so fad-ridden, so quick to change, so disposable, that it is hard to take high fashion seriously. Madame Dariaux insists on a further point. Those who can afford expensive clothes are less willing—and more embarrassed—to spend $2,000 on a dress. Communications have shown us the extent of poverty in many parts of the world; we are in closer touch with these realities—even by the secondhand means of a television screen—than any previous generation. A woman in her thirties or forties, therefore, can be rich, but she had better be committed to something: a job, a cause, a field. At the very least, she must be busy, for idleness is a disgrace.

Women who are even younger not only don't need fashion, they mock it. Hence the appearance of the antimode and of its American journalistic exponent, *Rags*, which appeared for a short time in 1970 and 1971. A counterculture combination of *Rolling Stone* and *Mother Earth News*, *Rags* focused on reportage of streetwear, on consumer rip-offs in clothes and cosmetics, on personalities, blacks, young designers. *Rags* printed ads using fat models and sent its photographers out to record the impressions of hard-hat construction workers on the subject of current women's styles. There was a general-ideas section of the magazine called Supermarket, one called Drugstore, which listed new beauty products, a column on astrology, and one on cooking called Doctor Eatgood. The whole package, though short-lived, was the closest look in print at *actual* fashion, the life-spirit of the early seventies. What made its achievement especially poignant was the fact that *Rags'* editorial board was made up of ex-staff members of *Harper's Bazaar* and some of the other glossies. Once magazines like *Rags* had helped to break down the journalistic arrogance of the sixties, once *Women's Wear Daily*'s goof on the midi turned women off clothes, high fashion *had* to throw in its lot with ordinary mortals. There was no alternative.

What, then, is the future of that lovely institution, haute couture? Years ago, in the twenties, Colette prefigured its fate: "The time is perhaps not far off when the haute couture, creator of a kind of sumptuous indigence, will become alarmed at the results obtained. It makes it easy for anyone with a capable pair of hands to cut a rectangle out of a piece of cloth, make two holes in it for sleeves, and then allow the embroiderer, weaver or even painter to do his best on it. A certain excess of refinement . . . exposes the creation to a danger that the properly jealous designer must always dread—facility."

That facility is now the stock in trade of all ready-to-wear manufacturers. Meanwhile, remnants of the couture tradition still exist, operating, for the most part, at a phenomenal loss. In 1973, only three houses managed to break even on their custom fittings: Dior, Givenchy, and St. Laurent. Even this was an accomplishment. One house has stayed open only at a consistent deficit of 25% every season. To make a dress in the old way costs some millions of francs. First there is the fabric itself and the trimmings. Then labor expenses, which have shot up prohibitively. The commission of the saleslady must be paid, and on top of that, the usual overhead, taxes, rent, decor, advertising, and models' salaries must be counted in.

Why do houses insist on staying open under such crushing payloads? There are two reasons. The first has been admirably expressed in an *Elle* article as an effort to avoid allowing their ideas to be overtaken by industry (*"pour éviter que leur inspiration ne devienne industrielle"*). The second reason exactly contradicts the first, though it does not apply to all high fashion establishments. It is that many do keep their couture division precisely in order to sell copies of prototypes to department stores and eventually to mass manufacturers. Meanwhile the semiannual showings are used for promotional purposes, to draw the attention of the press, and to sell boutique lines, prestige items like perfume, and goods whose production has been farmed out. Companies who buy a design in this manner pay huge sums for the use of the creator's name. Such licensing arrangements provide the financial anchor for most couturiers today.

What are the survival statistics of some of the large houses? Each is struggling according to its own particular style, though Maison Lanvin has a better footing than some. A look inside this venerable establishment is a trip back to the era of Art Deco. The door at number 15, Faubourg St. Honoré travels heavily over the carpet and clicks shut. Traffic noises vanish; there is a cushioned reverence about the place. The vendeuses are in black, hair pleated once a week by their local coiffeur. They possess an authority rare to behold in these days of trends and fads. Some have been here for thirty years, selling the four-piece knits, the beaded *robes de style* that are Lanvin's specialties. The couture house was founded in 1890 by Jeanne Lanvin and is run today by her nephew Yves. It remains one of the few family-owned names in the field. Jules-François Crahay has been the designer for more than a dozen years. His atelier is upstairs, next to that of Bernard Devaux, who does all the mass-distributed *prêt-à-porter* for Lanvin. Crahay is the house couturier, which means that he is in charge of everything from private fittings to designing the *prêt-à-porter de luxe*. The latter is made in Lanvin-designed or

Lanvin-chosen fabric, stitched by machine, hand-finished, and sold at forty boutiques bearing the Lanvin name. Devaux's products, on the other hand, may range from scarf designs to sunglasses, and are licensed to companies for eventual sale in specialty shops and department stores all over the world.

On the top floor of number 15 are six workrooms. Two are filled with young girls cutting patterns, sewing and finishing garments by hand. The other four rooms are empty. All together, Lanvin employs about fifty seamstresses who begin their apprenticeship as teen-agers and may continue with the firm for the rest of their lives. At the moment, Lanvin is on fairly solid ground financially. Part of its strength is a faithful clientele, built up over the years. Part of it lies in a reputation for workmanship. And there is another element, less a matter of prediction than of chance: Having lived its heyday in the late 1920's, when its famous perfumes were introduced, Lanvin finds itself in the midst of a revival of nostalgia that has given buyers a passion for everything Deco. Thus the house is ironically up to date without having to change its image. Even the original packaging for "My Sin" and "Arpège" remains intact, to the great delight of collectors. Aside from the perfumes, Lanvin has a men's wear division which accounts for half of the usual yearly volume of about $35 million. Compared with Dior's $90 million a year and St. Laurent's approximate $111 million gross, Lanvin is not a huge money-making venture. But it is holding its own.

Such figures are sometimes deceptive. Even less trustworthy is the fashion press itself, whose interests are served by optimistic accounting. Fairchild Publication's gossip sheet W reported that St. Laurent did $1,500,000 worth of sales to private clients in 1974; another paper recorded that his couture had suffered a million-dollar loss for that same year. But never mind. Broken down, the YSL empire brings in annually about $10 million on the three perfumes bearing his signature, $15 million on sheets and bath towels, the same amount on women's ready-to-wear boutique clothes, $20 million from the men's line, and a whopping $50 million from licensing agreements which cover handbags, jewelry, scarves, shoes, etc., and thus provide the major source of revenue for St. Laurent.

Who is he, this frail young man whom Dior used to call *"le petit prince"*? He is painfully shy; he is electrostatically intelligent. Both qualities contribute to making St. Laurent a great observer of social tastes. His radar is unerring. As mentioned, it was he who went down to the barricade to make sketches at the Paris student uprisings of 1968. He knows what's in the air, and his unique gift is that of translating these intangibles into the shape of a sheer wool chemise or the dash of a crushed-leather boot. He understands better than any other major designer the peculiar vitality of street clothes, the attraction of jeans, of the ruffled frontier dresses worn by American hippie girls, of the nostalgia revival and the love for all things Rétro. His instinct told him quite early in the seventies, for example, that there is something that allows the ugly bourgeois realism of kitsch to become high fashion—but only on the second time around.

His innovations are not enormous, yet they surprise by expressing with exactitude the style of life we lead, or emulate. St. Laurent's "trapeze" line, his first collection after the death of his mentor, Dior, was just this kind of success. Then, in 1958 he was already pointing toward the structured body cages of the sixties. His fisherman's shirts, turtlenecks, and pea jackets followed, much of their inspiration coming from outside the magic circle of haute couture. Army-navy surplus stores in New York intrigued him. African bush jackets and safari suits from sports outfitters took his fancy. He knew when the world was interested in Mondrian prints, and when women were ready for see-through blouses. With *le smoking,* an evening suit of black velvet, sharply cut like a man's, St. Laurent really hit his stride. Unconsciously, he had combined in that famous *tenue* a prefiguration of unisex, with his own gift for precise tailoring. Since then, it has been the raincoats, the pants, the hacking jackets that have built his reputation as a designer of basics. For he is, at his roots, a superb tailor, as opposed to a draper. (Most of the latter, not surprisingly perhaps, are women. Vionnet, Madame Grès, even the young Vicky Tiel, are examples who come to mind. The only famous exception was Chanel, who was really a ladies' tailor. Drapers tend to work with fabric directly on the body, tailors nearly always sketch, though often each will use both methods. But the roughly male-female division here is interesting.)

No rigid schemes blunt St. Laurent's ability to absorb what is in the atmosphere. Only one premise seems to guide him, and he is adamant about it: Clothes should set off the woman who wears them, not advertise her designer. Adhering to that notion has helped him grow as an artist. His flexibility leaves him subject to seduction by novelties (medieval monks' hoods one season, gun-moll satins the next), but he is wise enough to discard them after the fun has worn off. What he retains in his collections is a winnowing down of his idea of fashion that projects the wearer; and his clothes increasingly mean exactly what he intends.

St. Laurent is determined to maintain his couture operation

as long as possible. He employs 115 seamstresses and is deeply committed to their work and to the concept of *l'artisanat*—hand construction. Perhaps this explains the high seriousness of his new quarters on the Avenue Marceau. The building, an old five-story *hôtel particulier* of impossible grandeur, was decorated at a cost of $400,000 alone. It looks incongruous as world headquarters for one of the youngest and most modern of dressmakers. Perhaps the whole thing was engineered by his manager, Pierre Bergé. In any case, St. Laurent looks particularly small and anguished in this assemblage of red velvet drapery, *faux marbre* pillars, and full-length mirrors. His own office is tiny, almost claustrophobic, completely lined in a Proustian paisley fabric. Only his desk, a work table mounted on metal sawhorse legs and covered in gray felt, seems to give him any comfort. This little room is, one supposes, for interviews only, as St. Laurent chooses to spend almost all of his time at work in the ateliers. These are all painted white, full of air, light, plants, and chattering seamstresses. The girls are used to being looked in on by the portly Madame Buhchaert, who heads public relations. *"Bonjour!"* she sings as she opens the door, and they all chant back, peering out with curiosity, as though from a goldfish bowl.

Downstairs, one is back in the eighteenth century again, treading the green carpets made to look like moiré. The distances seem as vast as Versailles. On the left is Bergé's office, ten times the size of St. Laurent's. A glimpse of funereal rubber plants, a giant Warhol portrait of YSL, an ostentatious desk of metal and glass. Such is the importance of promotional genius these days. Without Bergé one wonders whether YSL sheets and bath towels would be sold in every linen department in America. Whether the eighty St. Laurent boutiques scattered from Pittsburgh to São Paulo would even have been dreamed of. Or, more important, whether the small but precious nucleus of his private customers would continue to be faithful.

Who are the clients of couture? At St. Laurent, the steady customers are Hélène Rochas, Olimpia de Rothschild, Charlotte Aillaud, Catherine Deneuve, Betty Catroux, Zizi Jeanmaire, and a host of other one-time-or-more purchasers. Dior sells to Jacqueline de Ribes, Sophia Loren, Princess Grace of Monaco, and Evangeline Bruce. Hubert de Givenchy dresses Audrey Hepburn, Rose Kennedy, Jacqueline Onassis, Gloria Guinness, São Schlumberger, and other faithfuls. But Givenchy's biggest volume? Sunglasses. Cardin claims 250 private clients for couture, including several princesses and additional anonymous trend-setters (known as locomotives in the trade), whose identities the house is apparently unwilling to disclose.

In spite of an estimated yearly wholesale volume of $400 million in clothing and accessories from all the French houses combined; in spite of Fairchild's editorial puffs in *W* and *WWD*; in spite of the calculated optimism of figures like Pierre Bergé (who is regularly quoted as saying, "The French couture is having its best season in years . . ."), it looks as though high fashion's greatest concrete value is in the inspiration it lends to mass production. Not even the Japanese can keep the Paris one-of-a-kind dress industry alive, although they are now the world's most faithful buyers of couture models for reproduction. United States interest in couture has fallen off markedly in recent years, although Ohrbach's, Lord & Taylor, I. Magnin, and Marshall Field still send representatives to the showings. *New York Times* reporting on the collections has been cut to a few paragraphs per season.

The couture has put some ingenuity into play in an effort to bring down the approximate $300,000 it costs to produce a collection. Cutting flat instead of on the mannequin, new machinery that replaces handwork, a general streamlining of production methods will help. But the result won't be high fashion in its traditional sense of made-to-fit-directly-on-the-body. *That* option is now relegated to home sewing or—if you can find her—to the "little seamstress around the corner."

A prestige couture house in financial trouble is not going to be extricated from its difficulties by a new breed of generous, enthusiastic clients. Virtually every maison which has managed to break even in the last few years has done so on the strength of money earned through licensing of its name. Some have managed on their *prêt-à-porter* combined with perfume sales. Others, like Courrèges, try to hit the press with new ideas, thereby drawing media attention (or ridicule) in a desperate attempt to generate steady sales of knitwear and accessories. Still others, like Philippe Venet, just settle for knock-offs— cheap reproductions of his designs for department stores. Most houses are operating by their wits, using a combination of whatever possibilities are at hand. Not surprisingly, the couture is facing a real identity crisis.

For some designers, this has meant an impasse in creativity. Cardin, Ungaro, Courrèges—and Rudi Gernreich in the United States—were all innovators in the mid-sixties. All changed the look of fashion beginning in 1963 or so; all were hailed as the avant-garde, as tastemakers of the future. Afterwards, each in his own way stopped dead. Cardin began to mastermind everything from theaters to umbrellas, Ungaro did one gimmicky collection after another, Gernreich quit clothes altogether and turned his attention to interior decoration, until the famous thong bathing suit, which is, after all, really nothing more than minimal exterior decoration.

André Courrèges is a more complex puzzle. The criticism leveled at him is generally that his style hasn't evolved in ten years. Each new season is a variation on the crisp white dress, the stiff silhouette, the plastic baby boots, the youthful cutouts and appliqués that made him famous in 1965. It is true that his capers tend to visual gags like telephones, the theme of his winter 1974 collection. And yet he is one of the few people designing today who pay attention to what happens to clothes in the weather. He still talks about a dress having "interior rhythm," like a building. He remains, more than almost any one of the futurists, an intelligent packager of modern woman. His uniforms for the 1972 Olympics were apt; he has done the same service for airline hostesses; he has designed a dashing interior for Simca-Matra's sportscar "Bagheera." His knowledge of the human body comes from two sources: his own aptitude for sports, particularly rugby and the Basque game pelote, and the architectural engineering studies he undertook at Pau, his birthplace near the Spanish border. His factory near Pau is one of his most splendid and characteristic creations: Like his clothes, it is a construct of sculptural undulations, standing gracefully against the landscape like one of Braque's white doves.

It can never be said that Courrèges doesn't hold to his convictions. Perhaps the eleven years he spent in training with Balenciaga gave him a sense of permanence about his own designs. He himself is resolutely modern in dress: Who else would wear a baby blue nylon zipsuit above little white boots to his studio on the austere rue François Premier? He explains the construction of this suit, peering intensely through clear lucite wrap-around spectacles. Next to the body there must be cotton. For breathing. Then a synthetic fabric on the outside to protect against the weather. Why wear two pieces of cloth when one length will do? Why not make a front door for the suit with a huge industrial zipper whose plastic ducklike squeaks would delight a child?

Courrèges has fun with clothes, but he disclaims designing them. *"Je ne fais pas de la mode."* What intrigues him are ideas. Like his own zipsuit, his dresses, his buildings, his surroundings are the result of a set of concepts. High heels give an unnatural thrust to the body, therefore he makes shoes flat to the ground. Human toes are rounded off: His boots won't have pointed tips. Women are built more athletically now than in the past: He gives them clothes to run, jump, ride bicycles in.

Courrèges is a cartoonist and loves to illustrate his thoughts with drawings. In New York to open his boutique in the fall of 1974, he was stunned by the "Year 2000" aspect of a building at 9 West 57th Street. It is a skyscraper formed like two vertical sweeps of the hand, like ski slopes back-to-back. So entranced was he that he declared, "Everything in the past must be forgotten. Versailles is a horrible nightmare, so unfunctional! Space travel colors our whole future. What is there to be gained by looking at history?" And yet Courrèges is a complex man. He and his wife, Cocoline, are restoring a medieval Spanish house all furnished with antiques, where they plan to live with their daughter Clafoutis. His aesthetic may be rigid, but it does not, evidently, exclude the past entirely.

To live in the future is very difficult. One has the feeling that Courrèges's notions fit this age, but not without some strain. His office is a space capsule: floors, ceiling, and walls painted dead white. The effect is marred by the inevitable smudges and streaks everywhere, like a banged-up squash court. No furniture except for the big draftsman's desk of white formica. No color at all save for a clutch of orange felt-tipped pens in a white cup and an orange baseball cap lying on the floor. As Courrèges speaks, his intensity fairly bounces off the walls, his tufts of hair twitch like antennae. His secretaries are forced to wear his designs. His assistants admit that he is a bit of a zealot. His mannequins do not inspire him as St. Laurent's seem to. Instead, they must fit into his scheme. There is an insistence on ideas in Courrèges work that puts one in the position of being an admirer but not a follower, someone glad to visit his territory but not to stay for long.

Courrèges is tired of trying to be twenty years ahead of current taste. In order to stay solvent, he has had to settle for the present, giving women what they want *now*—those Chinese pink or acid green status knits identified by his initials, or the clear plastic raincoats patterned with "AC." Other designers have done well on a smaller scale precisely by not overextending themselves. Louis Féraud is one of these.

Féraud is large, jovial, a man of the Midi who rolls his "r"'s and likes his glass of pastis in the afternoon, is afraid to travel in airplanes and never wants to own a car. He loves women and has married his present wife, Zizi, twice. He also adores garlic, painting, writing plays and novels. By his own admission he has had no formal education. His intelligence finds entirely articulate expression in his clothes, in their richly imaginative fabrics and simple cut. He loves the word *"flou"* the sound of which describes the rush of one of his long skirts as he swishes it from the rack. The selling area of his shop in the Faubourg St. Honoré is decorated with his paintings and managed by his wife. Upstairs in the workrooms his assistants lean over their drafting boards in blue jeans. Their banter flies above the constant sound of pop music; models drift in and out. It is Féraud's show and he loves directing this all-female cast. It is just the right size for him and he insists upon not expanding: "I have a house, a family, a dog, an occasional vacation near the Mediterranean, and that's all I care about." One almost has the illusion that this man is not really working at all, but just stage-managing a favorite hobby. The contrast with an operation like Lanvin is complete. The latter is serious business, run as smoothly as the ballbearings on the vaults at Chase Manhattan. La Maison Louis Féraud, on the other hand, is first and foremost an artist's atelier; success is merely an important by-product.

Féraud is part of a relatively new group of houses that, having begun in couture, are now almost entirely devoted to *prêt-à-porter*. Others are Karl Lagerfeld of Chloë, Ted Lapidus, Paco Rabanne, Jacques Esterel, the Japanese Kenzo Takada, and that of a young American woman, Vicky Tiel. All are characterized by couture training and a high-fashion approach to ready-to-wear. Vicky Tiel got her design education at New York's Parsons School, but her practical apprenticeship was served under Louis Féraud. He showed her draping, cutting, patternmaking, how to set up a workshop. He helped with the staffing of her atelier, and even presented her designs in the midst of one of his own collections, an unprecedented act of generosity in the competitive world of couture. Then he married Vicky's partner, Mia Fonssagrives, who had come with her from New York to try her hand at fashion too. The Féraud show stopper as well as the marriage, his second, was covered by an ecstatic press.

It was 1967. Proper French girls were still wearing kilts and pullovers. See-through lace dresses existed in the pages of magazines, went dancing at Castel's, but still were not being bought by the girl in the street. The Paris climate was right for two wacky Americans still in their twenties to invade the scene.

Before meeting Féraud, they had set up shop in a Left Bank garret which they painted orange and purple. In the kitchen sink they dyed their pantyhose and washed dishes. By day they outlined ideas and sketched; by night they did the nightclub circuit. At Régine's, New Jimmy's, Castel's, they met their first important contacts. No matter that these happened to be American film producers, not French clothes designers. The result landed them a whole-screen costume credit for the Peter Sellers' movie *What's New Pussycat?* Next they found themselves in Hollywood on an MGM contract, with a house in Malibu and a chauffeured limousine to transport them to studio headquarters every morning. Vicky describes them both as tanned, pink-lipsticked, and increasingly bored with the California syndrome. After a year they were back in Paris, several thousand dollars richer and a good deal wiser. Their costume credits now included *Candy* and *Grand Prix*. It was at this point that they began serious work with Féraud and met Richard Burton and Elizabeth Taylor. The Burtons helped them buy a charming shop on the rue Bonaparte, where they set up a boutique. At a time when properties in the St. Germain-des-Prés area were impossibly expensive, the two girls literally walked into the house of an antique dealer and offered him $50,000 in cash. He, on the verge of retirement, was delighted, and sold it to the crazy blue-jeaned Americans on the spot. Only later, when he discovered their cofinancier was Richard Burton, did he realize he might have doubled his profit.

Mia and Vicky set to work redecorating until they had an interior country garden: robin's-egg-blue walls, a white trellis, potted plants, and a caged canary. They were ready to open in the spring of 1968. With so small an operation, they had no choice but to work closer to the couture tradition than to *prêt-à-porter* methods. Vicky Tiel, who now continues the business in her own name, still follows the procedures set down by the Mia-Vicky team. An entire collection is sketched out on one large sheet of paper, so as to maintain a consistent theme. The models Vicky decides to use are cut out and redrafted. Swatches of fabric are pinned to the drawing, which is then handed over to Nicole, an experienced *toiliste*, who learned her trade, the making of muslin patterns from draping on a dummy, at Guy Laroche when she was fourteen. Vicky approves Nicole's toile, which is then tried on the house mannequin. Adjustments are made at this point, patterns are cut from the toile, and sent out to more than forty sewers. These are usually older women who have been dressmakers all their lives and are now either retired or out of work. The sewers skip the basting stage, which is one of the hallmarks of haute couture. Instead, they pin and sew directly on machines. Finishing, however, is done by hand as in the *grand ateliers*. Then the dresses are sent back to the rue Bonaparte boutique, where Madame Conté ships them out to the fifty or so outlets for Vicky Tiel clothes in France and the United States.

The Tiel prices are kept low by an astute use of fabric to reduce waste and by elimination of the hand-basting stage in production. Vicky's style is fluid and moves well. It is body dressing at its best. For this reason she finds silk crepe most congenial to work with. Not surprisingly, the Rétro style appealed to her as long ago as 1968. Her version of peasant dressing came the year after, with djellabas, saris, and exotic beads. In the fall of 1969 she made some headlines with the braless look, and for a few years after that she was known for her sexpot dresses. Film stars flocked to her: Bardot, Raquel Welch, Jacqueline Bisset, Sidne Rome, Julie Newmar—even Romy Schneider, who buys at Chanel also. Not just bomb-shells, but couture customers came as well. And showgirls from Le Crazy Horse Saloon. And Hugh Hefner's bunnies. Vicky Tiel, the owl-eyed brunette from Chevy Chase, Maryland, was beginning to make a name for herself in Paris.

Erotic escalation was the name of the game in clothes by then. Vicky played it well: Her 1969 collections were full of crazies like boots to the waist on bare-breasted models wearing Pocahontas braids. There were floor-length transparent lace caftans which looked like moving shower curtains. A dress that was nothing but a belt with long fringes made news, and so did a bra made of shells joined with chains, and bathing suits cut completely out at the sides and joined chastely up the middle. Nineteen seventy saw Vicky doing the first hot pants in Paris. Following these were crocheted bikinis appliqued with hands reaching around the breasts and on the crotch. The press went crazy. Everyone from *Cosmopolitan* to *Vogue* was at her showings. Even the staid *Jours de France*, the most conserva-tive—and most widely read—women's magazine in the coun-try, deigned to appear. Twiggy and Johanna Shimkus bought baby dresses from the collections. Elizabeth Taylor appeared in a Mia-Vicky at Maxim's, and fist fights broke out among the paparazzi who had to be constrained from breaking down the doors.

Today? The pop-locomotive era is dead and buried. Fallout from the sex explosion has diminished. Youth has stopped quaking. Vicky Tiel is older. She has married Elizabeth Taylor's makeup man, and they have a small child. Her summer garden boutique is just the slightest bit shopworn; the canary shrieks each time the front doorbell rings and scatters birdseed over the grass-green rug. Springtimes don't last forever, but Vicky Tiel knows how to adapt to the times. Her brown bangs and horn-rimmed glasses are exactly the same as in the mad years of the sixties, but now she is wrapped in voile scarves, shod in suede boots. She no longer wears a ring on every finger.

Mia is divorced from Féraud; he has gone back to his first wife. Burton still owns his half of the boutique. And Vicky has settled down to making her special kind of dress which flatters the body so well. It is a draped style which will not date, but the neck or hemlines will never cause a furor in the fashion press. She has her métier, and knows how to deploy her own particular skills in a field in which everyone else is busy copying Sonia Rykiel's sweaters, Lagerfeld's seamless cuts, or Chanel's suits. Her business is mainly wholesale, not so much for private clients as before. Wholesale is demanding; she no longer has much time to whip up a little something for any starlet who comes along. As a small enterprise she maintains complete control over whatever she designs, something that none of the big couture houses is able to do. Like Féraud, she is unwilling to overextend. With him, she may represent the kind of limited, decentralized dressmaking concern that will increasingly occupy the gap between haute couture and mass production.

Paris provides the perfect setting for small enterprise. There is no Seventh Avenue, and for the most part standardization is looked down upon. The designer doesn't have to put up with the tyranny of powerful magazines or rag-trade sheets like *Women's Wear Daily*. In France, journalists still report the collections instead of trying to influence them. A designer working in Paris is not greeted by daily pronunciamentos such as "Plum is in. You must do plum tweed suits." His look, his signature is what counts to the women buying his clothes, and every self-respecting designer strives for the difference that identifies him for his clients.

But what of his future? Is the couture designer, in particular, to be likened to some rare, flowering plant, as in the past, or to an endangered species? Has he completely lost the esteem once granted him as arbiter of taste in fashion? Perhaps not quite. The sculptor Louise Nevelson once said, "There are few people who understand themselves well enough to bring themselves to a high art." Many women welcome a fresh eye, a knowing touch, a new idea from time to time. At the very least, one needs to be rescued from one's worst faults. But the days of the designer and his Galatea are over.

Not that the visual results of the new way are always happy. As the cry becomes, "Dress according to your very own personality," the truth gradually appears that, unfortunately, everyone really does. The consequences can be anything from comic to outrageous one day, and can give an exact rendition of one's personality on the next. But the point here is that women will never learn about themselves unless *they* are the ones to experiment—not the designer at the drawing board. As for bringing oneself to an apex of self-expression via clothes, there are other means of accomplishing that feat, though some women find dress the most natural and convenient way. But the numbers who want to turn themselves into a free-standing work of art are relatively few.

Designers will serve more as transmitters than as oracles of taste. They are supplied with both an overview and a particular set of receiving equipment not possessed by most of us. They will function as indispensable intermediaries—if they are clever—between the real world of what women are wearing and the designer's own private imaginings of how women might possibly be persuaded to clothe themselves. Fashion today is a two-way shuttle between fantasy and street. The designer, rather than widening the gap between the lost glories of haute couture and the vitality of ready-to-wear, must act as a filter for the best of both.

chapter 13

status off
the rack

For America, the situation is different. Until recently, the yawning chasm between high-priced fantasy and working-girl attire was amply filled by the middle-class invention of status dressing. Although the American woman's attitude toward status is ambivalent, the designer look is definitely on its way out. Those "CD"'s and "V"'s over everything are no longer necessary plugs in the holes of our self-assurance.

Female confidence is one reason for the demise of status dressing. Another is that American women present the clothing industry with an entirely unique set of problems for which the status item provides absolutely no solution.

Not one of the independent designers working in Paris today would allow himself to be saddled with the responsibility for turning out garments to please a multiracial, multilingual, economically diversified hodgepodge of a hundred million American females scattered across 3,500 miles of coast-to-coast climate variations. That is Seventh Avenue's task. In the United States, such staggering conditions have to be dealt with; they determine the matter and manner of fashion around the country. But we have come to our own compromise with diversity—that kind of multiformity which, as is usual in America, takes the form of extremes.

On one hand we have Jonathan Logan and Sears, Russ Togs and J. C. Penney. On the other, we have designer clothes, America's answer to haute couture. At the lower end of the scale, Seventh Avenue's volume production still makes it possible to buy an acrylic pantsuit for $28 "at the store around the corner." The fabric will have been made by Dow Chemical Company, and the styling is strictly all-purpose schlock. The woman with slightly more to spend but nowhere special to go can even mail-order an entire mix-and-match four-piece weekend wardrobe for $72. It will arrive in autumnal grouse-shooting colors of country heather green with argyle plaid "detailing," and all its parts can be moved around as on a paper doll: green blazer with argyle A-line skirt, blazer with argyle pants, pants with pullover in green with argyle borders. And so on, until the arrival of next season's catalog. Meanwhile, the separates, once hopeful of leisurely country rambles or fall picnics under the maples, have either fallen apart at the seams or failed to live up to the promises evoked by the photogenic backdrops in the advertisements. Out they go, and a new spring is ushered in, also by mail.

Though the public at large is hardly a potential customer for status clothes, one still encounters small enclaves of exclusivity buying, especially in certain areas of cities like Beverly Hills, Dallas, and New York. This is the end of the fashion spectrum known as the "chain belt gang," which still haunts Neiman-Marcus, Saks, and the Madison Avenue boutiques in search of "class." One month it may be KJL's door-knocker earrings; another season it is YSL's link belt, or the Pucci lion's head clips, or the Dunhill lighter. Metal accessories, whether earrings, belts, chain pocketbooks, or gilt bits on shoes are really out front with status-conscious women. If by any freak of accident dressing by mail should become as reverse-chic as army surplus, Sears' mailbox would be stuffed with such orders. Meanwhile, Rive Gauche, Veneziano, Gucci, Charles Jourdan, and Ted Lapidus prey on status-bound whims. For it has long been axiomatic that status sells better in the United States if it has been made in Europe.

But winds of change have hit the world of status objects as well. Is it possible that American women—with the exception of a hard-core few—are willing to cast aside the Jackio O sunglasses, deposit the Gucci loafers at their nearest thrift shop, and do without Dior's signature written across their scarves? Have these erstwhile accoutrements of class been so overexposed that their value has diminished to the level of an unimaginative gift item? For in spite of the fact that the St. Laurent outlets hold their own in this country, the list of imported failures is surprisingly high.

One of the classic fables of status ventures in America is the rise and fall of Manhattan's first Valentino Boutique. Once hailed as a sure-fire proposition, it quickly became a multimillion-dollar vacuum. Its saga forms the most coherent illustration of the limits to status marketing in the United States. Part of Valentino's initial New York failure was due to death by overpricing, but the real reason lay in the subtle social changes that were taking place as we entered a new decade and, ultimately, a whole new state of mind about fashion.

True, money was beginning to be tight. By the autumn of 1970, charity balls were being abandoned in favor of spaghetti dinners at home; the great French restaurants continued to shut down one after the other. The recession had arrived and along with it radical chic and pointers for the very rich on how to cut corners in one's life-style, as manifested by an increase in jeans, bicycles, *Whole Earth Catalogs*, and do-it-yourself needlepoint. The furrier Jacques Kaplan began to wear denim suits and to spend his summers in small towns abroad, away from the shrill fashionables whom he dressed.

In a gesture of supreme—and ultimately suicidal—unconcern for American trends and American economics, Valentino Boutique opened at 801 Madison Avenue in 1970. In a hasty turnabout from my otherwise intellectually oriented career, I found myself recruited as a salesgirl to the Beautiful People starting on that fateful opening night in October.

The staff was a motley crew, singular by any standard. We were chosen for manners, a modicum of looks, our inexperience, and willingness to work for $2.50 an hour. Beyond that, our histories diverged radically. One girl was a scholar of eighteenth-century French painting, in flight from the confines of the Frick Museum Library; one was a sculptor; another had coauthored a book on modern American artists. There was a mysterious part-time Pan Am stewardess who lived on Park Avenue and spent her ample vacation time climbing Kilimanjaro, hang-gliding in Norway, or ballooning in Switzerland.

There was the daughter of a Greek newspaper magnate then out of favor, who was unable to find any other way to use her six languages. There was the genteel stock lady, a pale black whose various boutique jobs always took her only as far as the fringes of elegance. And Gordon, the big security guard whose remedy for abortion was a bottle of Spanish malt mixed with two pints of castor oil. A middle-aged cashier named Lucette, a black actress, veteran of Danish porno flicks, who was writing a cookbook called *How to Make It in the Kitchen*; an ex-model, a pot head, a flame-haired hooker, and myself rounded out the crew. Les Valentino Girls: Like an insane version of the Rockettes, we worked together but drolly out of step. We were there for the job, for kicks, for laughs, and to see what the world of fashion was all about. There we were, assembled for the all-star cast party of opening night. No advertising had appeared in the newspapers, no understated little ad in *The New Yorker*. *Women's Wear Daily* was the only publication that whispered any interest at all. But early in the festivities, the elevator at the brand-new boutique was grounded by a load of guests on their way to the roof; shrunken ladies in Sonia Rykiel sweaters shrieked hellos at everyone they knew; we salesgirls were flattened wallward by bearers of catered champagne; the rip-offs were tremendous and costly; the place was packed, in short, and "tout New York" was there. Valentino himself arrived—late—with his entourage, silent, uningratiating, severe. It was, after all, his fourth boutique. Though this was a first fling in America, Jacqueline Kennedy Onassis had been a best customer and his magic carpet to this country. Moreover, he was covered financially by Kenton Corporation, a young conglomerate whose stable included Cartier, Mark Cross, and Georg Jensen, among others.

By the time Valentino made his entrance that night, the five-story glass and steel shaft on Madison Avenue was filled to the brim. Like a toothpaste tube being squeezed from the top, its brown vinyl walls soon began to emit people onto the street. From there they could barely catch sight of Marina Schiano and of the wood-carved head of Naomi Sims as they modeled live under the neon lights of the display window. The architect, not a large man, had either escaped in his work clothes or had been trampled; Pilar Crespi, boutique coordinator for Valentino, though tall, had been lost for some time. The Howard Reeds, the Robert Gardiners, Geoffrey Beene, and the retail crew from Ohrbach's were, however, still very much in evidence. Many women sported identifying "V"'s. Most wore midis, in genuflection to the industry. If it existed at all, the sense of outrage about hemlines that later turned Seventh Avenue on its ear and gave the cheap little boutiques a new lease on life, was suppressed for the occasion. But much of that collective anger was as yet unrecognized. Though many women were waking up, there were just as many—especially among the rich—who still did not know how to see or trust their own image. They were ready as ever to fall back into the arms of their favorite designers for the usual head-to-toe treatment. Their paragon was—and still is—a certain Princess P. She was there, the personification of old-style hard chic, plastic skin radiant with all the scrubbed virtues of perfect grooming, resplendent in the unyielding architecture of her clothes. This gathering of intimates proved that the jet set is a true democracy. Where else would one find together princesses, taxi tycoons, entrepreneurs of art, and followers of fashion—all gathered to do homage to a poor boy from a village near Milan, who as a child daydreamed of the world of fashion?

In its first weeks the store continued to be mobbed: Barbra Streisand, Zsa Zsa Gabor, the elder Mrs. John Barry Ryan, the young Marquis de Romanonès, C-Z Guest, Rod Steiger. And a mink-clad Mafia doosie from Long Island, who bought a $2,000 fox fur coat in five minutes. Jacqueline Onassis appeared only after the crowds had subsided and, disguised in scarf and glasses, purchased one of everything, in each color.

And then winter set in. The great consumer freeze had evidently buried even the very rich. We paced the floors. It got so that when the front door opened the Burns guard would twitch out of his doze. There was rarely any noise, nothing but the thin aroma of stainless steel and glass shelves, and a fresh-glue smell that still came from the brown vinyl walls. Nothing to do. We settled into our sensualists' lair among the fur coats; some talked of Palm Beach; all watched the snow fall. An occasional customer would swim out from the shadows, finger a chiffon or a suede, reach for the price tag, exclaim, and exit. Helen became faintly hostile: Palm Beach was unknown to her and no film contracts were in sight. Brenda went on a bad acid trip and was fired. The Frick girl decided to get a divorce, painted her nails bright yellow, gained twenty pounds, and was fired. The expert on American artists got pregnant and stayed. There were frantic early-morning sales meetings. We were told that we must now use selling "technique"; we were told that the clothes were not astronomically priced by international designer standards. It was announced that, on the contrary, the Milan, Rome, and Paris branches of Valentino were grossing far more than we. The week's take from abroad was read off the teletype like a stock market report. A memo was distributed which began: "We are aiming for a $75,000 target in the next 10 days . . ." and ended with "Keep the faith!" But we could barely earn our keep, let alone anyone else's faith. Like girls of another profession, we began to pin our hopes on out-of-town guests. Uncertain men buying for their wives were a good mark: One could oversell on choices with a "send-back" proviso.

To make matters worse, in January of that year there was a flood, caused by frozen pipes. That morning, the sales staff made its way from the basement locker room through a corridor of blown lights, with the thud of water sounding on carpets overhead. The second floor sales area was dark and close as a rain forest. The only sound was of water coming rapidly from the ceiling like showers in a men's dressing room. That, and the whispered hiss of sums being counted from behind the cashier's desk. As we swam into her circle of light, there was Lucette staring over her demi-spectacles at a fistful of sales slips, lips moving in rapt calculation. Always at her post, come what may. Lucette, lone survivor of this new setback, was totting up the losses as usual. They were, as it turned out, formidable. Any other shop would have closed on the spot. Kept afloat by Kenton Corporation, however, the boutique maintained a fiction of survival, while the tally sheets continued to spell disaster.

So did our own books, at the end of each day. "No sales" were the only words appearing on most of them. A few girls were convinced that they were ugly or had halitosis and became profoundly depressed. Some ate. One or two of us launched into aesthetic dialogues about Isak Dinesen or

Bonnard, like refugees on a deserted island. It was then that we learned that Valentino Boutique was paying $4,000 a month for the privilege of its address alone.

Against all odds, spring finally arrived but could do little for our spirits or for the boutique's income. On the way back from the Pierre Hotel where the new collection had just been shown, we walked in silence. What we had seen was the beginning of Rétro, though no one had yet thought of the name. For us it was a literal regression, a trip into a particularly unpleasant past, a reactionary view of an era we barely remembered and would have been happy to forget altogether, a time of ration books and victory gardens, hair ribbons and sweetheart necklines. For reasons that we could not then understand, Valentino's second collection in America drew the entire fashion industry as for a wake: rapacious media doyennes in bronze fingernails, slung with ancient totems, metal fish on chains, cameras, their pens held within striking distance of note pads. Languorous models with shoe polish hair danced down the runway in forties beachwear, or in depression dresses, slimpsy, drowsy—like fallen parachutes. These were clothes for monsters, for braless bodies tall as stilts mounted with pinheads and painted smiles. Our silence was fraught: Each of us was thinking, How do I sell what I saw? In spite of fashion editor interest, nothing sold all that season—or the next.

That particular Valentino boutique closed in May 1974, amidst a tangle of bad relations with the now defunct Kenton Corporation and limitless legal squabbles that will probably continue until the year 2000. But the innate gift for marketing hot air on the part of the fashion press, that specialized talent for hype that has kept glamour afloat for so many years, that myth of dazzle—often paid for, cash down, by the designer himself, and flaunted by the magazines in the face of many a recession before this one—these tricks of the trade have not failed the House of Valentino. His name remains, in fact, one of the more illustrious in Europe, winning the expected press kudos and attracting a number of faithful old-school couture customers. Although a new Valentino shop has opened in New York, the venture into "deluxe ready-to-wear" on these shores has yet to prove a success. This may indicate that the head-to-toe tribute of consumer fidelity to a single designer just isn't going over any longer with American women. If so, it augurs well for the increasing number who refuse to associate being in fashion with buying labels.

How to explain it all? What has happened to status clothes and accessories is part of a progression that has sometimes seemed almost too quick for the eye and mind to record. Retrospectively, fashion has come a long way since Dior announced that the designer's function was to be a guardian of the public taste. The fact that he took this mission seriously, describing it as being "in the nature of an act of faith," shows us where women were, back in the fifties. Then the sixties guillotined most of the fashion aristocracy. From that moment, the few remaining kings of haute couture dropped their role of exterior decorator ready to dress the whole woman from hat to shoe. Class moorings were being loosened everywhere, and not least in matters of fashion. It was no longer considered a designer's right to create a total look for the woman to whom he sold clothes.

After the midi crisis of 1970, the world of high fashion became infinitely more mercurial. The design kings had to diversify or bow out of their métier. The dress business was in terrible shape, and couture slumped accordingly. On top of it all, the vengeance of a virulent trend toward anticonsumption had taken hold, with emphatic support from the women's movement both here and across the ocean. A burgeoning recession made the down swing final: Haute couture was already a relic of the more affluent past.

There were reasons other than economics to account for its demise. For one thing, couture was traditionally antierotic, and women were feeling their oats. Since Jackio O, there had been no major fashion leaders, except for a few bags of bones dragged out by *Women's Wear Daily*. The old-line fashion sharks, from magazine editors to entrepreneurs like Eleanor Lambert and the gossip columnist Suzy, were in thorough disrepute with their public. Dress design was no longer a genteel industry. It was a highly charged world of publicity, best-dressed lists, and commercial theatrics. People were more interested in other people than in clothes.

In the social shakeup of the sixties, the customary way of deciding a woman's rank by her dress may have gone by the wayside, but that is not to say that the fashion world was transformed into a democracy. The curiosity about people— about their backgrounds, schooling, jobs, husbands, and children—increased rather than abated, precisely because the outer signs were not so visible as in the past. Suddenly no one was wearing real jewelry anymore. Diamonds were duds. Mink was middle-class. Even Davidow suits went out of business.

Women in almost every society have given clues to their social status by the shorthand of dress. In Yucatán, for example, the huipil or basic white dress indicates its wearer's position only by whether the embroidery is in cotton or silk thread. American women, as we have seen, have not been noted for such nuances of social classification. During the sixties and early seventies they wanted the signals loud and clear: They went for gold. In a resolutely mobile society such as ours, the upward bound, having neither patience nor resources for head-to-toe Dior, were all too ready to settle for the Cartier tank watch or the elephant-hair bracelets from Hunting World. After the demise of real couture, accessories with designer labels provided the shortest route to class. In the early seventies, it was not uncommon to see an entire roll call of status items assembled on one Halston Ultrasueded body, from Gucci bit-and-chain loafer to Cartier triple-looped ring in three shades of gold. Today, however, sales aren't what they used to be. Although there are still plenty of women who would be unwilling to part with their Pucci signature scarves or Vuitton carryalls at the drop of an Hermès hat, such accoutrements are less and less apparent on the streets. Perhaps the status urge has been displaced onto art objects, shell collections, butcher-block and steel interiors, "honest" life-styles, socially committed jobs, or the search for raw power. In any case, what is left of couture and the status accessories it spawned is being snapped up by Arab oil sheiks, Japanese industrialists, and West German tourists. Perhaps they need its comforts more than we.

Even Dallas, status capital of the United States, reports less interest in designer labels than formerly, especially among the young. Neal Fox, who heads the couture and accessories division at Neiman-Marcus, says that a teen-ager may make a once-in-a-decade purchase of a St. Laurent silk blouse for $180, but she will wear it until she is thirty—with jeans or a cheap skirt. This sort of mixed-buying trend, which is not unusual throughout the country at a certain—but by no means high—level of income, is premised on one crucial ingredient: a new assurance in American youth.

Part of their self-confidence comes from the fact that there is no such thing anymore as suffering shame or embarrassment from wearing "inappropriate" dress. W reports its golden youth rolling up to the nearest McDonald's in $12 jeans belted with a $350 Indian turquoise buckle. Being over- or under-dressed for an occasion is impossible these days. Thus another weapon of social superiority has clattered to the ground. Broadly speaking, the dictum that anything goes must be based on the assumption that everyone is equal—in dress at least.

Hidden within that general rule, there are refinements, of course. Exceptions. Conditions. Special categories. Little changes. Take Andy Warhol's announcing his position as prime mover of the pop world by arriving at BP parties wearing a dinner jacket over jeans. His hybrid status was thus accurately confirmed. Indeed, he does belong to both worlds, but may have wanted to demonstrate his separateness from each. The heavy-breathing social aspirations of the past went out with static elegance as a sartorial ideal. Instead, we have new life-styles that connote movement—Warhol in transition from one world to another, or in flight from both. Action is what characterizes our age, forcing even the commercial badges of status to give way to style. That is, as long as style is personal and full of kinetic energy. For change is at the very heart of style. It is the trying on of many disguises, the multifaced persona, the inside talking to the world through masks. It is we as we more nearly *really* are.

Conversely, masks are also made to conceal realities. Clothes can give the lie to class. The fact that young freedom riders going south in 1965 and 1966 to enroll black voters wore blue jeans didn't disguise the invisible Brooks Brothers button-down beneath almost every work shirt. Farmer overalls don't make farmers any more than army fatigues make privates. It's all role playing: Pick your scene, choose your duds. Clothes don't necessarily make the woman—but they can provide her with camouflage.

The spectacularly rich, as opposed to the comfortable middle classes, don't have to bother with this level of disguise. Their problems are of another sort, more of the Marie Antoinette-playing-shepherdess variety. Because of the unspoken strictures against showing social position in the lavish manner of Renaissance princes—or even of Poiret's Paris—democracies have at their disposal the more convoluted methods of reverse snob appeal. This ethic reserves the word "sophisticated" for the wearing of outfits that belong to the rest of the world's poor: the common djellaba of North Africa, the Greek fisherman's shirt, the worksuit of Chinese peasants, the poncho of Andes Mountain people. What it really amounts to is borrowing. That peasant clothes are affordable by nearly everyone doubles their value to the very rich, providing that extra, unspoken pleasure of secreting one's identity instead of flaunting it. Perhaps the status battles of the future will all be fought in the lower price ranges. Women who can afford Galanos have been known to prefer Indian skirts from Bloomingdale's basement. True democracy in dress may still be far in the future, but when and if it comes, it may be the last refuge for the really rich. It offers the only social anonymity in today's media-hyped world.

chapter 14

---

people-packaging, american style

What about the women Seventh Avenue says it is designing for? How does the American fashion industry come up with ideas about how to clothe us?

It goes to France, for starters. Every firm from Sears and Montgomery Ward to Kimberly Knits and Adele Simpson has scouted the Paris collections for inspiration. Sometimes it's a straight steal, sometimes an "adaptation." Designer Victor Joris has been quoted as saying, "I can take that coat, make my pattern, and then change it any way I want. In 1960, Ricci did a green coat with an X collar. In 1966, we still had a version of it on our line. In 1961, Givenchy had a short, pink cotton coat.

It had a beautiful bustline. We bought it and put it in wool and one store sold 1,000 of our coat." *Our* coat, note.

So, in spite of repeated declarations of independence from France, the most convenient mine for American designers, merchants, and publicists of fashion is still Paris. For the most part, the French couture simply provides prototypes for mass production. At collection time, that single moment on the runway airs a designer's ideas, puts them out, so to speak, on the open market. Caution money or not, bought lock stock and barrel or sketched by a knowing eye, the dress is there with all its possibilities exposed.

Idea snatching from the couture has decreased, however, since *l'anti mode* took hold in France, rendering the Chanels and the Diors academic. In the last few seasons, Seventh Avenue rag-trade envoys have switched their attention to the twice-yearly Salon du prêt-à-porter, held at the Porte de Versailles in Paris. For those who aren't sent abroad, there is always the inspiration of New York. Certain members of the industry are known to cruise the little boutiques, army surplus stores, and thrift shops on a regular basis. Nothing wrong with that. Ideas have to come from somewhere when your job is to clothe a sector of the market consisting, say, of twenty-nine million young women between the ages of eighteen and thirty-five. But unfortunately few designers in that quasi-geographical entity known as Seventh Avenue are working in the comfort of their own unchallenged creativity.

What accounts for the persistent dazzle exerted by Paris? What leads Neiman-Marcus' top executive, Neal Fox, to say that "the fashion profits of the world are all in Europe"? Why are Americans still buying aggressively in foreign ready-to-wear, when our industrial methods at home continue far in advance of the Continent's? The answer of course is that if you are going to address yourself to a mass market as gigantic and heterogeneous as that of the United States, you are in for trouble and need any help that lies at hand.

One hears that the problem with American taste is its increasing standardization. Not true. The real difficulty, for a clothes manufacturer, is our almost incredible diversity. There are enough kinds of women in this country to keep the industry busy making everything from the dauntless miniskirt to pailleted evening chiffons. The temptation to come up with something for everybody is what keeps Seventh Avenue in a constant sweat. As though that weren't enough, American appreciation of the exotic has proliferated along with the back-to-roots movement among our minorities. So much so that the lure of clothes made in Afghanistan, Mexico, Colombia, or India has made a serious dent in the rag trade at home. In 1974, fifteen hundred members of the Amalgamated Clothing Workers picketed two New York City department stores that had outstanding sales of cheap imports. The union was right in suspecting that the attraction of these brightly colored and inexpensive clothes had probably cost about eleven thousand Americans their jobs.

Diversity hasn't always been a problem. Life was a lot simpler when a multiplicity of regional attitudes was the very last thing a manufacturer had to think of. When ready-to-wear began in 1830, its clientele could not have been more homogeneous. The name of the first ready-to-wear firm was Brooks Brothers, and it made clothes for sailors in New Bedford, Massachusetts. In that same year the sewing machine was invented by a French engineer named Thimmonnier. When its possibilities were later recognized by Singer, the ready-to-wear industry was really on its way. But for a number of years to come mass-production methods were limited to men's wear, specifically to uniforms. U.S. Army clothing was manufactured on the assembly line beginning in 1840. From that time on, sizes were standardized, thus establishing a working principle for ready-made clothing. Two decades later, Levi Strauss launched his denim pants for gold rush miners, and the Strauss factory in San Francisco was in operation. During the Civil War, ladies' sewing circles were supplied with machines in order to increase the supply of uniforms, but private use of the instrument was prohibited until 1876, when the patent ran out, and it could be traded on the open market. Meanwhile, paper patterns were invented in 1863 by Ebenezer Butterick, and the first women's magazines came into circulation. *McCall's* (which started out under the name of "Queen of Fashion" in 1873) was followed by *Harper's Bazaar* and the *Ladies' Home Journal. Vogue* began in 1893 as a publication expressly aimed at New York City's upper classes.

The 1880's ushered in the department store. It was a time of relative stability; the westward migrations had slowed, and women had the opportunity to shop at one location. Although Lord & Taylor had already been in existence for decades, its merchandise was limited. Until the department store came into being, even women in major urban centers did their shopping by mail-order catalog or bought from traveling peddlers. By the late nineteenth century, the garment industry was well enough organized to make regular deliveries to outlets, and clothes could be store bought as well as made at home on machines.

But it was not until the nineties that women's outfits became a regular feature of ready-to-wear. The trend was unexpectedly initiated by Charles Creed, a tailor who made riding habits for Queen Victoria. One of his suits became so popular that it was reproduced everywhere in England and America, assuming the role of a basic garment. The rage for ladies' "tailor-mades" soon swamped the industry, which in turn stocked the department stores with the desirable new merchandise. Availability, in this case, helped to create demand, and women's ready-to-wear was on its way to building a solid foundation. So solid, in fact, that there was room for specialization—the Neiman-Marcus empire in Dallas began in 1907 with a shop exclusively devoted to "ladies ready-made outer garments and millinery."

The rest of the ready-to-wear story is recent history: the unionization of female labor, mostly skilled and predominantly immigrant, with the formation of the International Ladies' Garment Workers Union in 1900; the trade publication *Women's Wear Daily*, which began in 1910 to keep the industry on its toes and up to date; the development of rayon and other synthetic fibers; the shirtwaist dress, which succeeded Creed's tailor-mades and became the first truly indigenous American fashion. Worn by upper, middle, and lower classes alike, the shirtdress thus helped to democratize fashion in this country at an early date. The twenties brought on the cult for youth and flappers; the thirties put pants in the picture and gave us both sportswear for day and Hollywood-inspired glamour for evening. This was also the era of Claire McCardell's American look, during which she carried on the great shirtwaist tradition while adding her own superb innovations to the repertoire. Her use of jersey, her insistence on comfort in a loose, unconstructed fit, her wrap-arounds, and pop-overs, and above all her concept of dresses made from a single length of fabric—these creations were marked by all the simplicity of genius.

By 1950, we had our rivals to French high fashion; Norell, Mainbocher, Trigère, Galanos were haute in price, though not couture in method. At the other end of the scale was the boom in mass-produced junior wear; Jonathan Logan, Bobbie Brooks, Russ Togs, Majestic, Sue Brett, were all firmly established in the marketplace. It was an era of conformity in dress partly fostered by the volume producers themselves, but bolstered by advertising and no doubt by a generous dose of postwar complacency. The typical junior miss wore billowing crinolines, belts like those sported by polo players, and drip-dry blouses. She collected, in every available color, those balletlike Capezios and Pappagallos that shoe salesmen embarrassingly called "your little flatties." The mid-fifties also saw a proliferation of Tyrolean dirndl dresses which took over on college campuses for a while and were labeled the schmaltz style. But the basic winter uniform was tweed skirt, cashmere (if possible) cardigan, and those outrageous midcalf socks which yielded to gravity every five minutes. The sixties had a lot to liberate us from.

As for ready-to-wear, it followed Paris just as unfailingly as we followed it. The early sixties saw our first attempt at a break with foreign design leadership. By 1963, the fashion focus had shifted to London, and Americans like Betsey Johnson and Rudi Gernreich were confidently cutting loose. While Carnaby Street turned out cheap goods, Americans led the way with body-skimming leotard dresses, bralessness, and the topless interlude. See-through blouses, pants for daytime wear, micro-miniskirts, jersey knits were in the works, with the rest of the world clamoring for *le style Américain.*

Meanwhile, "Seventh Avenue" had become synonymous with the entire U.S. fashion industry. Indeed most design is still centered in New York's garment district, a slice of Manhattan's West Side running along Broadway and Seventh Avenue between 34th and 42d streets. It is a confined area, a factor that increases the ingrown tendencies of its four thousand firms. Buildings here are uniformly gray and office-like, providing a mechanized atmosphere for dress production. But there is a lot of action outdoors. All day long porters push delivery racks past a motley collection of secretaries on coffee break, designers, models, pushcarts, delicatessens, and newspaper stands that are out of *Women's Wear Daily* at 10 A.M. but still have a *Times* at 6 P.M. Trucks weave in and out of the animal and vegetable traffic. The decibel level is certainly higher here than anywhere else in the city.

A marketplace as manic as this one has to have its subdivisions. On Seventh Avenue, specialization is the name of the game if you want to survive. Thus 1400 Broadway houses popular-priced manufacturers, while 1407 is chockablock with fabric dealers; 512 Seventh Avenue is coats and suits, 530 houses "better dresses" (Adele Simpson, Vera Maxwell, Malcolm Starr, Jerry Silverman, Mort Schrader); and down the street at 550 is where the top-price ready-mades are designed.

Perhaps it is overcrowding in limited areas that creates passionate traditions, habits, conventions. Whatever the reason, this tiny sector of Manhattan has developed its own intense street life, an explosive native vocabulary, a list of rigid food preferences, and a physical pace unchallenged by any other area of the city, with the possible exception of the floor of the Stock Exchange. Seventh Avenue has been known to project and elaborate a massive inferiority complex as well. It is filled with people who seem to be ashamed of their origins or their occupation or both. They know that to call a ripped-off copy of someone else's design an original is both incorrect and pretentious. They know that their products are, by and large, overpriced and badly made. Those who have made it big, like Larry Aldrich and John Weitz, prefer to be thought of as art collectors or playboys rather than as dress designers. It is not their fault that the profession commands little respect in this country. They will probably never be held in awe as French designers have been. But those who accept the dress business for what it is—a competitive, nerve-wracking brawl of an industry based on an all-pervasive profit motive—are at an immediate advantage.

Life on Seventh Avenue is so chaotic that in the past not even the star designers found time for much contact with the outside world. Except for Sarmi, who cultivated the Beautiful People, and Bill Blass, who went out on circuit, few made any effort to get a sounding of what women wanted in Akron or Des Moines. When the industry was nearing catastrophe in the 1970/71 season, most designers decided that personal appearances at O'Neil's or Younkers or Garfinkel's or Jordan Marsh might help. And it did. Now the airlines are full of Kaspers and Calvin Kleins and Diane von Fürstenbergs, making obligatory whistle stops and speeches, whirlwind tours and handshakes, just like politicians. And shuttle diplomacy works: It sells their clothes. Even magazine advertisements now quote them on everything from sex to how to make chicken cacciatore. In a country as big as this one, being a personality can win you a lot of sales.

What makes the scene inside a Seventh Avenue firm so frantic? At small shops employing even a single designer, everyone has ulcers. It's practically a requirement for the job. The manufacturer must supervise not only his designer, but also a houseful of sample makers, patternmakers, cutters, sewing machine operators, finishers, sales managers, bookkeepers, models, salesmen, buyers, men who take orders, men who make deliveries—and the telephone. Much of the noise level on Seventh Avenue is accounted for by that demonic instrument. Since very few deliveries in the entire history of the garment district have been known to arrive on time, the telephone takes a lot of abuse. Orders may be transmitted in a quiet voice, but the sound waves can vibrate unpleasantly when the manufacturer is on the wire with his notions supplier or dye house. Decibels really ring when his road salesman is at the receiving end of a long distance call, and the lines can be counted on to do a dance when an important buyer phones to say that the special cutting she ordered arrived in fuchsia instead of pale pink.

By the time Dubrow's Cafeteria has packaged its final morning container of coffee to go, the pavements are emptied of employees, and the trucks take over. From that moment until 5:30 P.M., the streets are only a little quieter than the offices. At 264 West 40th, designer Anthony Muto is already at work with his model. Her size eight figure is too bosomy for his sample, a crystal-pleated canary chiffon ball gown of the grand entrance variety, and there is some banter about her being on the Pill and throwing his sizing out of whack. Muto appears to have three sets of hands: one set for the telephone, one set for coffee, and a third for fittings. The dress has to be resized and repleated. While Muto goes back to his sketchboard, extension-wired telephone under chin, Joyce, the workroom manager, takes over. Meanwhile all hell has broken loose in the cutting section. One of the electric rotary blades—a sort of hedge clipper for shirred and deep-pile fabrics—has gone berserk. More telephone calls finally summon a repairman, and five cups of coffee later the machine is back in use.

In another corner of the workroom the patternmakers are busy cutting the marker. This is a hand operation and a crucial one, for the marker is really the blueprint that determines whether or not a garment will fit. Cardboard patterns corresponding to the various pieces of a dress are so laid on a long sheet of paper as to leave between them the least amount of space. Layers of fabric are spread under the marker, which serves as the master pattern. The cutter then delves through perhaps 300 layers of material, following the lines of the marker. If the cutting is just inside those lines, the end result is going to be a *small* size eight or ten, and the fit will be tight. This is what is known on Seventh Avenue as "shrinking the marker." It is done more often than any manufacturer would like to admit because it saves yards of fabric and, conse-quently, a lot of money. In Muto's shop such methods are recognized as shortsighted as well as dishonest. Reorders don't materialize once the results of a shrunk marker are sent out to buyers—*if* the buyer is on her toes. For, quite literally, the buck can stop dead on her desk. If she catches faulty sizing, the dress will never get to the customer, the customer won't complain about lack of fit, and the dress firm will recut correctly, thereby maintaining its good reputation.

The same rule applies to fabric. "Quality control," as it is known in the trade, should be enforced all the way down the line, from mill to merchandiser. When a blouse is returned because of shrinkage by a woman who has washed it once, the fault can be traced all the way back to the supplier. Fabrics shrink, they stretch, they run. They shouldn't be allowed out of production if they do. Materials are supposed to be inspected in the cutting room after delivery, and if the textile company is at fault, the mistake should be caught by the cutter. But the human propensity to let little things pass makes its entry at this point and gains a momentum all its own, infecting every stage of production. When business is bad, the temptation to take risks with the customer is enormous. The hunch is that the majority of women will accept faulty goods just because styles change so fast that they want whatever look is current *right now*. If you're really hungry, you don't send back the hamburger even if it's undercooked; your instinct is to eat it raw.

So most of Seventh Avenue has turned into a faddist's dream and a craftsman's nightmare. Many workers never see the completed product they've worked on. Assembly-line piece-work is a necessity. How can pride be fostered in what skilled hands can do, without a view of the whole, without any tradition of satisfaction in the labor itself? Customers are used to getting less, so they demand less. Manufacturers cut corners where they can. And you end up with a thoroughly demoralized industry. Part of the problem is the sheer behemoth size of the rag trade in the United States. It is unwieldy. It tries to react to every trend with quick ordering. It is like a fast-food chain totting up so many billion whamburgers to its credit, while trying to change the sauce formula every week. Numbers are everything. Survival means even more in an area with a one-fifth yearly attrition rate. The fast buck generates an impossible pace. When one asks a French designer like Louis Féraud what ails Seventh Avenue, his reply is money hunger.

To see the making of money as a threat to business may

seem a strange paradox, but even leading figures in the industry admit it is true. Abe Schrader, the sportswear manufacturer, says, "[In] piecework, everybody tries to make it a little faster. Instead of making five dresses a day they would like to make seven." Vincent Draddy, chairman of the board at David Crystal, adds, "There is always the pressure to make a dress for less." And the president of Saks Fifth Avenue finishes the thought: "There is only one way you can make it for less, by taking something out of it."

With everyone prey to haggling for the best possible price, why, if American production methods are so streamlined, aren't clothes cheaper? Bill Blass figures on $250,000 as a minimal cost to him of one collection. Like most designers, he does two a year. Each collection averages about a hundred designs, which means that one sample can cost more than $2,000. The deficit is taken up by the showing itself, and by discards, for inevitably some samples are not put on the runway if the designer feels they are apt to be duds.

A Blass dress selling for about $110 may bring in only a $2 profit to the design house. Labor is a heavy expense, accounting for perhaps $28 of the total purchasing price. Average wages for a garment worker were over $4 an hour in 1973, and have kept relative pace with the cost of living index since then. Overhead may come to $20. Fabric and trimmings are the least expensive ingredient, accounting for about $9. End cost to the manufacturer of making the dress is thus in the $60 range. The heavy expenses, however, are in the retail end of the operation. Store charges parallel what the manufacturer laid out to produce the garment. In addition to the wholesale price of the dress, markdowns, shortages, pilferage, alterations, salaries, costs of advertising, promotion, and window displays, overhead and administration billings can total as much as $108. Thus, at a selling price of $110, the Blass dress still gives its maker only $2 in profit.

Part of the problem of low gains resides in the general economy. One store executive reported a Con Edison bill of $36,000 a month in 1974, an escalation of $12,000 over the previous year. Before the fall of 1973, when business started downhill, Seventh Avenue garment workers numbered some 200,000. Firms were collectively grossing $7,000,000,000 yearly, and New York City was still boomtown for the clothing industry. But the effects of the recession showed up later that year, and quality companies, especially at the coat and suit level where wages are traditionally higher, started going out of business one after the other. The area was flooded with designers and workers looking for positions. Jobs had slipped to 160,000. Remaining companies tried to keep afloat by pushing for greater volume. And so began the whole vicious cycle that ends in the customer's distress with fabrics that shrink and seams that unravel. Naturally she is less than enchanted with her new clothes. Answer? The supreme logic of not buying anything. Or of buying thrift-shop hand-me-downs whose construction, though thirty or forty years old, is an unexpected treat when compared with today's. Or, there is always the possibility of wearing jeans and T-shirts forever. Or of getting out of the rag race entirely by making one's own clothes. Antifashion, in short.

As for Seventh Avenue itself, it began to react to the downhill slide with its usual brontosaurean lumberings. The reigning depression caused several firms to move out of New York. As a result, the industry is slowly decentralizing, and cities like Atlanta, Los Angeles, St. Louis, and Dallas provide the new homes for this migration and its dubious benefits. Gone are the days when buyers from all over the country crowded Manhattan hotels from the McAlpin to the Pierre: It's cheaper to send a buyer to Los Angeles if you're I. Magnin in Seattle. Labor is less expensive almost anywhere outside the Big Apple. Fashion writers no longer flock to seventy-five-odd showrooms in the famous eight-block radius to get the word for their copy. As the city's once-largest industry goes into its eighth decade, it is relinquishing its leadership in a business that accounts for $25 billion dollars nationwide. So be it; this is a big country.

Once removed from the East Coast megalopolis, the scene does change. Manufacturers and designers have discovered, if they hadn't known it before, that it's another world out there. At the Sanger-Harris department store in Dallas, pantsuits and wigs outsell Ultrasuede. Minis are still very much in the picture. Wash 'n wear acrylic evening dresses are as popular as color-coordinated housewares and bar sets. This is the land of Jonathan Logan, Russ Togs, and Bobbie Brooks, where familiarity breeds contentment.

At the other end of the scale of purchasing power, one finds that not even customers of the great Neiman-Marcus store take many risks with style. Here, too, fashion plays follow the leader. Obeisance to European design takes the form of two-week celebrations called Fortnights, during which Dallas turns itself into the Via Veneto, Bond Street, or the Faubourg St. Honoré. The carnival is cultural as well, offering representatives of the chosen country's music, theater, ballet, and paintings. Fortnights are the brainchild of Stanley Marcus, who retains his title as one of the world's great merchants. His penchant for theatrical retailing and pretty packaging for millionaires has turned Neiman-Marcus into an oasis for the oil, cotton, and cattle wealth of Texas and famous customers from abroad. Marcus is a specialist in ambience, and his touch sells. The art of making nothing look like something can turn a cake of soap nestled in a silver basket into a Cinderella story of retailing acumen.

But even Neiman-Marcus caters to tastes other than those of the remaining rich and status hungry. The store may not stock Bobbie Brookses, but it carries caftans of Indian manufacture. There are Chinese workers' uniforms among the Anne Kleins; Carol Horns and Stephen Burrowses among the Halstons. The word has reached even the last bastion of new wealth: Diversify!

Who are the new designers whose cues have come along the street-fashion route? The leading ones seem to be black; many are women. Black style is synonymous with motion. Black models changed the look of clothes when they were finally accepted in the late 1960's. For one thing, they fairly danced down the runways, making it look as though the fluid new dresses of silk or Arnel jersey were created especially for them. Runway modeling became their specialty at a time when magazines photographed an occasional token black in a large layout made up mostly of whites. But Luna, Pat Cleveland, Billie Blair, and Norma Darden were already making fashion news in daily women's columns for their presentations of the new style. Norma Darden once described in this way the difference between a stiff, traditional showing and the kind of jazzy demonstration of a dress that she's so good at: "It's like church. In a white church it's silent; in a black church, there's a lot of noise." Pop music was the new accompaniment for clothes; dance steps were part of the show.

Indeed, black designer Stephen Burrows acknowledges that his primary influence comes from dance movements. His easy living look, his unconventional colors, the flow of his fabrics, and the special trademark of his lettuce-leaf hems have put him at the head of a bright new vanguard. Burrows knows how to wield technology to advantage. For the famous hems he uses a zigzag stitch that puckers the fabric, ruffling it out instead of giving it a flat seam. It would not have occurred to most designers to employ stitching that destroys a line rather than straightens it, but Burrows liked the "mistake effect" and uses it to the hilt. Others in the fashion world were quick to acknowledge Burrows' particular genius and black style in general. In 1973, designer Karl Lagerfeld said, "If I open a fashion magazine here [in Paris] I don't have to read the caption to know it's a Rykiel or a Kenzo or a St. Laurent. In American fashion magazines I always have to read the captions. The only designer who seems to have a personality is Stephen Burrows. I think he has invented a whole new fashion."

When Burrows appeared on the scene in the sixties, only Wesley Tann, Jon Haggins, and Scott Barrie had any slice of the design pie which, by and large, was not being offered to blacks. But soon came the search for roots among black people who had read Malcolm X, had seen the new black films, and were responding to a deep sense of their own cultural background. The Afro hairstyle blossomed, followed by corn-row braids. Black business got off the ground with special makeup and cosmetic preparations. Already there were magazines like *Ebony* and *Essence*. Entertainers Diana Ross, Cicely Tyson, and Billy Dee Williams made the big time. The movies *Shaft* and *Sounder* put over the Superfly look. There was more money to spend; black fashion got out of Harlem and entered Bloomingdale's and Bendel's.

Women designers came back on the scene in the sixties as well. At their helm was Betsey Johnson, who started with Paraphernalia boutiques and still does her funky but functional clothes for the phenomenally successful Alley Cat. Betsey Johnson avowedly "hates fashion," but she was determined to show Seventh Avenue that "the crazies" could make money without costing the consumer much. Her crazies did make money and still do, though the original inspirations don't look so strange anymore. They look rather like the body clothes everyone is into: printed muslins with floppy sleeves, slinky nylon tricots to go to dinner in, T-shirts and T-dresses to wear all day long. A string of female designers followed in Betsey's wake: Liz Claiborne, Jeanne Campbell, Luba, Mary McFadden, Britta Bauer, Carol Horn, Maxime de la Falaise, Hanae Mori, Diane von Fürstenberg, Holly Harp, Cathy Hardwick, and Donna Karan, who took over for Anne Klein after the latter's death.

In the United States the current preeminence of female designers is due partly to the fact that they originate ideas for their own use. They are able to test out their own clothes and therefore know more surely than a man what is comfortable, what works, and what a woman wants. The other reason is that in these days of female emancipation, the ladies have shown that they can make it in business. As a consequence, men are more willing to back a woman designer financially.

Not that women have ever been excluded from fashion. The first dressmaker of any note was Marie Antoinette's Rose Bertin. The eighteenth century also had its Mademoiselle Pagelle, as the nineteenth had its Palmyre and its Victorine.

Then there were the pre-World War I Mesdames Cheruit, Paquin, and the Soeurs Callot. Jeanne Lanvin, Vionnet, Chanel, and Grès followed. But women disappeared from the fashion scene after World War II. Except for Schiaparelli, whose work was not structural but more like program music—a commedia dell'arte of witty trimmings and clever ideas—there was no one except the aging Chanel. And then suddenly Mary Quant exploded onto the marketplace, followed by Jean Muir and Zandra Rhodes. France has Emmanuelle Khanh, Sonia Rykiel, Jacqueline Jacobson of Dorothée Bis, Lison Bonfils, Renata, Chantal Thomass, Anne-Marie Beretta—the list is endless and bodes strikingly well for the future.

It is no accident that the top women designers are all in ready-to-wear. It is thus partly their influence, underscored by a lot of attention from the media, that has raised the level of taste in clothes everywhere. J. C. Penney and Sears ask them to design lines. Bobbie Brooks and Jonathan Logan scout them. Many of their ideas are "transposed" at much lower price levels. Indeed it is possible to say for ready-to-wear in general that what was lost in special finery for the privileged of the past has been compensated for by a general elevation of appearance in dress. Exclusivity does not foster inventions in mass technology; without new fabrics and advanced machinery, the garment industry would be unable to carry out new design possibilities.

The great dynamism of ready-to-wear is no secret. It is popular because it gives people what they really want at prices they can afford. It appeals to women of means as well, because they no longer want the responsibility of owning precious objects. Its technology is full of fabulous possibilities precisely because it can achieve an exact reproduction of an original model with dazzling speed. The result of this phenomenon, however, is that we are no longer sure of being able to distinguish between model and copy. The ease with which line-for-line reproduction can be done, coupled with a media life-style in which the picture of something or the publicity about it achieves precedence over the thing itself, since the latter is seen by very few people, has helped to displace our values from original to copy. The couture provides a perfect example. When ready-to-wear saturated the market in the sixties, it seemed to many that the handmade original dress was devalued by its mass-manufactured copies. What was the point of owning a suit fitted by Mademoiselle Chanel herself if the woman seated across from you at dinner was wearing the identical costume in a cheaper Ohrbach's knock-off edition? The smugness of the "only *you* know for sure" answer has by now worn off, and women are beginning to acknowledge that it really doesn't matter that much to own the original. A personal liking for superb craftsmanship and luxurious fabrics —yes. There is every reason to have a suit jacket lined with mink if one likes the feel and wants the warmth. But insofar as clothes are public—and they are to some extent always display items—no. It doesn't matter anymore because what has become important is the general look of a thing. Publicly, it is overall impression that counts. So ready-to-wear becomes a way of life; it also engineers a subtle shift of our own values away from appreciation of one-of-a-kind to involvement with its double.

There is no better example of this than the fantastic success of artistic multiples. Today almost anyone can own a Calder or Stella print. The question of where to place value has long troubled art dealers. Is the original the copper plate or lithographic stone? the artist's proof? the first few run-offs of the edition? Industrially, printed reproductions make value hard to locate. Mass availability seems to put an end to the cachet of possessing an original, whatever it is. In the arts we have witnessed this change as part of another phenomenon. Since World War II, the object itself has become vulnerable to the dangers of impermanence. We stood by in those years and saw bombs demolish people, countrysides, buildings, and valuable works of art. It is no wonder that art itself repeated this leitmotiv after the war, as in Jean Tinguely's "self-destroying" sculptures. The war made it suddenly clear that you couldn't create a beautiful thing and expect it to last forever.

Ours is an age destructive of substance. Memory, public images, *personalities* appear to be more permanent than things. Nowhere is this more apparent than in the clothing business. We will probably never see another Balenciaga, another Norell; their efforts would be considered misspent today by all but a very few. But the throw-away dress does not have to be ugly. When Seventh Avenue gets around to valuing creativity as highly as commercial success, American design can achieve preeminence in the market for mass-produced clothes. Already U.S. methods outpace those of the European *prêt-à-porter* by thirty or forty years. Our skills have always been those of technology and engineering. We know how to market. Since our sartorial destiny is going to be ready-to-wear, why not make the most of our heterogeneous resources, the strange and exotic bloom of our subcultures? Why not stop hedging our bets with classics, and take a few chances with style?

chapter 15

future
chic

The least-disputed axiom in the fashion field is that, just as change is inevitable, prediction is impossible. Or at the least, highly inadvisable. Conversely, since in fashion, as in most everything else, there is rarely anything *totally* new under the sun, not much is to be lost by a little crystal-ball gazing.

Speculation on the future of clothes can take us halfway around the world. From Manhattan to Morocco, from Los Angeles lofts to Paris salons, there is a small coterie of designers at work on the same problem: how we can look and live in a way that reflects us truly during the next decades. They are few, these artists, and very far between geographically. For the most part, they hardly know each others' names. Only one or two have other than local reputations. Each is eccentric in his own way; any one of them would be horrified to be linked with another in aspiration. They form no movement. But they are all wrestling with what is at the absolute dead center of design: the ways to translate into fabric what is going on in the mind's eye —their own, their customers', that of the public at large.

Essentially the failure of both haute couture and of Seventh Avenue has been the inability to understand that insofar as women today are concerned, we wear our *selves*. Fashion follows *us*. It is the zip code to our being. Since society's rate of change—velocity—has become so dizzying, fashion is hard put to keep up with us. The métier of clothes design in the seventies is based on the ability to anticipate and to get the jump on the zeitgeist. In the case of couture, dressmaking was tied to a static, "stately homes" way of life which has, quite simply, gone out of style. The fatal flaw in mass-produced goods, on the other hand, lies in trying to be all things to all people in a society whose components are unprecedentedly mobile and intensely unlike one another. In the sixties and early seventies, it took the combined underground force of a whole slew of funky one-man clothes factories with names like Truth and Soul or Roach Studios to move in with the stuff young people wanted. No wonder Seventh Avenue stood by openmouthed.

Ready-to-wear may be the only way to clothe America, but its hottest design ideas won't come off the drawing boards between 34th and 42d streets on New York's West Side. For while Seventh Avenue is still fiddling around with neckline detailing and sleeve treatment and interest on the belt buckle, along comes an American living in Morocco who has simply decided to revolutionize clothes. Okay, we've heard that before, right? First it was Dior, then Courrèges, then Gernreich back in 1964. Not too long ago it was Halston. A revolution a minute, which is what can make fashion such a drag and a put-on. And now who is he, this Peter Kent who isn't even *on* the fashion scene, who wings in to New York from Tangiers with all the answers? The man is very simple with a very complex history. So are his clothes.

He arrives at a time when the desire for simplicity has reached a hysterical pitch. The Rétro game is up. There is nothing more depressing than a way of decking yourself out that *began* by being old. Even the rag industry has finally caught on and has stopped bringing us reruns of every era except our own, so that at least the streets are no longer full of ladies who look like leftover extras from the late late show. Seventh Avenue seems to have made a policy decision to manufacture nothing but classics from now until doomsday— hardly a new ploy when you have to hedge your bets against the combined threats of a bad economic climate, an insatiable human instinct for change, and the well-known feminine capacity for reversing any decision regarding appearance. All anyone knows is that fashion has become a carrier for this craving to uncomplicate our lives, for the need to unlearn. In design, it is an advantage *not* to know how to construct a garment. Halston didn't know how, and he is currently emperor of a $30-million-a-year enterprise.

In the case of Peter Kent, you have a true neoprimitive American of the utmost sophistication. He is not interested in clothes, let alone fashion. To Kent, the notion that burgundy is this season's color or the Big Look that year's line is strictly from Mars. His "line" was put into production five thousand years ago, and his colors come from plants, minerals, and whatever else the earth is yielding this millennium in the way of dyes. Peter Kent is a lean, long Andy Warhol sans eyeglasses who lopes around his loft in Manhattan's Chelsea district wearing a Moroccan peasant's robe made from a length of fabric sewn up the sides, an elegant piece of eggplant-colored cotton. A sack, in other words. But Peter's modern sack is history incarnate—an end product of the whole saga of clothing in man's scramble up the reaches of civilization.

The logic of Kent's Design Community clothes is of the "why didn't I think of that" variety. Design Community was started as an attempt to reduce fabric waste in manufacture. He reckoned that pattern-making is not an a priori necessity, and he was right. Indeed, patterns have become, through the centuries, a degrading jigsaw puzzle. Design Community clothing is made up from a stock of four or five basic shapes, all of them of ancient derivation. There are Japanese "samurai" pants; long dresses based on the sleeveless Egyptian "kalasiris"; Hebraic, Assyrian, and Coptic coats and cloaks, all of which are cut from brown paper prototypes. Rarely does a Design Community garment require more than a single swathe of fabric.

Having begun on a shoestring, Kent and his co-workers had to circumvent all the costly hardware of contemporary clothes —including buttons. Their garments thus fasten with ties made of the same fabric as the dress or pants. Kent soon realized the beauty of their enforced decision: nothing in the finished piece detracts from the fabric it is made of. And so a second premise developed: the primacy of handwoven material and color, and the subordination of cut. The logic of these clothes is the doing away with body capsules—the tight fit, the high armholes, the swaddled look which has been so prevalent in the last two decades and was rightly objected to by the counterculture as being unhealthy for the body. What Design Community is all about is untailored clothes, or garments that require only the merest geometrical guidelines as patterns for their assembly.

This way of dressing has been in existence as long as man has bothered to clothe himself at all. Historically, weather and fabric have determined style. Adaptation to various climates produced the South Seas sarong and the Eskimo's leather-wrapped chaps. Many hot-country clothes developed centuries ago are still the most efficient: the Indian sari, the Mexican huipil, the North African burnoose. Mantles, shawls, and ponchos provide the simplest warmth at higher altitudes and permit weave and color to act as ornament. The draped trouser skirt of Thailand, the king's robe or bubu of Upper Volta, the Muslim woman's dress, and the Rumanian fota or folded skirt have fortunately all survived the "improvements" of clothes technology.

For even more expert instructions in how to work fabric one can always glance back at ancient Greece. To the Greeks, anyone wearing tight-fitting garments was probably a barbarian from the north. Greek chitons, peplos, and cloaks were, moreover, eminently unisex. Basic garments consisted of lengths of cloth that, pulled around the body, became clothes. Variety derived from the anatomy underneath and from a few ornaments—sandals, a fibula or pin to catch the fabric at a shoulder, a girdle around the waist or under the breasts. Draping of fabric plus the stance of its wearer were the keys to setting off the person underneath. Sociologist Bernard Rudof-

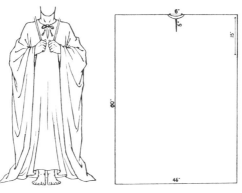

PATTERNLESSNESS. The ancient Egyptians knew how to make clothes of the simplest and most effective type, cut from a single length of fabric and draped on the figure. (From *Ancient Egyptian, Mesopotamian and Persian Costume*, by Mary Houston, Adam & Charles Black, London, 1954.)

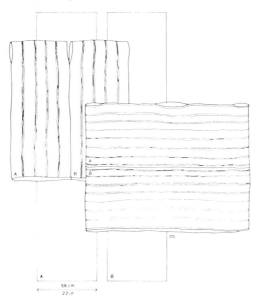

TWENTIETH-CENTURY SIMPLICITY OF DRESS. Peruvian ponchos cut from a swathe of fabric and folded. Their popularity today indicates that we can learn much from the return to patternless clothing. (From *Cut My Cote*, by Dorothy K. Burnham, Royal Ontario Museum, 1973, reproduced by permission.)

sky wrote of Greek costume that "the looks of the dress were entirely determined by the ability to wear it. Posture was inseparable from the ultimate effect. . . . The best dressed man or woman was therefore the one who knew how to wear the dress best, who embodied grace, charm and wit . . ." Norman Norell talked about these qualities not so very long ago, just before he died in 1972. But locked as we are into our tradition of body packaging and status buying, this true democracy of taste so far eludes us.

Will we ever get back to the importance of beautiful fabric cut in simple geometric shapes without the help of patterns, and draped on the body? Are we courageous enough about the human form to relax our dependence on clothing buttressed with "innards" and ornament and predesigned artifice? The liking for comfort, the demand for clothes that move, is a good sign. We are part way there, perhaps, when designers such as Karl Lagerfeld eliminate linings, facings, stiffening, and unnecessary seams in their clothes. At the upper price reaches of the ready-to-wear establishment, Lagerfeld has already made his mark: hemlines overstitched so as not to unravel, instead of turned up the bulkier way; seams joined flat by tiny zigzag threads; lightweight, clinging jerseys that can be layered on without heaviness. Lagerfeld openly admires the principles at work in the art of draping and is absorbed by the examples worn by ancient Greek and Roman statues in the Louvre. As far as he and his followers like Sonia Rykiel in Paris and Burrows and Holly Harp in the United States are concerned, the time is past for chopping fabric into tortuous little shapes joined by complex seaming.

It is far more difficult, however, to change the mind than the dress. Tailoring is an intensely Western craft, the results of which have provided us with our sartorial image for as long as anyone can remember. A suit of clothes has been the mark of Occidental man, setting him irrevocably apart from Eastern ways. A tailored three-piece used to be one of the glories of class; England's thimble-and-thread men made Saville Row a byword for privilege. In their *petits tailleurs,* their Chanels and St. Laurents, European and American women have carried on the tradition begun by Charles Creed, creator of Queen Victoria's hunting suits in the 1890's. But women have begun to see their lives differently in the last few years. As the body emerges from being something forbidden to constituting one's very self, it naturally predominates. We have long ago abandoned the notion of dress as cover, mere utilitarian protection. Now we are beginning to think of clothes as an intensification of the ego. Nothing does this so well as a dress that moves, that lends its own motion to that of its wearer, giving her a heightened sense of her body now become like that of a dancer. It is possible to speculate that according to this way of thinking, nudity might be considered another form of dress. One should be able to "put on nudity" as raiment.

If changing the look of clothes all starts in the mind, then who are the other fashion intellectuals and where are they hiding? Given the present system for locating genius, their lights appear to be obscured under bushels. Public relations people invariably look to what they know for news, and what they know is New York's garment district, its importers, its allied specialty shops and department stores. One needs a forked nose for fashion to skip over all the obvious sources and alight on talent from Morocco or SoHo or Los Angeles. Most of the still-young designers now scattered over the globe went through the fashion mill of the sixties. Their apprenticeships were served during the giant industrial takeover of street clothes by ready-to-wear. They saw it all happen, and the best of them survived to tell the tale. They did more—they struck out on their own; but that comes later. Here is how they would describe what happened.

Street clothes of the sixties and early seventies gave a lot of hype to individual dressing, especially at night. But in retrospect, it's clear that ready-to-wear tried to rip the "anti" right out of fashion. Seventh Avenue did an amoeba number on street-strutting individuality: It just absorbed that flash and stardust, ran it through the cutting machines, and spewed it out all over America in the shape of millions of "with it" Bobbie Brooks jean skirts or modified mod-rocker minidresses. It was the same story with cosmetics. Maybelline put murky art nouveau colors in every drugstore in the United States within what seemed like minutes of the originals' first appearance in London. Ready-to-wear does, after all, stand for access. Every woman can now buy—at assorted price ranges—what only the elite used to have a finger on.

The uptake of what began as antifashion by the middle classes in this country has been accelerated, of course, by what I have called velocity. Whereas a fashion revolution at Versailles would not have roused most of Louis XIV's subjects from blissful ignorance, a T-shirt today can change the look of half the world almost overnight. Whatever happens to styles now, from hot pants to the jeaning of America, inevitably affects how great masses of the world's population will look. There is a gigantic international fashion democracy, sponsored by travel, an omnipresent media, higher living standards, and the phasing out of dress as an indicator of social class. During the sixties, among politically aware young people above all,

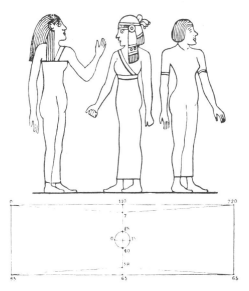

THE WAY IT USED TO LOOK. *Above*. Ancient Egyptian female costumes. *Below*. Hebrew nobles. (From *Die Trachten der Völker in Bild und Schnitt*, by Carl Köhler.

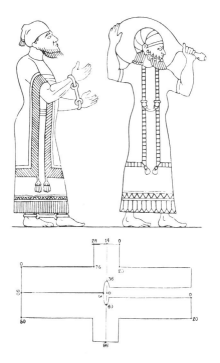

clothes already prefigured the kind of society to which they aspired. We have talked about their "thingless" instincts, their recycling of clothes, the uniforms of army surplus, work gear, jeans. Among urbanites, evidence of fairly standardized clothes for daytime wear, for work, has been around for some time. Such "uniforms," just like the classics of such disparate manufacturers as Jonathan Logan and Yves St. Laurent, are a basic condition of our time. They are the tabula rasa on which one can embroider one's soul. They are also increasingly unisex. The future has already shown us more auto mechanic's jumpsuits on city streets than at gas stations. But precisely because ready-to-wear has democratized everyday fashion to such an extent, the urge to improvise in the evenings will be that much stronger.

Come sundown, the drabbest khaki will be replaced by an outrageous boa, a malicious bodystocking, the glint of a silver eyelid. Fantasy will light the evening; nighttime itself will be an event. And here is where designers like Ben Compton come center stage. Compton is one of those survivors of the sixties' fashion factory who struck out on his own when it was clear that Seventh Avenue was turning itself into a copyist's sweatshop. His work is now idiosyncratic, painstakingly brilliant, and totally unclassifiable. A Compton creation is about as far from the everyday workaday outfit as one can get. His dresses are almost exclusively creatures of the night. He has already executed clothes "portraits" of personalities who particularly touch him, like Edith Sitwell and Madame Vionnet. He has come as close to reproducing in fabric the spirit of a gypsy or a figure in a Goya drawing or a night moth as human hands permit. His dresses are soul mirrors. To Ben Compton, fashion, especially night fashion, must capture all

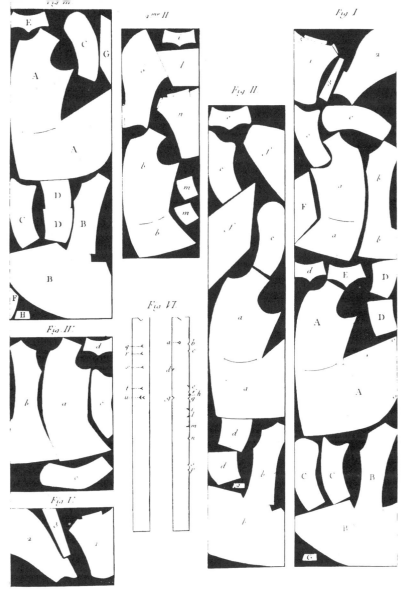

HOW IT OUGHT NOT TO BE. Fabric waste caused by the fragmented patterns of 19th-century European clothes. Unfortunately, this kind of cut still forms the basis of all "structured" clothes. (From *Art du Tailleur*, 1769. Used by B. Rudofsky in *Are Clothes Modern?* Paul Theobald, Chicago, 1947.)

the silvery undertow of personality, the dark side of the moon as well as the lighting of the lamps. Wearing a work of his is like putting on a full-length mask. The fascination of masks is that they reveal and conceal at once. That is exactly what Compton's clothes do. They are successful because they possess the particular identity of the woman for whom they were made.

Oddly enough, Ben Compton's work originates from the same intellectual precept as does Peter Kent's. Compton learned his trade on Seventh Avenue, but broke away in order to make "third world" clothes: patternless marvels of Indian and Islamic draping, simple African dashikis, capes and caftans. First and foremost, however, Compton was a theatrical costumer, and it shows. The theater heightened his sense of drama in clothes, and it was here that he grasped early the importance of honoring the fabric first, since the splendor of materials and color is what is projected from the stage. Compton's dresses are one of a kind, of course. In no way can this mix of imagination, humor, and expression of the wearer be commercially reproduced. But the concept is equally far from that of couture in that it celebrates the individual, not the designer. What Compton's work does point to are the possibilities for evening wear which are open to every woman who can put together a costume from a length of scarf or a web of nylon chiffon and a minimum of inhibition.

Rudi Gernreich, former guru to the avant-garde, reappears on the scene from time to time with important announcements. His latest words may be worth listening to, as he also had the first inklings as far as future fashions were concerned, back in the sixties. Gernreich, too, holds with unisex and with the prevalence of nonfashion, suggesting that the year 2000 may bring disposable look-alike clothes for equally hairless men and women. He sees the designer as more engineer than artist, putting into production the technical innovations at which humanity will no doubt continue to excel. A high-speed shuttleless loom has already been developed, accelerating the production rate of knitted goods tremendously. At the same time, both French and U.S. manufacturers are experimenting with nonwoven fabrics, like the pressed paper ones first used by French designer Paco Rabanne. Though there is little doubt that these would put looms out of business, the interest in such disposable fabrics is something to be watched. While American industry likes to rely on its own genius for perfecting synthetics, the French are at work on materials that react to temperature, keeping the skin cool in summer and warm in winter. And, thinking farther into the future, why not a coat wired like an electric blanket that can warm itself up? Or nylon webbing, sold in one size and pushed into shape by the wearer's body in the manner of the costumes of Alwin Nikolais' dancers?

The possibilities are endless, but what we already have is pretty breathtaking in the scope it allows design. Stretch clothes came about through the idea of transferring Lycra from girdles to outerwear. Gernreich's flesh-colored bodysuit has inspired a gamut of playclothes and even evening dresses with built-in bras or pants. Terry cloth has proved versatile because of its light weight and absorbent quality. Most interesting of all has been the improvement in fabric dyeing. The range of shades available is so immense that it is hard to remember the time when certain color combinations were thought unacceptable. If early Dacron appeared in a particularly insipid mint green with irritating frequency, it was because the first synthetics did not take many dyes well. Today, we think in terms of once-detested mixes like yellow and orange or pink and red. Weaving methods have lifted the ban on patterns worn together. Technology, in short, effects gradual but considerable changes in one's perception of what goes with what.

But not all design talent is protechnology. A considerable splinter group of handwoven natural fabrics enthusiasts has made its presence felt. So much so, in fact, that the mills are doing their best to turn out synthetics that look and feel natural. The demand for naturals is partly due to scarcity: Cotton production has remained more or less at a plateau for the last fifty years, and wool is actually growing less available and more expensive. The situation is such that, if there is to be a status market in the future, it may well be in the realm of natural versus synthetic fabrics rather than in Cartier watches.

That no such crisis has seriously threatened as yet permits designers like French-born André Murasan to continue hand-painting his silk dresses. Murasan is one of a scattering of artists who just happen to be working in the medium of clothes. Silk lends his colors the intensity of stained glass, a luminosity that comes from no other fabric. Though a painter by training, Murasan's concept of clothing corresponds, at its roots, with that of Kent and Compton. A characteristic dress by André Murasan floats squares of painted chiffon over a body stocking. Again the color-saturated fabric is preeminent, and its construction patternless.

New York City's SoHo houses a hodgepodge of design studios that are turning out handmade clothes worthy of the most discriminating connoisseur of what the French call *l'artisanat.* Patchworked velvets or appliquéd denim are used to make garments of extraordinary simplicity. Silk batiks, ikat, Rabat embroidery, intricate geometric weaves derived from Berber design are combined in clothes that feature richness of material above all else. Both here and abroad, *l'artisanat* has a sophisticated following, quite unlike that of the basic do-it-yourself-ers who have helped to popularize needlepoint, macramé equipment, and books on how to crochet.

Along with the new attention being paid to fabric is its logical accompaniment, the all-purpose pattern. The T-shirt and the caftan are perhaps the two archetypal forms of our decade. Guidelines for their construction have been manufactured and made available through the mail by Moisha Kubinyi's New Life Pattern Company, and by others. The principle here is the familiar one of no tailoring, no lapels, buttonholes, or set-in sleeves, and is therefore well adapted to home sewing. It is in effect what might be called flat draping. But behind the seeming ingenuousness of the idea lies a notion more comprehensive than anyone might suspect. This is the concept of communal clothes.

When one looks beneath the surface of Kent's work, that of Kubinyi or of a small cluster of other designers, one discovers that they are operating on radically new principles. Peter Kent is a sort of global nomad who has set up shop on the basis of joint participation wherever he happens to be. So far, wherever has included Spain, Egypt, Jordan, Iraq, Syria, India, London, the Aga Khan's complex at Costa Smeralda on Sardinia, Corsica, and now Tangiers. Here he and his family have taken over the top floor of the White Bear Hotel, which provides living quarters and workrooms for his "clothes factory," and a home base from which to commute to his New

York City loft. The distribution and sales department is at this edge of the Atlantic, with the bulk of production being done in Morocco. Why Morocco? Labor is cheaper and plentiful: The White Bear hums with seamstresses who know the ways of a Singer machine as well as how to hand-finish a hem. The hides are a fine quality and can be cured to order for leather coats, jerkins, and soft moccasins. And then, the Kents' life has been located somewhere along the Mediterranean for the past fifteen years.

Until 1961, living abroad was the last direction Peter Kent might have expected his future to take. An adolescence spent in the privileged and proper confines of Bronxville in New York's exclusive Westchester suburbs, college at Williams, marriage to a Holyoke girl, three children, a stint in the CIA, a junior-executive position at Reynolds Metal—none of it seemed to point to his auspicious disembarkation from the U.S.S. *Constitution* in Spain, belongings and family in tow. But he had left Reynolds and decided to taste Europe. So there they all stood on the dock at Málaga, wearing crew cuts, Madras jackets, and knee socks—well-meaning, well-scrubbed representatives of America abroad. Their household belongings, including a refrigerator with freezing compartment, were being examined with much amusement by deckhands and onlookers. The next week, while having an innocent drink at a cafe, their lives changed abruptly when they were initiated into the wandering life by a gypsy craftsman. From then on, it was clear that making things was to be the Kents' real work. In Torremolinos they met a California girl with a ring in one nostril and a Hungarian mother who had taught her how to sew and sent her to apprentice with a fine dressmaker.

Her designs still form the basis of the Kents' production, though she went her own way after twelve years of hammering out their joint concepts.

It may sound strange to speak of community involvement in a field that has nothing to do with landlord-tenant associations or neighborhood fund raising. But to Peter Kent, clothes are inseparably bound up with an organized group life-style that has received the catch-all nomenclature "commune." For the Kents, this means that they live with their family in a separate unit, but are joined in equal partnership with those who are involved with them in the clothes factory. Before the garments were marketed in this country, it also meant that the clothes were made and sold on the same premises. In Corsica, the premises included, in addition to the boutique workshop, a restaurant where in the evenings one could stop for a meal of home-grown vegetables and rice. Often one of the commune members would play guitar or improvise on the flute. Sometimes there was dancing. Conversation was likely to be in French, German, English, Spanish, Arabic, or Italian, depending on who the visitors were that night. There was a sense of ceremony in every act, from the pouring of red wine and the storytelling to the selling of clothes. Community members were chosen for their abilities: One was a superb suede craftsman, another made shoes. One girl knew ancient methods of dyeing, preparing her own vats of color from the herbs and vegetables grown nearby. Another could weave. Commune members were easily identifiable, as all of them wore like clothes—white homespun dresses cut on the bias, some with voluminous sleeves; the young men in haik tie pants, an ancient style that wraps the body instead of encasing it. By night the inhabitants of that candle-lit atmosphere were like shadow players, seeming never to walk, but to billow and glide instead.

By day they worked like bees in a hive. *The Whole Earth Catalog* was their supplier, their inspiration, and their pattern-book. It still is, and has served in the same way for countless others. Eventually, the Kents hope to put their own brown paper "patterns" in the public domain, with directions for making the basic garments in a range of sizes from infant to adult. In this way other communities can make use of them. Meanwhile, the clothes are being snapped up by chic women in New York, Southampton, and Dallas, among other U.S. cities. Little do the purchasers know that they are wearing primitive patterns made for today's people. Nor are they, in all probability, aware that these clothes are the product of a design ethic whose premise is the drawing together of people through a common necessity—in this case, clothing the body as well as nourishing it.

Communal clothes did not, of course, originate with the Kents or even with last decade's hippies. Lanza del Vasto, the Italian-born follower of Gandhi who started a religious retreat and self-sufficient farming community in the south of France in the 1940's, is one notable progenitor. Today his estate is flourishing. Its members spin and weave their own cloth, grow their own food, and educate their children. Del Vasto's followers are not limited to the Haut Languedoc, however. His way of life has inspired communes throughout Europe just as America's early utopians of Brook Farm or Vedanta laid the ideological foundations for our current rural exiles.

Nor is the notion of the social usefulness of clothes a new one. Popular French designer Tan Giudicelli has proposed a textile kibbutz, where one could go to live for a while and learn to make one's own clothes, the clothes of the future: seasonless, seamless, sizeless, sexless. Then one would leave with an entire wardrobe, hand-sewn, at factory prices. Ideas about the interchangeability of clothes are altering too. For example, the recent trend toward looser garments has made it possible to lend dresses more easily. The French *robe housse*, the jumper, the sack, or the Big Dress of 1975 vintage can be borrowed by anyone sized from the slimness of Twiggy to the amplitude of a Manouche. If clothes continue to be constructed in such a way as to allow this sort of transfer from one person to another, attitudes toward the ownership of our garments will undergo some radical changes. The more uniform, unisex, and unsized clothes become, the more they demand to be made personal. Implications for the accessories market are hopeful, should this trend take hold.

And meanwhile? Fashion has almost ceased to be seasonal. There are no more rules about certain fabrics for certain times of the year. Cotton is worn under furs, not just under the sun; corduroy is no longer an autumn word, and wool can be made gauzy enough to be as cool as silk in summer. The seasonal mode as an incentive to buying will diminish as it is found practical to restock stores on a constant basis, according to need. Eventually, the fall-spring tradition of collections will go the way of resort showings. No one will need them anymore except the fashion publicists, and where their popularity ratings will be by then is anyone's guess. The seasonal fashion cycle will more than likely be replaced by another polarity— the great difference in character between day and evening clothes already mentioned. The effect of such an A.M.-to-P.M. transformation will be to change a woman's sense of time insofar as how she looks is concerned. Sporting by day, feathers by night—it might even make her feel like two separate people sharing the same skin.

Still another fashion dichotomy is due to break down. As more people acquire second homes, and with mobility constantly on the increase, the look of country and city clothes will merge. Even now, the lines have blurred so that it seems ridiculous to think of heathery, tweedy outfits for one place and sharp little suits for another. Part of the city-country clothes merger is due to the craze for sports, which has established itself firmly in our lives. Everyone jogs. Tennis playing with machines when it is impossible to get to a court is proliferating in the cities. Soccer is enjoying a renaissance everywhere in the United States from Houston's Astrodome to New York's Central Park. Smashball, surfing, gliding, riding—indoors or out, we are a country of sports freaks. When the sky is blue, we'll be out under it. When it rains, we'll be at the indoor pool or rink or court.

Is it any wonder that sports clothes have their own attractions for us, quite apart from the activities they were designed for? As a nation, Americans love gear. L. L. Bean and Norm Thompson, Sierra Designs and Eastern Mountain Sports have to be doing something right to encourage the landslide mail-order business they are besieged with nowadays. The answer may be that active sportsgear is the thing for city streets. When even Bonwit's is selling terry warm-up suits for early morning joggers, you know that the out-of-doors is already big business. When sweatshirts and shooting bags make it as high fashion in the pages of *Elle* magazine, you know it's happening in France as well. Predictions are that in

1980, one in four French vacationers will spend his precious August out camping. And this means a whole new market of climbing boots and knapsacks, waterproof safari jackets, ponchos, and leg warmers—the very same items that are now walking the streets of Paris and New York.

For women have finally put their feet firmly into boots that don't leak in the snow and rain; their legs are often in stockings not of nylon but of heavy ribbed wool; their fingers no longer have to freeze in kid but are protected by interlined militia gloves or sheepskin mittens. Riding boots and crash helmets go to the office, tennis whites take to bicycles in summer, ski parkas elbow out fun furs during fuel shortages. Mackintoshes, hip waders, bib overalls, ear flaps, troop boots, rainsuits, lumber jackets, coveralls, canvas, rubber, khaki, flannel, olive drab, and pockets, pockets, pockets—they are all coming out of the mail-order houses, out of the surplus stores, out of the chicest specialty shops, and into the streets.

Is it possible that the camper's pocket knife will be the status accessory of the future, that the height of sophistication on city as well as country byways will be lunch-hour skating skirts, jodhpurs and riding boots, back-strapped knapsacks that leave hands free for packages, canvas totes that can go from forest trail to work? Will we see rugby shirts at typists' desks? There has already been a mini-revolution at foot level: Earth Shoes and their imitators have shoved all those T-strap quadruple-A sandals right into the sale bins at Bloomingdale's. When Seventh Avenue catches on to the sportsgear trend, it will no longer be an adventure to look for Icelandic sweaters at dockside stalls or stock shirts at the local riding shop. Ordering chamois-cloth shirts from Bean's will be old hat. But by the time everyone is into his new daytime sports uniform, we will at least have been comfortable, basking in the kind of warmth that only being slightly in advance of fashion can bestow.

Colette, with her unerring fashion sense, was already well ahead of the game in the mid-twenties. She knew, somehow, that sports were no mere counterfad to the fripperies of the pre-World War I era. In an essay called "Too Short," she denounced the dress designers of her time who made walking difficult for women who wore the tight skirts then à la mode. And she took a prescient look into the future: "If we want to get about, on foot or on horseback, climb a mountain or traverse a marsh, it won't be you, Couturier, that we'll consult, but specialists that you despise, the technicians of the waterproof raincoat, the puttee, the ski boot and the Saumur riding breeches." Now it seems that fashion may be about to go full circle as it always does, back to those once-ignored "specialists"—but this time for inspiration and advice in chic.

Speculation does not, of course, have to be limited to sportsgear. The clothes of the future may well turn out to be your living room couch. In an uncertain economy, nothing one puts money into looks so stable as furniture. Fashion may be forced to take a back seat as penalty for its frivolous reputation. In some ways interior design affords a broader barometric reading of social change than does clothing. Homes are more enduring than dress. Not that we are embedded in our living quarters like pebbles in cement, but where and how we live does provide us with a firmer social matrix. We move, but when we do, we take part of our matrix with us in the form of furniture and household equipment. These things express us in our relationships with people—not in the same direct and intimate way as do our clothes, but in a similar manner.

Furnishings register change more slowly, perhaps, than style of dress, but register they do. So that given an alternative for self-expression, the American woman may well choose to seize upon transforming her kitchen rather than herself.

It is possible to discern a subtle transfer of energy going on in this direction since the sixties. In our country it is somehow considered more acceptable to spend time and money fixing up one's abode rather than adorning one's person. Perhaps the reason is a residual puritanism, a finger-shaking attitude toward vanity; perhaps it is just common sense about money. But the balance has swung to concern about life-style and consequently to the appurtenances of how one lives.

The seventies are servantless; restaurants are expensive; we cook at home more. Technology has provided us with comfortable seating, no-stain upholstery, and inexpensive artworks. Paint and supergraphics combined with elbow grease and a little imagination make it possible for anyone to create a setting for his interests, activities, and day-to-day existence. Even fashion has followed suit by flooding the stores with at home wear. And we find Cardin in the bathroom and on the beds, if not in the closets.

Atmosphere. Clothes are part of it. Toasters and wallpaper and chairs are part of it. Anything that belongs in a home, that can be opened, shut, pushed, pulled, tacked, glued, molded, bolted, or braced is part of it. The objects we choose to live with, just as much as the ones we choose to wear, have a significance beyond mere convention. Increasingly, it looks as though our houses will *not* become "batteries for utility people" as Konrad Lorenz once predicted about mass dwellings. We have chosen to refuse this. Instead, we decorate like a nation possessed, in an effort to put our signature on everything. Of course we are swayed by fads, we have gone through stages.

Inevitably, along with the mode Rétro went the tinsel trimmings of silver wallpaper and peacock feathers and peach satin slipcovers. Once the thirties had become the rage, Ruhlmann lamps like funerary urns sprang up in our homes, along with the flashy tat, the Aztec dash, the haut bourgeois thrill of Puiforcat silver and of plaster wedding-cake moldings and sideboards of Corbusier-like construction that turned drawing rooms into stages for MGM spectaculars. All this single-minded concentration on interior chic ended abruptly in death by overdose of sophistication. And so we started again from scratch, this time with scrubbed butcher-block, blue and white pottery, and unbleached muslin. But don't forget that before we were smitten with Art Deco, we had been entwined in the tendrils of Art Nouveau. And before these ventures into the dreary past, we had been resolutely up-to-date in a 1950's sort of way with Billy Baldwin as the *metleur-en-scène*. Was it any better, having one's tabletops littered with tortoise-framed snapshots of family and the autographed famous? Were ice-blue walls and butler's tables really the last word in borrowed chic, and what about all those full-blown roses on the wallpaper, and the yards of glazed chintz? What about the *clutter*? It was hopeless. All that "good taste," that department-store-decorator cachet, never solved any of the problems of daily living.

So we had to do it ourselves. For once, people are beginning to worry about the design of mass-produced objects. Like ready-to-wear clothes, such products are getting better and better as we realize that what comes to hand on a daily basis affects our lives even more strongly than special occasion utensils. Think of how the shape of spoons has changed within the last century. Cutlery was on a bigger scale when people ate more. Teaspoons had longer, deeper bowls, meant for sipping. Think of chairs: the straight-backed wooden-pegged sitting instruments of our upright ancestors—and the ones of today, blown up like plastic clouds, into which you can plunge. What does the squashy beanbag say about contemporary posture, about our mania for being relaxed? One does not sit. One deposits one's body passively in modern chairs. Or think of symmetry, the placement of objects. The eye is trained by exposure and we have learned to live with Oriental asymmetry as easily as with our native insistence on having everything lined up like tin soldiers on the mantelpiece. The order or disorder we create, our instinct for what we find in nature, our feel for space and shape are all partly formed by everyday instruments and objects. As our teaspoons are calibrated to today's needs, as even our beanbag chairs are made in practical bright coverings, as we teach ourselves to arrange flowers or porcelain in new ways, so the quality of these things in turn improves our lives.

The same aching for simplicity that has affected our way of dressing invades our houses. The uptight rigors of formal entertaining have given way at last to a casualness that, far from being careless, is really more gracious than the past's overload of Louis Quinze and crystal chandeliering. It is so because our style now centers more on people, our guests, our families, and less on things. Owning fewer objects is partly responsible, and our irrepressible mobility accounts in some measure for our desire to own less. Once we have settled somewhere for any length of time, using a room for several purposes instead of walling it off only for dining or for receiving is another sign that we can afford to be more people-centered and less manipulated by our surroundings. We make our environment, not vice versa. Even the prospect of wall-less houses becoming the norm is not inconceivable.

Along with the American woman's newly acquired self-confidence in clothes goes an assurance about her personal setting as well. Oh, professional decorators are still in business. Status still sells among the insecure upper-middle classes who have never learned that a home is where one's collective history is, not a show one puts on for the neighbors. Stage management for the house or apartment dweller still makes up a sector of the $21 billion and some a year that Americans spend on decor. Natural in the sense of straw and hemp and unbleached linen, hand-hewn logs and raw wood surfaces, flagstones and rock collections, shells and plants and wicker—this sort of purchasable natural represents a kind of seventies status that can be just as dead-handed and phony as down-home patchwork tea-cosiness, or the comfortable promise that you *can* go home again if your decor is honest. But it is still a far cry from the pretentions of Deco sleek. And if there have to be trends at all, the effect made by even studied naturalness is a lot prettier than most. But basically we are less involved in the mad scramble for objects that characterized other eras. Deep down we are more literally at home with what we have, and harbor a new respect for the well-designed articles we use.

Then, too, men are increasingly in the picture. Women are more a part of their lives as they are more a part of ours. We allow their bicycles and baseballs in the hallway because we play too. They are permitted in the kitchen to concoct their own specialties because the fun of cooking is no longer confined to the female of the species. As many men find that their satisfactions derive less and less from their jobs, home provides an outlet for the hand talents of carpentry and gardening, cooking, and even making clothes. And the women's movement has established once and for all that such activities are far from effeminate.

So home may be where the new heart of fashion lies. At the very least, it is an integral part of the atmosphere of clothes because clothes are no longer separable from one's life-style. However, there is a crucial factor missing in decor as a means of personal expression. Clothes and cosmetics permit direct involvement with the body. Although a home is a shell, a womb, a sort of second sheath like that of a dress, it is of a kind once removed from immediate physical contact with skin, muscle, movement, and all the properties of a live human form.

For the liberated *body* is what fashion is all about these days. Body pride is underneath most of the changes women have experienced since the reawakening of the movement in the sixties. Body pride underlies how we live, what we eat, our new slenderness and athleticism, our fitness, our clothes. And our clothes, conversely, mirror nothing less than the interior decor of our minds: They are what we think, they are our inner furniture made visible.

Whereas fashion used to be, as the painter Vertès once said, "public opinion expressed in dress," it has been transformed by today's women into style. And style is *private* opinion expressed in dress. Style is the visual answer to the question "Who am I?" It is not concerned with that old bugaboo, "Who do I want to be in the eyes of others?"

Because style now corresponds more closely to inner verities, because it is so much a reflection of what is on women's minds, it is less vulnerable to outer directives than ever before. For one thing, style's new heroine is more independent. She is the young woman committed to a very active way of life, a modern mesomorph who has outgrown the endless adolescence promoted by the youth maniacs of ten years ago. Her body is no longer possessed by that sour look of a Twiggy-grown-older which haunted those who followed fashion with a vengeance in the swinging sixties. The modern mesomorph makes a mockery of youth-infatuation. She has other fish to fry. Her energies have been transferred from preoccupation with her appearance to concentration on her performance, whether that means running companies, raising children, or perfecting her tennis game. Snobbery about youth has already diminished, and it will disappear as the female population grows older. Whereas in the last decade the "youth sector"—those between the ages of fifteen and twenty-four—was increasing at a rate of twelve million a year, the seventies have slowed down the rate to five million, and the eighties will see the proportion of young actually on the wane.

The woman in her mid-thirties who is now the market for the clothing and cosmetics industries also constitutes a different magazine readership from her fashionable progenitors. As *Vogue, Harper's Bazaar*, and the Fairchild publications release their hold on manufacturer and consumer alike, practical advice on how to make it, how to do it, what's a good buy and what's a rip-off will win hands down over the fantasy press. Style is in the streets, in the photojournalism of everyday life, in the faces of women without names. The old-fashioned journalism of sustained euphoria and outrageous vocabulary—the romancing of this look and that look and the seasonal, mindless excitement drummed up from nowhere—has knocked itself out in an acute fit of overconsumption. Fashion advice? Who needs it? Unbiased consumer criticism of clothes as they come off the production line, commentary on street styles, fashion news in the sense of what's coming up next, a supermarket of ideas—yes, perhaps there is a place for all that still. But can one even condone its being relegated to women's pages, especially when we know that as many men as women read the Family/Style section of, say, *The New York Times*? And anyway, as for "keeping up" with fashion—that will be out of the question.

This effort to catch up with and entrap time by being à la mode may have had its day. Its past charms are undeniable, as it has been the element that has made fashion so valuable as a register of social values. The appetite for it is still there, as is only natural. We must remember that only human beings choose their own hides. Only they of all the animals wear mental concepts. We humans are creatures of imagination: Even our body coverings begin as dreams, and flower in sketches on drawing boards. When finished and viewed from a distance, clothes are like details on a frieze, details that trail, as we pass them, the unmistakable fragrance of an era. But in the future, clothes may not provide us with so many clues to the life of our own time.

The nature of the seventies makes this so. The sheer number of things going on simultaneously has almost changed the nature of time itself from a progressive concept to a multi-layered phenomenon. We shall have to learn how to keep several—often contradictory—notions in our heads at once. Fads and fashions that seem to oppose each other will appear on the scene together. Adjusting to one look and then another would be fatal. Instead, women will be increasingly forced to settle for *their* look from the plethora of choices available.

A good thing, that. Yves St. Laurent has wisely said about personal style that it is something that, once found, should never change. He has even gone so far as to pronounce that adherence to one's style gauges a woman's security and sense of well-being more accurately than anything else she does.

That same assurance is what has led us not just to accept, but positively to relish plurality. We are tuned to the excitement of events, to the sense of endless alternatives, countless messages. Our lives are flooded with imagery, with choice. We are alive in the midst of a harvest of cultures, an incredible, multicolored wealth of influences—black, Mexican-American, Indian, Oriental, Puerto Rican—whose originators will compose one-sixth of our population by the year 2000. This makes one thing about style quite certain: the time for a single standard is over. In the future, looking good will take on as many faces as there are women.

index

Clara Pierre grew up in Philadelphia, went to college at Sarah Lawrence and got her M.A. in International Law at Columbia University. After several years of writing about foreign relations she found herself hired as a salesgirl at Valentino's boutique. This experience provided the idea for *Looking Good*, her first book. A free-lance writer, Ms. Pierre has written articles for *New York*, *House and Garden*, *Saturday Review*, *Cosmopolitan*, *The New York Times*, and the *Village Voice* among others. She lives with her husband in Manhattan.